Not on My Watch

Not on My Watch

Alexandra Morton

How a Renegade Whale Biologist Took on
Governments and Industry to Save Wild Salmon

RANDOM HOUSE CANADA

PUBLISHED BY RANDOM HOUSE CANADA

Copyright © 2021 Alexandra Morton

www.penguinrandomhouse.ca

Random House Canada and colophon are registered trademarks.

Library and Archives Canada Cataloguing in Publication

Title: Not on my watch : how a renegade whale biologist took on governments and industry to save wild salmon / Alexandra Morton.
Names: Morton, Alexandra, 1957- author.
Identifiers: Canadiana (ebook) 20200281798 | Canadiana (print) 2020028178X | ISBN 9780735279667 (hardcover) | ISBN 9780735279674 (EPUB)
Subjects: LCSH: Morton, Alexandra, 1957- | LCSH: Marine biologists—British Columbia—Biography. | LCSH: Pacific salmon—Conservation—British Columbia. | LCSH: Salmon farming—Environmental aspects—British Columbia. | LCGFT: Autobiographies.
Classification: LCC QH91.3.M67 A3 2021 | DDC 578.77092—dc23

Text design: Talia Abramson
Jacket design: Leah Springate
Map design: Talia Abramson
Image credits: front jacket photo courtesy of the author; (coastline on jacket) Artak Petrosyan / Unsplash; photo of orca courtesy of the author

Printed and bound in Canada

10 9 8 7 6 5 4 3 2 1

To my children, who were unwavering in their love,
support and kindness as we lived this together.
And to the Ahta River: you were the spark
in my heart that would not be dimmed.

CONTENTS

Part IV: The Uprising

Photographs of events described in this book can be found at www.alexandramorton.ca

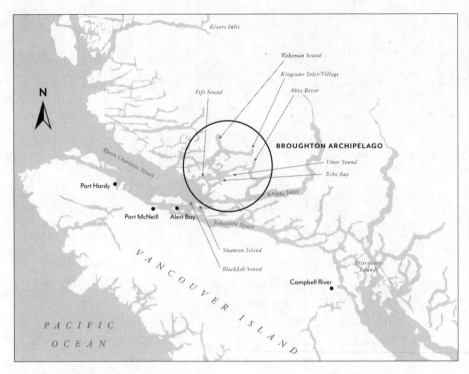

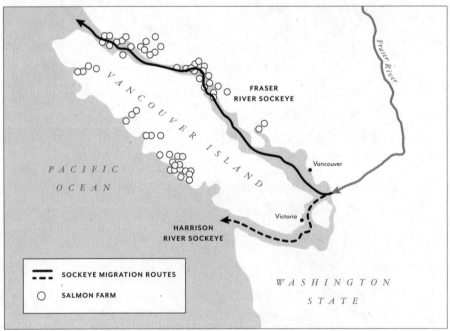

North Vancouver Island

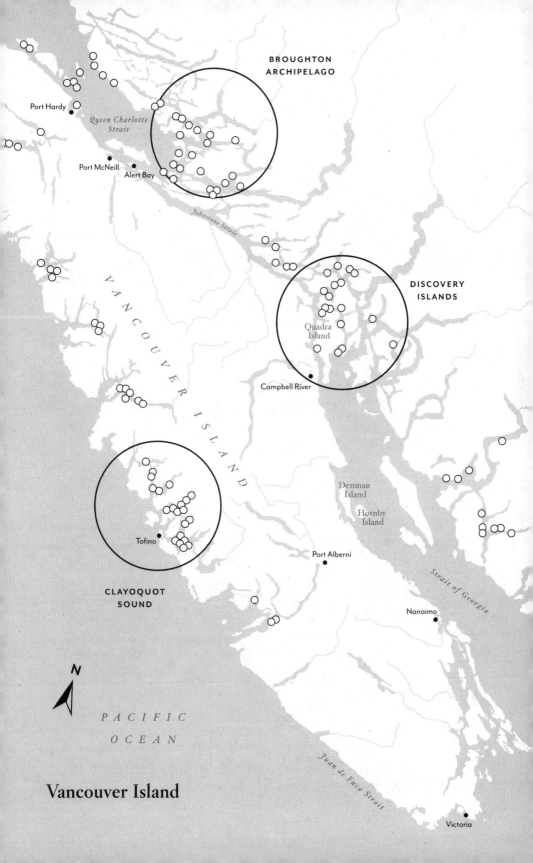

Wonder and Resistance

WHEN I WAS a child I was drawn to animals, especially the wild ones, and to the ponds and forests where they lived. I was curious. I tracked them and watched them. No matter whether I was looking into the gold-flecked eye of a frog, or at the way a deer held her ears as she stepped out of the forest at sunset, animals were mysterious, beautiful and wise. When I turned eight, I knew wanted to become a scientist but I wasn't sure how. The only picture of a woman scientist that I had seen was of Madame Curie, and I was afraid to become that person in the blurry picture wearing a white lab coat. At the same time I realized that only small children "played with animals." A growing dread consumed me. To grow up I needed to stop spending time in the woods and marshes. I still remember the sensation of stopping myself from looking under a piece of wood where I knew a snake almost certainly lay coiled.

Then just before Christmas 1965, I received an issue of *National Geographic* with Jane Goodall on the cover. I stared at it. The outer world paused and went silent as I sank to the dark brown carpet of my mother's study. I pored over every picture of this beautiful woman, looking perfectly happy, who studied chimpanzees in the frightening jungle. Was she real? I felt an explosion of joy as the walls I was building around myself crumpled and the inner compass I was trying to redirect slipped free. I would follow in the footsteps of Jane Goodall. That was my promise to me. Seeing those pictures of Jane gave me my life. Thank you so much, Jane, for allowing *National Geographic* to expose your work and your paradise, no small sacrifice, I realized years later.

Over the next decade, I read every book about scientists who, following in Goodall's footsteps, went into the wilderness to study an animal. And I saw a pattern. While they began as people driven by curiosity and the need to understand, they inevitably became "activists," though none of them used that term back then. The more they understood the animal they had chosen to study, the more urgently they felt the need to stand in the way of the crushing advance of human appetite for the land on which the animal relied or for the creature itself. I felt sad for these scientists. They had to abandon the dream they had worked so hard for. They had to leave the jungle, savannah or ocean to confront the people who were causing the damage. Once the scientists found the perpetrators, they had to figure out how to stop them.

Dr. Jane Goodall did more than reveal the origins of our humanness through her science; she demonstrated that becoming a groundbreaking scientist didn't require a loss of compassion. Other scientists criticized her heavily from the start for giving the chimps she was studying names instead of numbers. Today she admits in her lectures that she went into a conference on primates a wildlife biologist and came out an activist, when she refused to accept the methods of her colleagues, who, in the name of science, were torturing primates in a way that horrified her.

I took this all in and decided I was *not* going to be shoved off my life's path. I was going to plug my ears, ignore the "issues" and follow my dream to the end. I was going to decipher the language of some large-brained non-human species, creating a Rosetta stone of sorts to end the solitude of my species. We needed to hear what another animal on this planet was saying, I thought, because it seemed that we were going mad in our isolation. A lofty aim for a teenager, I know, but this is what I wanted to do. Of course things are so much simpler when you are a child, and so I failed to stay true to my fifteen-year-old self. What I didn't realize back then was that if I ignored the impact humans were having on the animals I had chosen to study, I would end up studying their extinction.

It gets even more complex. Scientists who go to learn about animals in the remote regions of our planet also meet Indigenous people. While the peoples and cultures that evolved over thousands of years in one place are adapted to their home environment, the scientist is, in many ways, an introduced species.

When I first arrived in the remote archipelago on the west coast of Canada, where I still live, to study whales—my chosen large-brained mammal—I didn't understand the land, the animals or the people. I had no idea how to respond to storms or predators or where to find food. I didn't immediately recognize the difference between the nomads of the planet, meaning people who moved generation after generation, and the people who spent thousands of years in one place. Over the years I have encountered instances where my Indigenous companions have heard and felt things I don't. Asking them questions didn't help. I was simply not adapted to the place and did not have the internal hardware to perceive some things.

However, the act of doing science—decades of continuously count-ing the number of birds or fish, the minutes between whale blows, the date the herring arrived, the amount of rainfall—leads to a gradual understanding of a place. I learned to expect the rush of black and sil-ver herring schools roiling beneath the surface of the Pacific Ocean, pulling huge spring salmon in their wake, with the A-clans of the northern resident orca on their tails. As I began to feel the pulse of this place, I perceived the difference between "normal" and exceptional. For example, a healthy run of salmon as opposed to a run of salmon that never arrived. Seeing the missing pieces is important, too, because they affect the world as much as the things I can see.

No scientist can spend ten thousand years becoming finely tuned to a place, but the constant counting, measuring and weighing, then analyzing data to reveal the trends of life, can bring scientists into align-ment with Indigenous viewpoints. As a result, when the big machines of industry advance on us, whether clear-cutting forests, damming rivers to flood valleys or exterminating animals for profit, scientists can see the running cracks as they form, undoing the entire web of life. We see the disappearances. We are emotionally hurt by the loss and naturally move to take a stand with the people of the place, the Indigenous people. In all the books I read as a child I didn't notice this alliance, but when I went back to them as an adult I realized it was there. It is not an easy relationship for many reasons, but saving our planet and acting in accordance with Indigenous tradition are one and the same.

Salmon and people came back to the coast of British Columbia together ten thousand years ago as the glaciers receded. The land had been scraped down to bare rock by the crushing weight of the ice. Salmon, swimming up the rivers by the millions to spawn and then die, helped rebuild the soil, feeding trees that eventually decayed, became soil and fed new forests. As much as killing was important to the survival of the humans, so was stewardship. They had to make sure they left enough for tomorrow, for their children, for the future.

Alliances between scientists and the people of the land are forged because in very different ways we personally experience the changes, we feel the death of the land and this urgency drives us. Thinking I could ignore the urge to push back against the destruction of the place I came to think of as home was a child's view, because standing in this place, the harm was advancing on me as well.

I have so many questions. Do world leaders and CEOs of oil companies, manufacturers of pesticides and myriad other destructive industries experience niggling concern for their own children? Do they worry whether their gated community can withstand the brute force of the runaway fires, floods and storms of this new climate regime they are creating? If so, they must hope, if even for an instant, that someone is going to throw on the brakes and make sure there is enough left for their children to thrive. Can they see that they are behaving like addicts to rising share price, that they are on a treadmill with no off switch, harming their own, as they take us straight to Armageddon?

Do these questions strike you as extreme? If they do, you might find that by the time you finish my account of this fight to save the wild salmon, the whales and ultimately the humans of the Pacific Northwest Coast, you might be asking even more pointed questions yourself. Especially given that as I'm finishing this manuscript, the world is in the grip of a viral pandemic that is revealing the cracks in the artificial web of life we hastily constructed and now depend on.

A recent prime minister of Canada, Stephen Harper, said that environmental activists are "terrorists" and he began legislating how such terrorists would be dealt with. He miscalculated. Canadians, for the most part, did not accept this characterization and pushed back in the most wonderful way, by realizing they were activists too. This grass-roots support took the target off our backs and allowed us continue our work to keep natural systems alive.

Activists are trying to protect all our children. If we, as a society, fail to bequeath a planet to future generations that can support human civilization, we will be the target of hate as hate has never been felt before. It is not hard to see that we are stealing the ability to thrive from future generations, but even as the destruction continues, the tide is turning.

Paul Hawken, in his book *Blessed Unrest*, calls activists Earth's immune response. Jane Goodall, a beacon, assures scientists that it's okay to be an activist—that, morally, you *have* to be an activist. I now can add that it feels good to be an activist. It feels good to refuse to allow yourself to be chased—to turn around and meet those who are killing the planet with everything you are.

To undertake this journey from whale researcher to front-line activist was not a choice. The other option was to go numb and pray that I truly was powerless, that there really was nothing I could do. However, *nothing* is very big. Doing nothing requires thousands of decisions to look the other way, withdraw your hand, clench the change in your pocket, scoff, duck, lie and feed the very thing that is killing us.

The governments and industry I've been facing off with over the impact of fish farming on the marine waters of British Columbia had a game plan. They knew what and who was going to get hurt, and they knew how to feign concern while their actions and inactions pushed wild salmon and all the beings that depend on them towards extinction. Did they think the changes caused by the devastating pathogen spillage from industrial salmon feedlots would be better for us all in the long run? I don't think so. But I do know that some people had made a decision to support the industry ahead of all other concerns. I learned that ministers of government had almost no idea what is going on; their senior bureaucrats, working in offices a couple of flights downstairs, were the architects of what happened here. The ones who ignored all the evidence must have known they were up to no good. While they were careful about leaving fingerprints, once they caught my interest, I followed them through access to information requests for their internal communications like I had once followed whales. You'll see that I did not find innocence or good intentions.

Many scientists are sending increasingly urgent messages to society that we are hurting ourselves, the way our fingertips send messages to the brain to pull our hands out of a fire. Bureaucrats try to insert themselves like sponges, absorbing our messages and wringing them out into sealed receptacles, making sure no one notices and can react. They tell their bosses and the world that we are activists, not *real* scientists. Our funding dwindles, we endure financial ruin, our careers do not advance and our own colleagues and allies step away from us. We are slandered and our science is smothered, unless we can outsmart them.

This is my story. I tell it because we learn from stories such as mine. During the first two decades in which I tried to save the ecosystem I live in, I refused to use the word *fight*, but I have adopted that term now. This is the story of a fight to keep part of this Earth alive.

I have seen a lot, worked with people who could not be more different from each other and from myself, and watched in wonder as decades of failure mysteriously blossomed into a movement, an uprising, and caused change. I don't know yet if that change will be enough—I am waiting to hear from the wild salmon on this—but I know the survival of this part of the planet depends on this fight and everyone who stepped into the ring.

I have been on the front lines now for so long I don't make plans. I'm part of a wave of unstable, raw energy, the ruthless grinding of evolution in play. How can I possibly know whether I am available Tuesday at 2 p.m., three months from now? There might be a die-off in a salmon river to be investigated, an infestation to measure, a front line I have to stand on with my allies. I am careful with my energy now because there is always too much to do. I have opted to be the small mammal, not the big dinosaur. I try to be strategically nimble so that I can respond to the shape and direction of the wave. I have intentionally kept my voice free from big institutions so the opposition can't find and cut off my supply line, a braided trickle of support from a diversity of sources. I realized that when I was responsible for the salaries of other people, I had to be careful not to scare funders away by speaking the unvarnished truth. So I now work with allies, not employees.

These allies are like wild horses, a tough, raw crowd. We experience a lot of casualties—hurt feelings, misunderstandings, the collision of egos, sudden departures—but we are inexorably moving in the same direction breaking the grip on the pulse of life. There is no leader negotiating on everyone's behalf, who can be haltered and led into a barn, then silenced.

I am part of the resistance movement against extinction. The movement spans the globe. We are a force of nature. Like a river, we well up, slip around, bore through and dive under obstacles. We don't stop.

Not all of this story is mine to tell and so there are some gaps. I have also withheld the names of people who have already suffered too much in this struggle. I hope my book will help, in at least a small way, to bring the species that we named *human* into ecological compliance with the planet we live on. This is not the time to give up.

Part I

Into the Wilderness

The Path to Activism
Was Paved with Science

THE SEVENTEEN ROYAL Canadian Mounted Police officers surrounding me were dressed in tactical gear—layers of textured black. Black belts, black helmets, black vests, black shoes, black pistols. I was a sixty-one-year-old woman dressed in jeans and runners. The rising southeast wind funnelled down Knight Inlet, the longest inlet on the coast of British Columbia. The *Viktoria Viking*, a vessel that delivers fish to salmon farms, was sidling up to the aluminum cages of the farm I was standing on. As soon as she was docked, her crew swung a large black pipe out over the metal walkway into the net pen suspended in the cold waters of the inlet, and young Atlantic salmon infected with piscine orthoreovirus, PRV, poured out of the boat into the pen. After seven years of studying this salmon blood virus, I knew how dangerous these fish were to the part of the world I call home.

"Step past us and you will be arrested," one of the officers said. I slipped past him and approached the boat. The knot of men followed me, but none moved to restrain me.

The one who had warned me asked, "So how do you see this going?"

"Arrest me, put me in one of your black Zodiacs and take me to Port McNeill," I replied.

The Musgamagw and 'Namgis Indigenous people of the Broughton Archipelago, which stretches towards the northern tip of Vancouver Island along mainland British Columbia, had occupied two other salmon farms belonging to the same Norwegian company, Mowi, for sixty days. Even though they had been saying no to the fish farming industry for thirty years, the industry had only grown, the wild salmon in the region were in collapse and the First Nations no longer had wild salmon to catch. They had lost their most nutritious source of protein and, since salmon permeates their culture to the point that they are not Musgamagw without salmon, they were losing themselves. Winter was on us and I feared for the young women who were occupying the other aluminum salmon farms, big as football fields, as storm-driven waves crashed through the pens. Mowi, which used to be called Marine Harvest, had laid charges against me for trespass the previous year, because I boarded one of their farms with members of these nations as they performed a cleansing ceremony, and took underwater video of their fish. Those charges were still before the courts, but I decided that unless I took the same risks as the people of this land, I was not doing everything I could to bring the standoff to a productive conclusion without anyone getting hurt. The nations were demanding that all the salmon farms be removed from the territories of the Musgamagw Dzawada'enuxw, Mamalilikulla, Kwikwasut'inuxw Haxwa'mis and 'Namgis.

Several RCMP officers moved away from me to huddle with employees of Mowi, then the officer who had talked to me returned. "There will be no arrests today," he said, and I nodded, walked up to the ship and laid my hand on it as it loomed several stories above me. Next I scooped up hundreds of the scales that had been knocked off the fish as they tumbled down the pipe and were drifting in the water. I would send these to a lab to document the presence of the virus in these fish as they arrived fresh from the hatchery. This is how I confirmed that hundreds of thousands of Atlantic salmon infected with an Atlantic blood virus were pouring into the pens in an inlet that once supported millions of the five species of Pacific wild salmon.

Once the fish were unloaded, the ship backed away and the police departed, following it down the inlet in their black Zodiacs. I messaged my friend John Geraghty, who had dropped me off on the farm, that since I hadn't been arrested I would be staying the night. He pulled up in his boat and threw me a garbage bag stocked for what lay ahead of me: sleeping bag, heavy Cowichan sweater, water and granola bars. Without trying to talk me out of it, for which I remain grateful, he left. I can't say I was happy to be occupying this salmon farm, but it had to be done.

I had tried everything I could think of for over thirty years to protect this part of the BC coast from the impact of industrial salmon farming. Everywhere in the world that this industry operates, wild salmon stocks vanish, with devastating impacts on whales and many other species, as well as on human communities. I had done seventeen years of research, co-publishing findings in the journal *Science* and elsewhere that predicted the collapse of the pink salmon of Knight Inlet due to the sea lice that were spreading from farm salmon and eating young wild salmon to death. I was the scientist who published the first paper on the arrival of the Atlantic Ocean virus, PRV, into these Pacific waters, which could only be explained by the introduction of millions of Atlantic farm salmon into the province. I'd travelled to Norway to speak to Mowi's shareholders, trying to persuade them that the impact of their industry was unacceptable. I took the industry and government to court four times to try to stop the harm it was doing, and never lost. I had done a lot more too, as had the allies and First Nations.

None of these things convinced government to protect wild salmon from the flow of pathogens from these industrial marine feedlots into the ocean, which has mystified me for the whole time I'd been involved in trying to get them to stop. When it comes to the oceans, it seems that anything goes.

———

Whales were the creatures that brought me to this point.

From the moment I decided to follow Jane Goodall's path and study language in a large-brained animal, I had to make a choice: primate, elephant or whale?

I picked whales. Sometimes I wished I had picked elephants, because most of the time spent studying whales is just staring at the surface of the ocean waiting. When whales do surface, all you usually get to see are their fins and backs. Terrestrial biologists can observe a wealth of information: facial expressions, hackles, body posture, body condition, intimate interactions. The study of scat, alone, provides detailed information on diet and health. Terrestrial animals leave tracks, nests and trails. You can set up observation platforms and sit quietly and learn.

Watching whales means travelling constantly in boats that are tossing about in every kind of weather. I once met a government biologist who in his spare time studied Sasquatch, the legendary super-sized, human-like primates that may exist along the coast of the northwest American continent. As I listened to his stories of the evidence he had accumulated but never confirmed, I realized here was someone who had chosen an animal that was even harder to study than whales. However fleeting my observations, I could see them.

Whales can never build a nest or curl up in a cave, since they have to return to the surface of the ocean for every breath, no matter whether the water is calm or rising in mountainous swells. Their life at the dynamic boundary where air meets water means that a whale's only home is their family. With drones as a new tool, we now know that whales touch each other often. Orca travelling abreast will leave a space for members to fill as they rise to the surface to breathe. They use sound to stay in touch in the near darkness in which they live. A mother rounding a point of land will charge back calling to her three-year-old who has strayed out of earshot, relaxing when she re-establishes acoustic contact with her little one.

Whales don't have the thick pelts of sea otters, seals and sea lions. They have to maintain a thick insulating layer of fat to stay warm. Their huge brains, about five times the size of ours, are built with the same information-rich network wiring as human brains, an expensive piece of biological machinery to maintain for an animal that spends much of its life holding its breath. Brains require an abundant and steady supply of oxygen, and so do muscles. Because whales have to use their muscles continuously from the moment they are born or they will sink and drown, their brains and muscles compete for every breath that they hold in their lungs between surfacings. If whales were not using all of this massive brain, evolution would have produced a downsized model that was more oxygen-efficient to run. Whales were clearly thinking with those great big brains, and I was drawn to try to figure out what they were thinking about by studying their sounds.

In the grip of urgency to begin my research, I skipped the last year of high school, winning early acceptance into the American University in Washington, DC. After I graduated with a Bachelor of Science, I headed west to the University of Southern California in Los Angeles, closer to the ocean. An academic adviser suggested I start with studying communication in a smaller species that would be easier to work with, suggesting fish in a tank. I balked and chose, instead, to begin my studies with captive dolphins. I'd missed several prerequisite courses for graduate work in my undergrad degree, and so while I attended those make-up classes I began my research at Marineland of the Pacific just south of Los Angeles.

Marineland gave me the permission to lower an underwater microphone, called a hydrophone, into the dolphin tank. While I was in the process of figuring out how to study the steady stream of clicks, buzzes and whistles uttered by the ten bottlenosed dolphins zooming around that tank, the female orca at the park gave birth to the first whale conceived in captivity. The curator asked if I would move my gear to the whale tank and record the sounds of the newborn whale. I eagerly agreed, and this is how I came to know Corky, the female orca, and

Orky, the male, both captured off the coast of British Columbia when they were about five years old, in 1968 and 1969.

When their first calls came over the headset, I drew in a long breath. They were so beautiful. Unlike the dolphin sounds, these calls were squarely within my hearing range, which meant I could listen in real time, instead of having to play back the tapes at a slower speed. The calls completely captured my attention, hitting a resonant frequency throughout my entire being. I knew instantly that orcas were the animals I wanted to spend the rest of my life with.

When humans greet each other we utter specific sounds: variations of "hello" in every language. We make a different set of sounds when we part ways, eat or tuck our young into bed. Matching the sounds whales made to identifiable behaviours, like playing, greetings or feeding, seemed a good place for me to start trying to understand the orca. Human language is a portal to our thoughts; since orca are so vocal, I hoped that correlating their sounds with their behaviours would allow me to start the journey into their world. I wanted to know what they were thinking about, what was important to them—what was going on in that huge Cadillac of a brain of theirs. As I watched Corky's eight-foot baby whale, I felt extremely lucky. I would study how this newborn learned the language of whales and I would learn with her.

To my untrained eyes everything looked normal. Corky was very attentive to her baby. She taught the infant how to breath, adjusting her own oxygen needs to those of her newborn. The baby learned correctly to open the blowhole on the top of her head when she heard the whoosh of Mom releasing a lungful. This meant the baby only breathed in when her blowhole was above the surface of the water so she wouldn't choke or drown.

Along with the marine park staff, I waited for the moment that the baby would nurse, absolutely crucial for her survival. But it never happened. The tank was small and circular. This meant Corky and her baby could never swim in a straight line. While the little one was learning how to steer she slammed repeatedly into the wall, opening and reopening a wound on the tip of her lower jaw. As Corky repeatedly rushed to get between the baby and the wall, protecting her, the little whale became fixated on Corky's white eye-patch and tried to nurse on the crease of Corky's mouth. It seemed to all of us who were watching that the baby had been born with an innate set of instructions to locate a white patch and nuzzle there. She had found the wrong white patch.

Corky was consumed with protecting her baby from breaking its delicate lower jaw against the concrete. There was no opportunity for her to glide and roll over and show the baby her mammaries, embedded in two slits near her tail. There was no attentive female relative to nudge the baby to the source of rich, creamy milk. Orky, the male, appeared to have no knowledge of what to do.

And so whales and humans watched together as the baby starved to death. Everyone said, *Corky is a new mother, this was to be expected, she will do better next time.* That sounded good to me.

Over the next two years, I spent twelve hours a day one month and twelve hours a night the next month watching and recording the whales. I divided their sounds into sixty-two different calls and gave each an alphanumeric code: A1, F2, C3, and so on. I labelled calls that were basically the same, but with different endings or beginnings, the same letter and a different number. I categorized the whales' behaviours—unison swimming, spy-hopping vertically out of the water, resting, grinding their teeth on the submerged platform (the same way other animals respond to the stress and boredom of captivity by inflicting pain on themselves). For every hour I spent recording—288 hours in total—I spent two or more coding everything the pair said and did. The most fascinating calls were the ones I dubbed the F series, which the whales used to initiate and sign off each "conversation."

I graphed all of this and saw that certain calls dominated specific activities. I assigned each sound a colour and transcribed whale conversations into ribbons of colours. Given that humans are predominantly a visual species, and orca an acoustic species, it seemed to me that it made sense to create visual representations of their calls to tap into the extraordinary pattern recognition capacity of the human brain.

It took time for me to slow down to the rhythm of whales, but once I did, I saw things that hinted at their rich culture. In the pale pink of a Los Angeles pre-dawn, Orky and Corky casually squirted mouthfuls of water against a spot on the tank wall as they swam past. When the sun rose over the bleachers that surrounded their tank, the spot they were dousing was always where the sunlight hit first. As the sun moved through the seasons, the whales adjusted for it. Once the bright streak of light appeared, the whales not only squirted water in the right place, they gently pressed their huge soft pink tongues against it.

During a rare lightning storm in the middle of the night, Orky raised his head above the water and drifted with his mouth open towards the brilliant flashes, making an eerie groaning noise. Every now and then during exhibition hours he picked a child to follow, swimming alongside them. The children caught on immediately and delighted in the attention of the whale. He even lifted his barn-door-sized pectoral fin inviting the child to touch him. I regret that I was too shy to approach the parents to ask for details about these children. Why did Orky pick them out of thousands? Were they special in some way or wearing colours the whale was attracted to, or was Orky simply in the mood to train a human every now and then and found the young ones easier to educate?

Corky loved sex, like many in the dolphin family, and she was a deft seductress. In the private hours near dawn she would swim past her sleeping mate, gently grazing him with her pectoral fin from his head to his tail. If he kept snoozing, she slipped under him and ran her fin down his throat, past his belly button, along his genital slit to his tail. If this failed to do the trick, she just rammed him so hard his dorsal fin shivered at the impact, and he would take off after her.

I loved the long hours with the whales, particularly when the park was closed and Orky and Corky did things no other human knew about. They were so exposed to me I could see and hear everything they did, and I did everything I could to absorb and learn from them. I was sure that if I watched long enough and analyzed enough data, I would crack the code and learn what they were saying. Sometimes they floated side-by-side at night and had long conversations, like a human couple talking in bed. Other times they practised behaviours in perfect unison, such as laying their tails on the training platform and raising their pectoral fins—something that dumbfounded the trainers when I showed them the pictures. I so wanted to believe that these whales were content, I missed the underlying message for years. And when at last it hit me, it hit me hard: everything was wrong with this situation.

Corky gave birth to one stillborn and six live babies and none survived. Some of her babies were taken from her while they were still alive in the hope that the park staff could force-feed them and eventually return them to their mother; others died in the tank with her.

I recorded the wispy newborn voices growing raspy and desperate as the babies slowly starved over a week to ten days. I recorded the call Corky made as her babies were guided into slings and winched out of the tank with large cranes. One moment the baby's frightened calls filled the tank, and the next that little voice was gone forever as the baby was removed from the water. Corky's response haunts me to this day. She suffered terribly. There was no other way to interpret her behaviour.

While she never hurt the people who entered the tank to guide her babies into the slings, she attacked the trainer platform with such force that the whole stadium shook. She flung her body again and again against the spot where humans stood to command her to perform jumps, wave her fin, give them a ride. Then, each time, she sank to the bottom and made the same call over and over for days, stopping only to grab a breath at the surface and then return to the bottom of the tank, where she lay on the drain. Orky swam alone on the surface. Every few hours he vocalized. I recognized his call as F1, *pituuu*. When Corky didn't answer, Orky fell silent and resumed his circling.

After several days, he would get an answer from her, in the dark of night. Even though I was hidden, the whales kept track of everything around them. They knew I was there. I don't know if they resented my presence, but I noticed that their most intimate interactions took place when there were no crowds, no trainers, no veterinarians. With only me as witness, Corky at last would respond *pituuu* and rise to the surface, where she moved close to Orky. Breathing in perfect unison, the two whales would call back and forth, *pituuu, pituuu*, as they circled the tank for hours. Later that day Corky would begin to eat again.

One morning, I arrived to find water pouring across the park, everything awash. Heart pounding, I ran to the whale tank, which rose three storeys high, with glass viewing windows encircling each level. I found Corky with a deep crease on the point of her face, her delicate rostrum, facing away from the window she had shattered. It was the window into the storage room where hundreds of stuffed toy baby orcas were stacked. I walked downstairs to where the stuffed whales were piled in drifts from the force of the water. The significance of Corky's action doubled me over in grief. I sat on the wet floor and cried. Then I picked up a chunk of the broken, inch-thick glass and put it into my pocket to ensure I never forgot perhaps the clearest message I have ever received from a whale. There were dozens of windows around her tank, but Corky broke the one that separated her from the tiny stuffed replicas of her babies. Did Corky recognize their resemblance to the babies that she had lost? Did she long for her babies so much that she could not bear to see the stack of little whales sitting behind that window? We had no way to answer that question, but the park staff moved them out of her sight.

The last time I undertook a science vigil over the birth of one of Corky's babies I had my own three-month-old child. My son fascinated Corky and she watched me holding him as I watched her. By that point I knew something of the depth of a mother's love. I knew that everything I had observed suggested Corky felt an emotion at least as intense as the love I felt for my baby.

Shortly after the birth and death of this baby orca, I left Corky to go study her family, which I had found in Canada. At the time, I was so dedicated to not being an activist that, even recognizing agony in the whales I had come to know and care for deeply, I abandoned them. I was hell-bent on my research and was concerned that becoming an advocate would derail my science. Trying to save animals is so hard that it drains your resources, consumes your time and burns the bridge to science's inner sanctum: the respect of your peers. Sleep is lost, you risk obsession. In my defence, I will say that it's easier to draw hard lines when you are young. The blindness of having little past makes things appear simple.

Afterwards I learned that when SeaWorld bought Marineland some years later, Orky was taken away from Corky. He was a rare adult male orca in captivity, and SeaWorld's owners wanted to use him as a breeder to make more whales for them to profit from. As with the babies, the water in the tank was lowered so the staff could manoeuvre a huge sling that was slipped underneath Orky. Corky knew exactly what was going down and tried to climb into the sling with him. Orky died shortly thereafter. We know from research on wild orca that the males rarely survive the loss of family. Corky is still circling tanks amusing people for profit, though now there are people working to persuade SeaWorld to allow them to bring Corky back to British Columbia for her retirement.

At this time in the late 1970s, Canadian researchers were just discovering that each pod or family of orca uses a unique set of calls—a dialect. The calls between closely related families are more similar than those between distantly related whales. Because I had spent hundreds of hours learning the dialect used by Orky and Corky, I hoped to find their family and continue my research on wild whales that used the calls I had become familiar with.

I knew Corky and Orky had been captured off the coast of British Columbia, and so I reached out to a Canadian scientist with Fisheries and Oceans Canada (DFO), Dr. Michael Bigg, who had been tasked by the Canadian government to find out how many whales could be

captured annually to satisfy the demand by oceanariums without risking their population. Whales were viewed as another fishery requiring management. In the process of counting whales, Mike had made
the remarkable discovery that every orca has a unique pattern in the
grey whorl behind its dorsal fin. This meant that instead of estimating
how many whales used the waters of British Columbia, he was able to
count each one. As his research continued, he realized the whales were
organized into highly stable families, or pods, and that these pods had
extended communities of whales that used a very similar dialect and all
exhibited predictable travel patterns. Mike collected all the photos he
could find that had been taken during whale captures; since the young
whales targeted by the marine parks stuck close to their mothers during
the terrifying roundups. In this way, Mike was able to figure out where
the captive whales came from and who their mothers were.

When I contacted him to ask if he knew what families Orky and
Corky were from, Mike said he had no usable information on Orky,
but that during her capture, Corky had shadowed a female who was
clearly her mother. That female was now known as A23, or Stripe, and
was a member of the A5 pod from the group of pods known as the
northern resident orca. Mike generously sent me photocopied pictures of Corky's entire family and said, "Go to Alert Bay in August and
you will find them." So in 1979 I did, and the summer after that I didn't
go back to California.

2.

Finding Home

IN OCTOBER 1984, I followed an orca matriarch known as Scimitar into the network of waterways between Kingcome and Knight Inlets, known as the Broughton Archipelago or Musgamagw Dzawada'enuxw territory. It was a cool rainy day. My husband, Robin Morton, a local documentary filmmaker whom I'd met during my second summer of research in British Columbia, steered our inflatable, while our three-year-old son played under the makeshift canopy over the bow and I kept my eyes on the whales. For now we lived on a boat which we chartered out to others to make a living, but we were also hunting for a place to use as a home base. We wanted whales, a few neighbour children for our son to grow up with and, with luck, mail service.

I watched the whales as they split into two groups at the western entrance to Fife Sound. Scimitar, the matriarch and a grandmother, took one group to the north side, as her daughter and grandchildren veered off to hug the southern shore. The sons went up the middle, leaving the more productive shorelines, where salmon tended to school, for the females and young ones.

The blows of the whales reached up to meet the low-lying clouds and the dark green water, the colour of an ocean rich with plankton, mirrored the steep green hillsides. I held the chart under the canopy, out of the rain, and inched my finger along our route; there were so many islands I was afraid we would be lost if I lost my place on the chart. There were water and whales everywhere and, while I was unaware of it at the time, a river of life flowing under the boat carrying my small family. Chum salmon, also known as dog salmon because they grow large curved canine teeth during spawning, were returning to the seven rivers of this archipelago, carrying the energy of the sunlight that hits the open waters of the Pacific Ocean. Sunlight allows plankton to bloom, small fish and shrimp-like organisms eat the plankton, salmon eat these little creatures and when their clock rings *time to spawn*, the fish head for the coast, carrying this energy up the rivers to their spawning grounds.

We followed the whales as they foraged the length of Fife Sound and then entered what looked like a gigantic amphitheatre, ringed by mountains that rose all around us. My chart showed this was the crossroads for the four major waterways—Kingcome Inlet, Tribune Channel, Cramer Pass and Fife Sound—that were the spokes of the wheel of this archipelago. The whales called to each other with the distinctive F1 call they used to synchronize their movements. The three strands of the family drew together and headed straight for Tribune Channel, which circles Gilford Island—the marine access used by migrating salmon to reach the Ahta, the Kakweiken and the other rivers of Knight Inlet. I would learn in later years that the A-clan pods of the northern resident orca, which Scimitar belonged to, often used Tribune Channel as a place to sleep. Orca keep swimming as they sleep and Tribune is apparently a good place to do this with its deep quiet waters.

It was turning to evening and Robin and I needed to find a campsite before dark, which wasn't easy. There weren't many spots flat enough to erect a tent that also had the right kind of bay to anchor the boat. As I scanned the shoreline through binoculars I saw a plume of smoke coming from what looked like a floating house. The chart said this place was called Echo Bay. We turned towards it and picked up speed.

A young woman was splitting kindling for her evening fire on the deck of the floating house. At our approach two little girls shyly moved to stand behind her. When we slowed and pulled alongside, my son emerged from his den in the bow and the older girl didn't waste a second before asking him, "Do you play cards?" I don't think my little boy knew what cards were, but he was more than ready to get out of the boat and bravely replied yes, and then the woman invited all of us into her warm house.

That was my introduction to Echo Bay, which became our home. I have since apologized in every Big House in the Indigenous communities in and around Echo Bay for not asking their permission to study the whales in their territories. I did not understand until decades later that these waters and the surrounding lands were governed by nations of people who had never given up this responsibility and right. Looking back I find it stunning how much I didn't know, couldn't see or ignored, when the whales first dropped me off here. The evidence of First Nations history and presence was everywhere. The dark green islets were ringed in white clamshell beaches, the debris from villages thousands of years old that depended on clams as a food source.

Over the years my perception of this piece of wilderness has changed dramatically. The risk of getting lost vanished as I explored the shoreline of every bay, channel and sound, and walked nearly every beach. Some days I hurried to a river mouth to arrive at the beginning of the flood tide, turned off my engine and drifted silently for hours as my boat rode the rising tide into the river. I became flotsam, just another floating log. Fish, bears, seals and birds paid no attention to me and so I could learn from them. I followed wolves as they trotted the rocky shorelines of small islands, entered the water without breaking their gait, swam to the next island and then the next. There were days where the whales' voices called out of the speakers in my boat as loons and wolves called in the air, a symphony of predators.

It was easy to move to Echo Bay. We simply tied our 1939, sixty-five-foot wood boat, *Blue Fjord* to the government dock. We left periodically to make money from charters, and at times Robin went alone to make industrial marine films. The community suited us well. It was off-grid, with no phones, no ferry or roads other than logging roads, but it did have a post office that received mail three times a week by seaplane. At the time, about two hundred people, including workers in the nearby logging camps, lived in Echo Bay. There were several families with young children and we became friends. At the head of the bay a one-room school taught grades one to seven, the children arriving in the morning by boat. The sound of our ship's generator annoyed the local Echo Bay Resort owners, Nancy and Bob Richter, so they invited us to tie up and plug into their power for free if we would keep an eye on the place when they went away. That was the kind of place it was.

Every day I headed out to look for whales, sometimes with Robin, sometimes just with our son. Before I learned their habits, it was very hard to find them. I asked every tugboat owner, fisherman, log salvager and crew boat that I encountered if they would call me if they saw whales. Some did, some didn't. People were suspicious about us initially. There were rumours that we were picking up drugs from offshore vessels. The RCMP vessel stopped us often, and I always asked if they had seen whales.

While the community was very small, it was extremely social. Potluck dinners happened weekly. The finest seafood—crab, clams, salmon, cod, halibut, prawns—was normal fare. Central to the community was the Proctor family, Billy and Yvonne, their daughters, and grandchildren: three generations born and raised in the archipelago. They hosted the big events like Easter and Halloween. They knew everything about how to survive in Echo Bay and were generous with their knowledge.

Near the end of our second year in the community, my husband drowned while filming whales. Whales make bubbles as a threat gesture. So, thinking he could get closer to them if he didn't use scuba gear, which produces bubbles, Robin used a rebreather. Rebreathers recirculate exhaled air, scrubbing out the carbon dioxide and adding oxygen. Any rebreather malfunction is dangerous because our bodies have no alarm system to warn us of rising carbon dioxide levels in our blood.

I was in the boat spotting whales for Robin with our son. Robin dove as Eve, a matriarch of the A5 pod, approached him. Then Eve surfaced, speeding away in the opposite direction. Something wasn't right. Robin had told me many times not to ruin his shot by bringing the boat in too soon. I waited for some long moments, then I tied myself to the boat, dove in and got him. But it was too late.

Enormous loss changes your chemistry. When the emotional floor collapsed under me, a whole other layer was revealed. This kind of sadness was never part of me before. I am sure I would have been lost without my son. Eventually I climbed out of the hole and rebuilt the floor. I likely appeared to be the same, but I was different; I guess I better understood the terms of my existence. Things can and do vanish forever.

After Robin died, I sold the *Blue Fjord* and my son and I moved into a small cabin behind the resort. I still had the Zodiac to get around in. I lived off the money from the sale of the boat, wrote articles about whales and sold whale photographs. It was helpful that the animal I was studying was so loved by people that I could help support us with whale stories and photos. In 1989, though, I needed to take a job as deckhand on Billy Proctor's thirty-eight-foot fish boat, *Twilight Rock*, to earn enough that we could stay in Echo Bay. The fishing season was only eight weeks long, so that left most of the year for whale research.

Billy's boat was a "combination boat," a troller and gillnetter. It was a little controversial for him to hire a female deckhand, especially one who had to bring along her eight-year-old. The first day out, I knew I'd made a big mistake. I felt terribly queasy and dizzy. I couldn't eat or drink coffee. I never got seasick on the waterways of the archipelago, but as the small boat started creaking in the open ocean swells, burping wafts of diesel fumes from the fuel tank vents, all I wanted to do was get back to land.

We headed for the Yankee Bank east of the Scott Islands off the northern tip of Vancouver Island. At night Billy didn't anchor—we just drifted out there. I found that terrifying at first, though the skipper seemed relaxed; his snores shook the boat. They were accompanied by giggles from my son, who had never heard anything quite like Captain Proctor snoring. That entire first ten-day trip I was plotting how to find Billy another deckhand as soon as we went back to port to deliver our catch. Then he handed me my first cheque. Without that money, I would have had to leave the archipelago. My son and I fished with him for three summers.

I bought an old floathouse, painted it periwinkle blue, and joined the rest of the community floating around Echo Bay. I learned to run a chainsaw to cut firewood, to preserve salmon for the winter months, to feed us on the abundant rock cod, clams and sea cucumbers. I rowed my son to the one-room school every morning, and my daughter, too, born fourteen years after he was.

I loved living on the sea. The house rested on two logs, called skids, and the skids sat on a flat bundle of about fifteen big logs tightly lashed together—the float. Otters spent time under the house, grunting and crunching on their catch; my cat caught fish and brought them into the kitchen. There was one frightening day when the wind hit from a direction I was not prepared for and the ropes running to the anchors on land began to break. The house swung away from shore, straining the remaining lines to the breaking point. I knew that in moments we would be drifting down the channel. I started up my boat, tied the bow securely to the float and put her into gear. As I accelerated, the house reversed direction and nudged up against its "stiff legs"—more logs that ran from the float up the beach to a big rock or tree in order to keep the house near the shore, but off the beach. I left the boat in gear, climbed back out onto the float and lashed my house securely to a stiff leg. Wilderness living with children was all about anticipating what might go wrong and dealing with it before disaster struck.

We travelled home from social events at night in my speedboat. Sometimes dolphins rode the bow wave, creating a light show in the brilliant phosphorescent zooplankton. As a single mom, I had no room for carelessness. I only ran my chainsaw when the weather was calm enough for me to be airlifted to town in a medevac if need be; I inspected the ropes and chains that held my house in place regularly. I loved heading out in the early mornings to look for whales, a child curled asleep with our dog in the bow as I sipped coffee. I often went on "wanders" where I had no destination. I let instinct pick my routes. When I found a lovely point, I often wondered what I would see if I sat there for ten years.

I never ventured deep into the forests. I still won't; I think people who do so are terrifically brave. I am so cautious on the water friends dubbed me "chicken of the sea." But there was no 911 to call—in fact there were no phones. In 1992, when I bought a twenty-two-foot cabin cruiser with a ninety-horsepower outboard, I considered naming her the *Light and Variable* as that is the weather I like to venture out in. In the end I decided to call my boat *Blackfish Sound*—since *blackfish* is the local name for orca, I studied their sounds and nearby Blackfish Sound is one of my favourite bodies of water because it supports so much life.

I lived all summer in my boat with the children. I got up around 4 a.m. with the sun and roamed the water until midday. By then my little crew was awake, fed and restless. They got to pick where we would tie up: nearby Telegraph Cove, Mitchell Bay or Hansen Island where there were other children. As they ran off with their friends, my boat became my office. I spent the afternoons entering the data I was collecting into databases, working on scientific papers and writing.

The whales were wonderful teachers, but I came away from every encounter with more questions than answers. I took some of those questions to Echo Bay's fishermen, who are also salmon predators, like the orca, but who speak a language I can more or less understand. They helped me understand why whales did certain things.

"Why do you think male orca travel up Kingcome Inlet in spring with six inches of dorsal fin out of the water?" I asked. They looked like sharks cruising along. I had no idea why they behaved this way and only in the spring in Kingcome Inlet.

"Oh that's an easy one," said Chris Bennett, the owner and operator of a fishing lodge he'd built out of salvaged logs. "They are hunting for spring salmon that travel just below the six-foot layer of glacier meltwater."

It seemed so obvious once I knew.

I learned that in the winter months, the archipelago served as the exclusive fish forage territory for the northern resident orca clan known as the A5s, Corky's family. A deeply scarred female, Eve (A9), was the matriarch. Instead of hunting the large migrating schools of salmon in the big channels where they hunted during the summer months, in winter Eve took her family to specific kelp forests among the tiny islets of the archipelago. There the whales put on sudden bursts of speed, carving up the surface in plumes of spray, clearly chasing something, but what? I asked Billy Proctor about this. He said, "I'll pick you up tomorrow at the start of the ebb tide and I'll show you."

It was always fun going out in Billy's speedboat. He liked to scare people, swerving suddenly, for instance, to take his boat through a tiny gap between two boulders. There were always chunks of fibreglass missing out of the bow of his boats where he'd clearly hit things, hard. Born and raised in the archipelago, Billy was in his fifties when I met him—a living encyclopedia. Part of the reason Robin and I settled in Echo Bay in the first place was his answer to our question, "Do you see whales in the winter?"

"Oh Christ, ya, they like to head up the inlets before a storm. We called 'em blackfish, though, didn't start saying orca until the hippies starting coming around here."

Billy loved a good story. "Was crossing to town a few years back, when I saw a float drifting free, no boat pulling it. I went over to see what it was and Christ if it wasn't a guy naked, hair to his ass, playing a flute. Said he was calling the orca."

I hadn't told Billy where I'd seen the whales hunting, but that morning he headed straight for one of the whales' most popular winter destinations. When we got there, Billy picked up a spool of thirty-pound test fishing line with an octopus-looking lure called a skunk hootchie attached to the end and threw the line out.

Soon he landed a beautiful, fat, bright coppery spring salmon. He called it a "winter spring," by which he meant a chinook or spring salmon he caught in the winter months. Since these fish were not preparing to spawn, their high-calorie diet made them exceptionally good eating, which I discovered later that night when suddenly I couldn't eat another bite because the flesh was so rich. This is why the orca hunted winter springs in the kelp forests: they were loaded with the fat the whales depended on to keep warm.

Everyone thought I would leave this place after Robin died, but when my father called to say that he was coming to take me and my son home with him to New England, I told him I *was* home. Robin Morton was like a hurricane who'd swept me off my feet, derailed my plans for graduate school and dropped me exactly where I belonged. I should have completed my degree, but if I had, I would have arrived in Echo Bay too late. I would have missed an essential lesson: I would not have seen, smelled and tasted the abundance of this place. It would have been impossible for me to fully imagine the enormity of life that thrived here and thus to understand what was being lost. Had I not experienced this first-hand, the importance of this ecosystem would not have got inside me and I would not have fought so hard to keep it alive.

3.

The Invisible Fork in the Road

LOSING ROBIN HAD hit me hard, but life in Echo Bay was such a perfect fit for me—the hard work of homesteading, the beauty of this wilderness—that I was able to regain my balance and return to studying the mysteries of whale communication. By 1989, my research was breaking new ground every time I encountered whales, particularly in the winter months, a season in which scientists had not observed what orca on the BC coast were up to.

Most whale research took place in the summer for obvious reasons: the weather is calmer; young scientists are on summer break from university; and many orca families congregated in areas like Johnstone Strait, near the Broughton Archipelago, to feed on migrating salmon. I was learning that the mammal-eating orca pods, the Biggs orca, originally called transients, were not transient at all; they were highly present on the coast in the winter months. The fish-eating orca pods—the so-called resident whales that I was studying—were also occasionally present in the winter, but they broke down into their smallest divisible units, Mom and the kids, probably in response to the reduced inshore salmon presence compared with the summer's mass migrations.

In summertime, Johnstone Strait became a superhighway for salmon along northeastern Vancouver Island, hosting millions of salmon that pulsed through in huge waves, moving from open ocean feeding grounds to their spawning rivers—the finest food an orca could wish for. Since the eating was easy, the orca clans could gather in numbers, maintaining their relationships and their culture. Yes, *culture* is a word that applies to some animal societies. For orca, like many of us, what they eat influences everything from how often they vocalize, to where they travel and how big their groups can be.

The sounds I recorded from the wild members of the A5 pod in the deep inlets of the Broughton Archipelago were technically the same as those made by Orky and Corky in captivity, but the wild orcas' calls echo off the submerged canyons to define the space the way the music from an organ fills a cathedral. They interacted with their echoes to the point that I could not guess how many whales were vocalizing.

As I recorded the A5s—Corky's pod—I realized that, although she had been taken as a youngster and had been in captivity for over ten years before I dropped my hydrophone in her tank, she had preserved her dialect perfectly. The call that Corky and Orky began their conversations with, F1, *piiittttuuuu*, was used similarly by the wild whales. It was also prominent when whales arrived at an intersection where a channel forked into two or more waterways. I noticed that as the whales approached and passed me, this call sounded different. As they came towards me I heard a staccato *piii ttttuuuu*, but as they were going away from me, just a *ttttuuuu*. Did the whales hear it the same way? If so, the call had a directional component to it. The listener would be able to tell if the caller was coming or going.

When a family swimming down either side of Fife Sound cruised out into the expanse of the amphitheatre-shaped centre of the Broughton, they repeated *pituuu* back and forth, drawing together as they called. The whales are likely able to decipher the travel trajectory of the calling whale down to a matter of degrees.

Orca are precise, they are careful, they adore their families, and they are highly suspicious of any individual that doesn't speak their language. For example, the fish-eating resident orca use entirely different calls than the mammal-eating Biggs orca, and they do not associate with each other. Similarly the fish-eating orca off southern Vancouver Island, known as the southern resident orca, use a different dialect than the northern whales, and they do not associate.

I placed a stationary hydrophone on an island at the east end of Fife Sound, where I knew the whales often vocalized, and broadcast it into my house via a VHF (very high frequency) marine radio signal. When I heard them calling, I was in my boat within minutes. My children became expert at making instantaneous play dates over the radio, knowing which friend to call depending on the direction their mother was headed in. If that failed, my daughter, who loved to read, grabbed a book and my son his Legos. One time I overheard my son say that he was raised in a Zodiac. I felt bad. He and my daughter were both troopers. Studying whales is a very slow process that requires limitless time among them.

In the spring of 1989, Billy Proctor came to me, for once, with a request. I am sure I leaned towards him, with an earnest expression, ready to do my best, so proud he was asking me for something instead of the other way around. He got right to the point. He wanted me to write to the Department of Fisheries and Oceans to tell the federal government that they were putting the new fish farms in all the wrong places.

The year before, this new industry of salmon farming had appeared in the Broughton Archipelago. Each farm was a series of floating aluminum walkways arranged in a series of rectangles with a net bag hanging down from each one into the water; they were anchored to the sea floor, with ropes running to the shoreline as well. Floating feedsheds, floats with bins to hold the dead fish, called mort floats, and living quarters for the workers were also attached to the farms.

Those first farms were run by IBEC, a company owned by the Rockefeller family that had mostly been raising pigs in the US. The province's salmon enhancement hatcheries sold chinook salmon eggs to these commercial operators at bargain basement prices. While the enhancement hatcheries, funded by the federal government, released their young fish into the wild, the salmon farms were now raising fish to harvest size and selling them to markets. Each farm held approximately 250,000 chinook salmon.

Echo Bay had so few people our public school was constantly threatened with closure. Like other parents in the neighbourhood, my first reaction to the new farms was to hope they would bring families with children to the area and help keep our school open. School enrolment was so low that if a single family left, the school might close, and we all knew that the school was the heart of the community. So I liked the farms but knew I had to hear Billy out. He was one of my most respected teachers.

I picked up my pen and took notes as he started listing the places where fish farms shouldn't be allowed yet were going in. Greenway Sound, for instance, which was a spring salmon nursery. Billy had fought to get that area closed to commercial fishing in 1968. He took a lot of heat for this stand from the other fishermen, but he knew the young salmon needed to be allowed to mature undisturbed. Because he ran the local enhancement hatchery, working to rebuild wild coho salmon numbers in the archipelago, Billy also knew that crowding fish in pens leads to disease; before anyone else articulated this, he knew the farms would be a threat to our ecosystem.

He ticked off more places. Sargeaunt Pass was where spring salmon rested on their way up Knight Inlet. Sir Edmund Bay and the Burdwood Islands were two of the best prawn fishing spots on the coast; the waste from the farms would smother these fishing grounds. Humphrey Rock was where millions of adult pink salmon waited for rains to raise river levels so they could enter the Ahta, Glendale and Kakweiken Rivers to spawn. Putting a farm in these places was too risky to the wild salmon.

Fish farmers were also shooting seals, sea lions and otters that were attracted to the salmon in their pens. Billy said the young workers on the farms didn't know how to handle a gun or that bullets can skip on the water for a long way; he was scared of getting shot by a stray bullet as he passed in his open speedboat. I nodded. I had already experienced guns going off on both sides of me while I was drifting in my boat for long periods of time recording whales.

"Those kids on the farms are bored," he said. "They have no idea what they are doing out here. And they gotta stop stringing ropes every-where trying to keep them farms from blowing away. I nearly lost my goddamn head coming around the corner from Smith Rock. There was a black rope right at eye level and I ducked just in time."

Most worrisome, Billy said, was that the resident overwintering chi-nook salmon, which were so important to the orca that I was studying, had just disappeared.

That night I organized Billy's concerns into categories—places where wild species needed to be protected, firearm safety concerns, hazards to navigation—and on the only word processor in town, typed my first letter to DFO on the need to reduce the impact of salmon farms on this area. I listed Billy's concerns, leaving out his anger over the way this new industry had just waltzed in, ignored everyone already making a living here, grabbed the best fishing grounds and behaved so carelessly they put lives at risk. Looking back, maybe that was a mistake. Anger might have succeeded where logic and reason failed.

I tucked the printed pages into an envelope, threw it on the dash of my boat and took it to the post office. This was the fork in my road.

The answer came a few weeks later.

"Dear Ms. Morton, thank you for your letter, the health of wild salmon is DFO's highest priority, salmon farming in British Columbia is heavily regulated . . ."

Not one of Billy's concerns had been addressed. I wrote a second letter.

They wrote back: "Dear Ms. Morton, there is no evidence . . ."

This was the theme. I wrote ten thousand pages of letters. I mean that literally: I kept track by drawing a line with a thick black marker above my printer for every package of five hundred sheets of paper I used.

What made this so frustrating was that I was sending DFO evidence from on-the-ground observers that the new industry that they were issuing permits to was causing growing problems that warranted attention. My community was an early-warning indicator of the serious risk and conflict ahead.

I had assumed that everyone who worked in the Department was like the whale scientist, Dr. Michael Bigg, who had generously sent me directions to Corky's family. I still called him frequently to share and discuss the whale behaviours I was observing. However, Mike's role in the Department was whale research, not fish. He couldn't help me reach anyone in DFO who would give serious consideration to the issues my community was raising and come out and evaluate the situation.

I kept writing as the evidence of impact grew. When the industry switched from raising chinook salmon, which were dying of disease before reaching harvest size, to Atlantic salmon, people found escaped Atlantic salmon in local rivers. Coho salmon in the local enhancement hatchery erupted with boils that became open sores and killed them; no one had seen this before. The farms got bigger and one day Billy was spraying down his boat with seawater when his lips started to burn— evidence of Echo Bay's first red tide, the bloom of an organism called *Heterosigma*, which is a classic indicator of pollution.

I did not have proof that all these things were caused by the farms, but my letters should have triggered a government response. For a time, I was convinced that if I just lined up my words in the right order, someone at DFO or from the province would realize they should come out to the Broughton and investigate. I copied each of my letters to fishermen, environmentalists, officials in different levels of government and the foreign scientists I'd found who were studying the impact of salmon farms. Managing the farms was a responsibility of the provincial government, but the impact they were having was on wild fish, which are a federal responsibility. The province told me my concerns should be sent to the federal government, and the federal government told me that the province was responsible for the farms so I should contact the province.

What I didn't realize at the time was that salmon farming in Canada existed in a legal grey zone because no one in this country is allowed to own fish that are in the ocean. These farms were simply net pens in the ocean, and it followed that the salmon in them were in the ocean. In addition the law says no one is allowed to fence off parts of the ocean for their private use. Marine laws going back to the Magna Carta in 1215 protect the right of vessels to travel over *all* marine waters—no fences allowed. Therefore, the laws of Canada do not recognize that a piece of the ocean in a pen belongs to a company. Even though our governments have ignored the fact that fish farms are privatizing ocean spaces, salmon farming is an unlawful private fishery. The federal government realized that it had no clear right to issue licences to the industry, so it gave this fishery to the provinces to regulate as "farms." But they aren't actually farms. Twenty years later I went to court and untangled some of this; the court defined the industry as a "fishery" and gave regulation of the industry back to the federal government. But when I was writing these letters, trying to find someone to take responsibility for this circular mess, it was like watching a tennis match. The province sent my concerns to the feds and the feds lobbed them back to the province. I kept writing to both the federal and provincial governments, but out of ignorance at the time I omitted the most important governments of all, the local First Nations governments.

All of this correspondence was before email. For each letter, I started up the generator in the shed beside my floathouse and printed one page at a time, making ten copies of letters that often stretched to ten pages. The postmistress of Echo Bay, who processed armfuls of my mail month after month, said the volume was a factor in keeping the post office.

I am more than a little irritated with myself for being so slow to realize I was going about it all wrong. Yes, I needed to write the letters to lay out all the evidence and examples clearly, but I didn't need to keep pushing on the most buttressed door in the fortress. That door was never going to open. It didn't even have hinges. The Department of Fisheries and Oceans was never going to admit there were problems.

They were already invested in covering up the fact that the laws of the land did not permit this activity.

Undaunted by their strategy, which seemed designed to wear me down, I eventually thought I figured out their lack of action. DFO didn't want anecdotal evidence, they wanted published scientific evidence. So that is what I set out to give them: published science on the harms the industry was causing.

One of the complexities of being a biologist today is that we don't know how much time an ecosystem under siege has left before it collapses. I did not imagine that it was actually possible for the abundance of the Broughton salmon and herring to drain away. However, I remembered walking on the shores of Saanich Inlet on the southern tip of Vancouver Island back in 1981 with Robin and one of his friends, who said, "We used to catch spring salmon here, but no one even tries anymore. There are none." This was shocking to me—the idea that the powerfully abundant salmon could disappear. I remember wondering if anyone knew why and if they'd tried to stop that disappearance. I thought about what this would be like if it happened in the Broughton; every animal and human would suffer. Salmon were so abundant and both the out-migration of the young fish headed to sea and the in-migration of the adults returning to spawn were so consistent that over a hundred species, including humans, could depend on them. Out-migrating juvenile salmon fed nesting marine birds and in-migrating adults fed bears preparing for hibernation, allowed orca to gather in numbers and maintain their culture, fed eagles struggling to nuture their growing chicks and provided people with food that could be stored over the winter.

It was the whales who had led me to Echo Bay in the first place that bumped me up to the next level of response.

In 1993, I was following a subgroup of the A4s, close relatives of Corky's family, west out of Tribune Channel. Mike Bigg told me he thought Corky's mate, Orky, might have been part of the A4s. When Orky was taken as a five-year-old, every whale in his pod either died or was also sold except one, an adult male. That male was never seen again. Everyone who studies wild orca knows that losing his whole family at once is more than enough to kill an adult male orca, who often dies shortly after his mother dies. Orky also suffered this fate when he lost Corky. Family bonds between orca appear to be a life or death matter, even stronger than such bonds in humans.

That day, the A4s came west out of Tribune Channel into the centre of the archipelago, where the four major waterways converge at the Burdwood Islands. I manoeuvred my boat ahead of the whales and dropped the hydrophone overboard. A loud staccato chirping screeched out of the headsets. I clicked off the recorder, thinking it was malfunctioning, but the noise was so loud I could still hear it through the hull of my boat. I pressed record again and turned my attention to the whales. They were all "spy-hopping," cruising along with their heads at a forty-five-degree angle out of the water. This was a new behaviour. What were they doing? What were they looking at? The sound level needles on my recorder were slamming past the red zone, and I turned the input levels down to the lowest setting.

The Burdwood Islands were a local jewel where we held school campouts and picnics and our children's birthday parties. We skinny-dipped on the beautiful beaches. The province had promised to keep these islands salmon farm free, but when salmon in a nearby Simoom Sound farm started dying from one of the toxic algae blooms in the 1990s, the farm was towed into the Burdwoods, where it stayed.

I looked back at the whales, and realized they were swimming with their ears out of the water. Whale ears are entirely internal, with only a little dimple to mark their place behind the whale's eye. They proceeded on the route they had followed for thousands of years, right past the Burdwood fish farm, owned at the time by the Weston family who were grocery magnates. That would be the last time I saw the A4s in the Broughton Archipelago. This refuge, rich with food and quiet sleeping channels, was now an industrial zone. When they turned the corner into Fife Sound, they finally dove and silently abandoned the place.

A quarter of a century has passed since this whale family—two sisters and their kids—have been seen in the Broughton Archipelago. The sound that drove them away was made by an Airmar acoustic harassment device, or AHD, which broadcasts its signal at 198 decibels, the volume of a jet engine at takeoff. AHDs were designed to repel harbour seals, which had learned how to catch and eat farm salmon through the nets. Wily seals swam up to the nets and scared the Atlantic salmon into diving to the bottom of their pens, where the seals grabbed hold of the fish and sucked their soft flesh right through the mesh. I had raised two seal pups and they seemed to me as smart as any dog. They figure things out, especially if there is a food reward to be had.

The noisemakers were the fish farmers' solution to deal with these natural salmon predators. As it turned out, the seals appeared willing to accept hearing damage in exchange for easy access to an exceptionally high-calorie fish. Over the next few years all of us locals nearly hit seals, likely deafened by the AHDs, with our speedboats when they popped up in front of us. They appeared to have no idea that we were coming at them until we were almost on top of them, at which point they exploded into frantic splashing, trying to dive below the boats as we tried to veer away from them. This was not normal seal behaviour.

The only species that turned out to be repelled by the AHDs were the resident orca and the porpoises. Exposing their ears to the seal-scarers would be like us walking into a hallway where needles were zinging towards our eyes. One by one the resident fish-eating orca families left the area and never came back. The Biggs orca, which eat marine mammals, came up with a different solution. They rerouted themselves so as to keep an island or headland between their ears and the farms that were broadcasting the noise. Since this shift meant more of them came directly past my floathouse in Cramer Pass, it was easy for me to notice the change. Putting salmon farms in prime wild salmon habitat turned out to be as much a threat to the whales as to the salmon.

I wrote another letter. "Dear Minister of Fisheries, I have been researching killer whales in the Broughton Archipelago for five years and would like to report that the acoustic harassment devices on the farms appear to displace the resident orca."

And I received the usual reply. "Dear Ms. Morton, There is no evidence . . ."

This time, the impact I was witnessing was squarely in my wheelhouse. I had years of data on A-clan presence before seal-scarers were installed and I collected seven years of evidence after the seal-scarers began blaring. Gathering and analyzing my results, I published "Displacement of *Orcinus orca* (L.) by high amplitude sound in British Columbia, Canada," in the *ICES Journal of Marine Mammal Science* in 2002, in which I compared whale presence before and after the seal-scarers. I also reported on where the whales had gone. I collaborated with Helena Symonds from OrcaLab, a remarkable facility located in Blackney Pass, between Blackfish Sound and Johnstone Strait, that tracked the whales over a large area through a series of remote hydrophones. Helena had become highly skilled at identifying clans, pods and subgroups simply by hearing their calls. From her data, we knew the whales hadn't died, but had been displaced from the Broughton Archipelago, twelve-hundred square kilometres of important habitat.

Displacing whales is against the law in Canada.

I sent the paper to DFO, which ran an experiment to test my conclusions. The Department anchored an empty fish farm in nearby Retreat Passage, prime harbour porpoise habitat. Then they turned a seal-scarer on. The porpoise left. When they turned it off, the porpoise came back. But the noisemakers had a dinner-bell effect on seals. When seals heard the devices they swam to the farm, even though there were no fish in it; they had learned to associate the noise with the fat fish they had developed a taste for. Pods of orca had been displaced by a piece of equipment that didn't even work. DFO did nothing in reaction to our paper or the experiment that proved our results. They did not enforce the Fisheries Act and charge the companies with breaking the law.

The fish farmers themselves abandoned the devices when they realized they were actually attracting seals.

Orca have tolerated so much from us: the dramatic rise in boat noise, gunshot wounds, depletion of their food resource, displacement from all the bays that cities and towns took over, the rise of the whale-watching industry. But they could not tolerate the seal-scarers. Whenever people say that the whales or salmon will persist despite our unneighbourly ways, I reply that these creatures do have a breaking point. Unless we think carefully about what these animals need to survive and watch them closely, we won't know where that point is until we've exceeded it.

4.

This Was No "Mistake"

I HAD A lot of respect for Billy and the other fishermen in the area, who were growing increasingly angry about the salmon farms. But for the longest time I wanted to believe that they just didn't like salmon farms because they were new or because the farm salmon would compete for their market. Until salmon farms came along, fresh salmon was only for sale during the fishing season and came only from fishermen. But now that the farms were affecting something I knew about, the whales, they got my attention and I started to study the impact of salmon farms in earnest.

Salmon farms are a type of feedlot: they raise as many animals as possible, as fast as possible, in as small a space as possible, on an unnatural diet. Feedlots break all the natural laws that keep wild populations healthy, largely because they breed out genetic diversity, they crowd creatures together and they prevent predators from removing the sick and dying. As a result, sick animals linger in feedlots, dying slowly and shedding disease particles as they go, infecting those around them. This not only causes an exponential increase in disease organisms, it turns the pathogen world upside down, encouraging viruses to become more lethal. In the wild, virulent pathogens are snuffed out because they kill their hosts, but in feedlots the hosts just keep coming and so virulence escalates unfettered. All other feedlots, except salmon farms, are sealed off from the natural environment. Chicken feedlot operators prevent wild birds from landing and taking off from their feedlots, because the threat of spreading avian flu is too great. Yet the province of British Columbia and Canada, as a whole, allow salmon farms to release streams of waste and pathogens into the pristine habitat of the once-abundant wild salmon.

When wild salmon enter the rivers to spawn, bears, eagles, wolves and other predators catch them and carry them into the forest to feed on. As these fish remains decompose, nutrients are released into the soil. Nitrogen-15 is found almost exclusively in the ocean and so when it is detected in trees along the rivers where salmon spawn, we know it came from salmon. Researchers studying BC forests report that the larger the salmon run, the more trees grow. They measure this by taking a tiny core sample from the tree so they can compare the width of the tree's growth rings for each year. Nitrogen-15 is carried far beyond the river valleys, into alpine meadows, by eagles and other birds. The growth of trees is linked to the health of this planet. The more trees grow, the more they absorb carbon dioxide, drawing down the deadly level of this greenhouse gas that is putting our entire civilization at risk. Scientists struggle to describe the impact of climate collapse as human activity pushes our planet past one life-threatening goalpost after another at rates faster than anyone had thought possible. Despite this, governments like the ones I am dealing with remain intent on allowing the natural mechanisms we need to survive to be broken, such as the harm being done to the wild salmon migrations that feed the forests that help reduce greenhouse gases and stabilize our climate.

With no human intervention, the BC coast is capable of producing hundreds of millions of wild salmon, but to achieve this, fish have to keep moving. If they pause in one place, they overload their surroundings and nature sends in the parasites, viruses and bacteria to restore balance, thinning the crowd to viable levels. This is nature's response to salmon farms too. A million salmon from the Atlantic Ocean going around in circles in places only wild Pacific salmon know how to use properly is an abomination that nature cannot tolerate. And so she begins her relent-less attempt to restore the equilibrium that life depends on, sending in the predators and an army of pathogens.

The tragedy when it comes to feedlots is that nature can't get at the source of the problem. As the pathogens escalate in number and viru-lence, killing fish on both sides of the nets, only the wild fish die off. There is no consequence to the farms, as the pens will be refilled again and again.

Life is easy in the pens; disease can persist in the farms at a steady, unnatural background level because salmon's natural predators can't get in and remove the slow, weak, infectious individuals, halting the spread of disease. The farmers see disease as normal, the cost of doing business. I see their mort floats sink lower in the water as the dead stored there wait for the tug and barges to carry them away. A loss rate of 1 percent on a farm sounds low, but when there are a million fish in the farm, that's ten thousand fish lost. In nature ten thousand fish dying of a contagion in a single bay is an epidemic. In a salmon farm it is business as usual.

Making the situation worse, the presence of fish crowded in a farm activates natural corrective measures, like sea lice and bacterial outbreaks, but these feedback loops only decrease the wild popula-tions exposed to the farms. The farmers argue that most of their fish live until they are harvested, suggesting there is no disease problem, but this doesn't tell us anything about the shedding rate of pathogens from "acceptable" levels of farm diseases, such as mouth rot, and how this is affecting wild fish. Unlike wild salmon, farm salmon can remain alive even when they are too weak to swim, because no predators can reach them. Predators such as eagles hunt wild fish from the sky, and whales, other fish and sea lions hunt them from the water, feasting on slow swimmers.

With predators out of the picture, every pathogen in the farm is amplified and then broadcast into the ocean at high, unnatural levels. Predation cannot turn off the fire hose of contagions washing out of the farms. The surface of the water around the farms in the archipelago becomes greasy with the oily feed and rotting fish. The sea floor blanches monochrome grey with waste, unable to decompose for lack of oxygen. And the tides carry billions of infectious viral and bacterial particles.

The industry's mother country, Norway, knew that British Columbia's wild salmon would be put at risk by the introduction of this industry. In 1991, Jon Lilletun, from the Norwegian parliamentary committee on environment, travelled to Canada and testified in front of the Canadian Senate, saying, "We are very strict [in Norway] about the quality and the environment questions. Therefore, some of the fish farmers went to Canada. They said we want bigger fish farms; we can do as we like. That is a very hot subject, I think." Canada was warned.

The BC and Canadian governments did not admit the obvious and they still don't. Setting up enormous fish feedlots in the pristine wilderness was like pouring diesel fuel into an engine that can only burn gasoline. They were breaking the coast.

In 1998, a scientist at the University of Oslo named Dr. T.A. Bakke called salmon farms "pathogen culture facilities" in a scientific paper published in the *Canadian Journal of Fisheries and Aquatic Sciences*. It doesn't get more blunt than that. He went out of his way to place his article in a Canadian government-run scientific journal, and still Canada didn't hear the message that you can't have both wild salmon and farmed salmon in net pens on one coast. No one has managed this anywhere in the world. The decision to swing the door wide open to salmon farms was a decision to slam the door on wild fish.

The more I read about the industry, the more I realized that the people in charge of farms in the provincial ministry of agriculture in the late 1980s and early 1990s knew about this risk and they were more than willing to take it. They are the architects of the chaos and damage that ensued.

Down at sea level out in my boat, trying to find whales that were no longer there, I didn't understand the scope of what was happening, but Geoff Meggs, editor of the BC Fisherman's Union paper, *The Fisherman*, did. Meggs was there when it all began on April 19, 1984, six months before I first came to the Broughton Archipelago, when the Science Council of Canada unveiled its "industrial aquaculture development plan." The council's mandate was to ensure that Canada kept up technologically with the rest of the world. While this aim seemed well-meaning, Meggs prophetically wrote, "The days of common property fishing are over." Implementing the fish farm plan would affect thousands of people throughout rural British Columbia, on the coast and up the rivers, as well as whales, bears and even the forests, which eventually would be starved of the enormous energy wild salmon carry upstream.

A major hurdle for the fledgling industry were the Canadian laws that prohibited ownership of a fish in the ocean, private fisheries and privatization of ocean spaces. As I've mentioned, since salmon farming presumes to do all of these, the federal government handed management of the industry to the provinces on both the east and west coasts. No one involved identified this industry as a private fishery; these were farms, and the provinces knew what to do with farms. This was why my requests to government to reduce the impact of these farms drifted in circles, never landing fully on anyone's desk. The provinces oversaw the farms, even though the farms were in the oceans, a federal jurisdiction.

Meggs reported that the public hatcheries built to benefit wild salmon runs were being pressured into providing eggs to the salmon farming industry. When I visited one of the salmon farms owned by IBEC in Blunden Pass, near my floathouse, in the late 1980s, it was full of chinook salmon that were an abnormal shade: white. No one would say why they were that colour or where they came from. The industry was insulated by such secrets.

After a few unsuccessful years, IBEC abandoned the Broughton because their fish kept dying. In the early 1990s a succession of Norwegian salmon farming companies moved in: Stolt, Scanmar, Marine Harvest (which became Mowi), Cermaq, Grieg. The Norwegians were not interested in farming Pacific salmon, because they were too finicky. Back in Norway, they had bred Atlantic salmon that could survive crowding and grew fast in pens. They planned to stock their new farms with Atlantic salmon.

To all appearances, the transition to Atlantic salmon went smoothly. My neighbours and I were unaware of it until after the fact, but in *The Fisherman* Meggs chronicled the internal government brawl over the introduction of millions of Atlantic salmon eggs into Pacific waters.

In 1990, the highest-ranking DFO official on the west coast of Canada, the regional director general Pat Chamut, wrote to his counterpart in the Pacific Rim and Trade Policy Division of DFO. He pointed out that continued large-scale introduction of Atlantic salmon to British Columbia would eventually result in the introduction of exotic disease agents that could damage wild salmon and "devastate" the economy of those who depended on wild salmon. Chamut went on to say, "Unlike terrestrial animals, where complete containment and isolation is possible, fish are difficult to contain as well as isolate. Once an infectious agent becomes established in a wild population of fish, it is impossible to eradicate."

On the other end of the spectrum, Dr. Dorothee Keiser at the DFO Pacific Biological Station, who sat on the Department's Fish Transplant Committee, asked at the November 6, 1985, meeting of that committee if she could grant salmon farmers an exemption from DFO oversight when they move fish from hatcheries where the fish are born and spend a year, into the marine farms where they would finish growing. This would mean farm salmon would not be screened by government before they were transferred into ocean pens and into contact with wild salmon.

Meggs wrote in *The Fisherman* on April 18, 1986: "The Rockefeller-owned IBEC farm operation near Port McNeill has already imported eggs from a Scottish hatchery which provided eggs now blamed for a disastrous bacterial furunculosis outbreak in Norway." Did the DFO Fish Transplant Committee screen those fish before they went out to the IBEC farms in the Broughton?

The more I read, the more I realized how right Billy Proctor was when he had asked that DFO exempt the chinook salmon nursery area in Greenway Sound from salmon farming. When the Department replied that there was "no evidence" to support his concerns, they already had the evidence; and it sounded like at least some of them were as worried as Billy. In 1991, a DFO veterinarian, Gary Hoskins, wrote a memo confirming that "the risks of introducing an infectious agent with Atlantic salmon eggs is high, as well as real."

Norway, in the North Atlantic, halted the importation of Pacific salmon into their country in the early 1990s, fearful of introducing disease, but Canadian government departments were fighting among themselves to open the door to Atlantic salmon in British Columbia. Why was the Canadian government ignoring the concerns of its own Department of Fisheries and Oceans staff?

It turns out there was something to consider that they thought was bigger than the health of Canada's wild salmon populations and the economic welfare of people who depended on them: international trade. In a report to their state senator, Slade Gorton, Atlantic salmon-egg producers from Washington state complained "that there would be great market potential for their Atlantic salmon eggs in British Columbia if existing import restrictions were removed." Pat Chamut from Fisheries and Oceans Canada responded, "[D]espite allegations that restrictions were introduced to limit trade for the benefit of BC producers, our foremost and only concern was to protect our wild and cultured stocks from exotic disease." Chamut lost this fight and Norwegian companies farming BC waters imported 30 million Atlantic salmon eggs. "At stake are staggering profits for those who wind up in control," wrote Meggs.

In the midst of this bedlam, the Science Council of Canada quietly ran up a warning flag. Aboriginal Title to fish could thwart the "full development" of the salmon farming industry in British Columbia. The Council urged the same government that was blithely tossing the

THIS WAS NO "MISTAKE"   41

gravest of biological warnings out the window to "consult with Indian people." The government did not.

Somewhere in Norway, a map of British Columbia lay on a table. Thousands of kilometres of pristine, salmon-rich waterways lay exposed and vulnerable. A circle was drawn around the Broughton Archipelago: Musgamagw territory, wintering feeding grounds for the orca matriarch, Eve, and her family, birthplace of millions of wild salmon, my home. Phone calls were made. The invasion began.

5.

The Clearances

IN THE SUMMER of 1989, provincial officials showed up in Echo Bay in a large white speedboat, saying they were conducting the Coastal Resource Interest Study, or CRIS. They asked us all to come to a meeting in Alert Bay, the town where Mike Bigg had first sent me in search of Corky's family, to tell them where the best fishing grounds were. The officials said that after we identified these areas, they would be designated red zones for which no fish farm application would be accepted. This was great, I thought, they heard our concerns. My letters had had some affect. I rallied my community to go to the meeting, even though fishermen are not at all keen to put their best fishing spots on a map.

Much of the community piled into Billy Proctor's thirty-eight-foot *Twilight Rock* and headed for the evening meeting, a three-hour trip each way, most of it in the dark. The archipelago screamed a gale at us. The night was black and hostile. It was as if she was saying *Don't do this!* Billy navigated by instruments; all we could see was the ocean hitting the windows of the wheelhouse. When I think back, I hate that I went to the meeting myself, and even more that I encouraged others to go.

A few months later we got the resulting map in the mail, showing the archipelago coloured red, yellow and green, indicating where fish farms could go. Many of the areas that my neighbours had asked to be protected were now red zones where the province stated no fin-fish applications would be accepted. But as the fish farms kept arriving, I noticed more were appearing in the red zones than in the green or yellow zones. The province was permitting farm tenures in the locations my community had said should be off limits so as to protect wild salmon. More to the point, they were putting them where their own map indicated they wouldn't allow them. If they had wanted to use us to identify the places on this coast where fish survive best, why bother with the whole charade of creating red zones? I was shocked. I wrote to the government asking why most of the fish farms were being given tenures in the red zones.

First the bureaucrats responded that before they issued those permits, they had talked to the local groups that had provided the input and that these groups had changed their minds about the need to protect the red zones. I pointed out that my Raincoast Research Society, which I had formed to study whales, was listed as one of those groups on the back of their map and I certainly had not been consulted again or changed my mind. Neither had anyone else on the list; I'd asked them.

Then the bureaucrats said that the red zones had been painted with a "broad brush" and the farms in question were too small to make a difference. I pointed out that the red zone at Sargeaunt Pass, where spring salmon coming and going to Knight Inlet rested, was so small that the fish farm not only completely filled it but extended beyond it on the map.

Then I got the truth. The bureaucrats revealed that any site that had been applied for prior to the completion of the study was grandfathered in; the industry had anticipated these restrictions and had applied for every bay that was even remotely suitable.

Echo Bay wasn't the only community to ask government to be more careful about where they were situating salmon farms. The community of Sechelt, near Vancouver, was even more upset than we were. The response from government to our objections was always that the industry was "good for small coastal communities." My community was as small as it gets, but other than hoping for a few more children in our school, we had no need to be saved by salmon farms. Echo Bay was a thriving, diverse place. As well, the First Nations communities of the region had made it clear from the start they did not want salmon farms.

None of this mattered: as the government kept repeating, the industry was "here to stay."

At the end of my first season of fishing with Billy, I'd decided to make my floathouse legal, so I went to the provincial capital, Victoria, to get a foreshore tenure, a contract giving me the legal right to tie my house to the shore in return for paying the province an annual fee. My neighbours had told me not to bother. Most of them didn't have tenures, and it wasn't like the place was crowded. However, not every bay is a good place to tie up a floathouse; most are not. You need a stream for drinking water, good protection from the wind and preferably some periods of sun each day; I also didn't want to be too far from the school. With bays being snapped up by salmon farmers, I didn't want to lose my tie-up in a protected, sunny little bay with good water.

I remember clearly how this encounter went. The man behind the desk pleasantly informed me that the province had decided to no longer tenure residents' floathouses in the archipelago, but to only allow tenures for log storage, the floating fishing and wilderness lodges that were popular with tourists, and aquaculture.

I leaned towards him. "You realize my whole town lives in floathouses."

He nodded, still cheerful. "Yes."

"We have a post office and a school—we are a community."

"Yes," he agreed.

I asked him how it was possible that the government was not going to allow people to live in a community that had been there for over a hundred years. Echo Bay was the only town in the archipelago with a post office, a fuel dock and a small store. A short distance to the north was a logging camp, Scott Cove, and to the south another logging camp in Shoal Harbour. A short speedboat ride away was the First Nation village of Gwayasdums. All the children from these places went to school together in Echo Bay. People living in the outlying bays were fishermen, log salvagers, artists and old-timers who had been here their whole lives. There was a floating church and at the head of Echo Bay a community hall where we held concerts and other community events that brought together people from many kilometres around, our speedboats rafted two or three deep to the little dock.

At that point the man behind the desk said he didn't know why I shouldn't be able to get a tenure to continue this life, but he couldn't give me one. While the Province of BC was telling us that salmon farms would be good for us, they had rescinded our right to live where the farms were moving in.

Over the following months, the provincial agency in charge of tenures, Crown Lands, photographed our floathouses from the air. Some people had several floats tied together, supporting buildings like boatsheds, workshops or greenhouses. Crown Lands sent me pictures of my neighbours' floats, asking me to describe what all the structures were used for. I refused and so did my neighbours when they received similar requests. Given that their tenures were on sites that the fish companies might want, the owners of the floating fishing lodges, one of the groups most concerned about the impact of salmon farms, fell silent on the subject; the same bureaucrats were in charge of tourism and salmon farm tenures. Tourism is a much bigger employer in British Columbia, but each of the lodges was a small concern. The lodge owners I talked to certainly believed that the less they said about salmon farms, the more likely their foreshore licences would be renewed.

We learned to keep our heads down, hoping not to be noticed, hoping we would be allowed to continue to exist. No such luck. Tenures for Echo Bay's residents were systematically denied and obstructed; gradually the families left and no new families moved in. This independent community in the wilderness was extinguished. The provincial government came in and burned the school down, on Billy Proctor's birthday in 2009, on the grounds that destroying it was less expensive than maintaining it with so few children left. The mayor of nearby Port McNeill, which at first embraced salmon farms, called us "misfits" in the local *North Island Gazette* because we resisted the ruthless industrialization of the area. Around our dinner tables, afloat in small bays, we came to the conclusion that the government was making it so hard for us to stay because the salmon farmers didn't want witnesses. People who love the lands and the fish inevitably become a problem for the fish farmers and apparently they had persuaded the government to get rid of us.

I bought a piece of steep hillside from Billy Proctor, who had generously subdivided his property and sold the parcels at a very affordable price to people who wanted to stay on in Echo Bay. He was trying to hold his community together, trying to counter the government clearances. Billy agreed to pull my old floathouse up that hill to its new place. The floathouse had been Billy's childhood home, built in 1919.

On the first day of this endeavour, the cables from the skids under the house to his tractor broke and the whole structure ran back to the sea. When the skids hit the beach, the floor joists kept going for a bit and stopped at an angle where they remain to this day. A lot of my glass jars of preserves fell to the floor. Pickled beets mingled with canned salmon and tomato sauce. The tide came in and cleaned up.

On day two, we tried again. Constructed of fir framing, siding and flooring, the shack was a lot heavier than anticipated, but up the hill she came at last, groaning and creaking, several windows shattering as the house buckled and bent in the process. Once we had her in place, she sprouted a porch and an addition. I purchased the first solar panels and house batteries in the community, planted a garden and fruit trees and really began to settle in.

From 1989 to 1992, the industry had allowed its employees to live in Echo Bay. We had become friends, our children went to school together and we gathered over dinners of local seafood, venison and home-baked desserts in our floating homes. After a beer or two, the stories came tumbling out. One farmer told me he didn't like working on the farm, but at least it was better than working in a potash factory. Many employees were from eastern Canada, refugees from the collapse of the North Atlantic cod due to DFO's refusal to heed the warnings of its own scientists to reduce fishing.

Some of the farm workers said they were told to keep throwing feed into the pens even after the fish had died and been removed. They guessed this was so it looked like there were still fish in the pens to the people back at head office. Others said they liked to fish and caught wild chinook salmon right outside the pens. Then they noticed the same sores on the wild fish as they saw on the farm salmon. Soon, they said, there were no wild fish to catch. Dying fish was a theme with the farmers; generally they said they didn't know why any of it happened.

After a few years, the companies tied floating bunkhouses to the farms and prohibited their employees from "fraternizing" with the locals in Echo Bay. However, fish farm workers kept seeking me out, desperate to talk to someone who might do something about the disease and death they were witnessing. Sadly, after unburdening themselves, almost like they had come to confession, they invariably asked me not to tell anyone. They were afraid of repercussions for revealing what went on in the farms. I always kept their confidence, but I think now that was a mistake. I wouldn't have protected someone who confided that they were going to hurt someone, so why did I hide people who were part of the harm being done to every living creature around these farms?

One young guy called to say he'd asked his high-school teacher who to talk to and she'd recommended me. He said that when government health inspectors were expected at the farm site he worked on, his superiors told him to attach long sewer pipes to the underside of each toilet. As part of their checklist, the inspectors poured dye into the toilet, flushed and went outside to see if the dye came up in the pens. It never did, because it was trapped in the long pipes. Nothing could actually flush out of a toilet when it was attached to a long pipe running deep underwater, so as soon as the inspectors were gone, the workers removed the pipes. He said the fish in the pens eat everything: the little fish that get through the mesh, cigarette butts, and when they flushed the toilets, the fish ate that.

"We are going to kill someone with this shit," he said, but he wouldn't tell me which farm.

I told him that I couldn't report that some guy on some farm told me this. He was going to have to report it himself. I don't know if he did.

When the first outbreak of furunculosis occurred early in 1991 in the farms, it spread rapidly farm to farm. Furunculosis is a bacterial disease that ruptures into open sores that broadcast bacteria into the water where they drift until they infect another fish. IBEC tried to keep the outbreak secret. They instructed staff not to talk about it on the VHF radio, and at one point, management dropped instructions on how to deal with the situation to the crew from helicopters to avoid anyone finding out what was up. We found out because some of the workers were still living in Echo Bay at the time.

I wrote to DFO about this outbreak, when it spread to the local Scott Cove coho enhancement hatchery that fall of 1991. Most of Echo Bay volunteered at that hatchery. I saw more than a quarter of the big silver fish erupt in sores and die from the infection. DFO gave us the antibiotic oxytetracycline and instructed us to inject every adult fish in the hatchery. The open sores healed and the rest of the fish survived, but the Department never checked to see if the bacteria were still present in the wild stock. They never tested the young salmon we released in the spring or the wild salmon in the creeks that had also been exposed to the infected farms. Were we spreading farm salmon diseases via the young fish we were releasing? We flew thousands of the young coho raised in the hatchery out to several Broughton rivers. The sheer lack of concern from DFO is unforgivable, given the warning from their own scientists, officials and people such as in my community.

Two years later, in 1993, boils lifted the skin of the coho again in irreg-
ular pus-filled lumps that covered large parts of their bodies. The boils
burst and once again the bacteria that cause furunculosis, which are
known to survive in wet wood, permeated the hatchery. The water from
this hatchery, loaded with bacteria, poured out into the watershed. This
time the drug DFO sent to us didn't work. While fuelling my boat in Echo
Bay, two fish farm boats pulled up at the gas dock and I overheard the
workers talking about having a "triple dose of furunculosis" at their farm.

Our local hatchery, in a building in the nearby logging camp in Scott
Cove, had several large tanks for holding the adult fish and stacks of
mesh trays that water ran through to incubate the eggs. While it was
run by local volunteers, it was part of DFO's Salmonid Enhancement
Programs and so DFO provided the instructions on how to collect
and raise the fish. When I told the manager of the hatchery what the
men had said, he contacted DFO and found out that what they meant
by "triple dose" was that the bacteria in the farms that year was triple-
antibiotic resistant—in other words, resistant to every antibiotic drug
approved for use in fish farms.

Our local DFO advisor sent us another drug, erythromycin, but
once again, no one from the government undertook an investigation
as to where this disease had come from or expressed concern that we
might be spreading it. No one in the hatchery had any experience with
this level of disease. For the ten years prior to the first outbreak, only
3 percent of the fish in the hatchery died. Now we were facing outbreak
after outbreak, losing up to 28 percent of the broodstock, and DFO was
showing no curiosity as to why. During a provincial review of salmon
farms in 1995, I submitted the details of these outbreaks and while the
authors of the review did not interview anyone from the hatchery, they
wrote that the disease outbreaks at the Scott Cove facility were simply
due to a change in fish handling procedures.

At the time, my focus was still whales, but in the early 1990s my
neighbour, Glen Neidrauer, who counted how many salmon returned
to the archipelago each fall for DFO, reported that thousands of

chum salmon had died on the banks of the Viner River near the Burdwood salmon farm one fall. No one had any idea why. Billy Proctor and Glen Neidrauer were very concerned. After he reported it, Glen said no one from DFO came to check. The salmon in that river began vanishing like water down a drain.

As the crushing footprint of the fish farms descended on the archipelago, the companies began buying each other up. BC Packers, a local company owned by one of the richest men in BC, Jim Pattison, ran farms in the Broughton for a while; eventually those sites were bought by Cermaq. Marine Harvest bought Stolt and then turned into Mowi, and Grieg squeezed a few farms into the Broughton's southern reaches. All these companies were from Norway. Clearly, Canada wanted Norway to use our coast.

The farms unerringly lodged themselves in the vital organs of the archipelago—all the places wild fish need to thrive, the red zones as the province named them. It wasn't only salmon that were affected. Local prawn and rock-cod fishermen were soon displaced as the companies dropped their spider-web array of cement anchor blocks and chains to keep the farms in place directly on their fishing grounds. DFO did not compensate these fishermen for their lost income.

At one point I did a study on the ocean currents. I made homemade drifters out of small squares of wood with netting that hung down so that the blocks would move with the currents, not the wind. I spray-painted them bright orange. I numbered the drifters and threw fifty into the water near the farms. Over the next few days I searched to see where they went. This is when I realized the farms were sited where the biggest tidelines formed in the archipelago. Tidelines are where the flood tide meets the outgoing water, and at the turning of the tide, the two water masses—one from the ocean, the other from deep in the inlet—slide along each other for a few hours. Because they keep pouring towards each other, everything floating ends up sandwiched in a line between the tides; logs, seaweed, garbage and larval fish collect in the tidelines, and my blocks showed up there as well. I could see clearly that one end of these tidelines, which predictably formed in the same places daily, poured into the maw of the farms, flushing out tons of feces each day from every farm as it brought oxygen and tiny larval fish and shrimp into the pens.

By 1995, I developed a twitch under my left eye as I stayed up late night after night trying to explain in endless letters and briefings to government the terrible things that were happening to this beautiful, generous place. Just six years into this invasion, the whales I was studying had left, the fat winter springs had vanished, dark red and brilliant orange algae blooms had become common, seals and sea lions were being shot and the local coho salmon had erupted in boils.

I began to make a point of going everywhere people pointed to problems with fish farms to see the situation with my own eyes so that I could write accurately about what was happening. A shrimper called me to report what he called "extraterrestrials" that were stuck in the eyeballs of the flounder that came up in his net. The parasites had bodies that looked exactly like tiny hot dogs and holdfasts that penetrated deep into the fish's eye, rupturing the eyeball as they grew roots. Some fish had several in each eye. I spent the next winter fishing seasons going boat to boat, jumping aboard as they pulled in their catch, to learn more about this parasite, which was called *Phrixocephalus cincinnatus*.

I searched for experts on this parasite, which none of the fishermen I talked to had seen in the Broughton. It turned out it was associated with places where the sea floor was fouled, such as the industrial harbour in San Diego, California. An expert on this parasite from Mississippi told me mine was the first report of the parasite near salmon farms anywhere, and that the number I was finding per fish was unheard of. Two researchers on the US Gulf Coast, Reginald Blaylock and Robin Overstreet, and I published a paper on this.

This became my method. When I ran into something I had never seen before, I searched for experts to collaborate with and worked as the field end of the team. Most were happy to join forces with me, because getting into the field was expensive and I was prepared to provide the samples they needed and also help write up the results.

One winter evening my VHF radio picked up a conversation between two sportfishermen who had caught three Atlantic salmon in the nearby Wakeman River. I picked up the VHF radio mic, and said, "To the guys talking about catching Atlantics, could you come back to the *Blackfish Sound?*" (In marine radio protocol you identify yourself by your boat name.) There was silence.

I tried again. "Hey, really sorry to barge in on your conversation, but I am wondering, did you keep those fish?"

One of the men answered. "No, we released them. Just habit I guess."

"Any chance I could go back into the Wakeman with you tomorrow and try to get those fish?"

It's never hard to talk fishermen into more fishing. They agreed. The next day we headed to the Wakeman together in my boat and walked up the river.

"Right here is where I hooked the big doe," said one of the fishermen.

One cast and he had her again. It was the same for the two males.

I bent down to look at them carefully. The males had tiny, wavy parallel lines all over their heads: teeth rake marks. The only fish in the river in the middle of winter large enough to make those teeth marks were steelhead, which was what the fishermen had been after. It appeared these Atlantic salmon had been fighting with the local steelhead, which are the closest relative to the Atlantic salmon found in the Pacific. Unlike all the Pacific salmon species, Atlantic salmon and steelhead don't die after spawning and can return to the ocean and then spawn again after a period of time. When I opened them up, I saw that they were very mature. Had the males been trying to mate with steelhead females, as well as the female Atlantics?

———

In the summer of 2000, I decided to count all the Atlantic salmon caught by commercial fishermen in DFO fishing Area 12, which included the Broughton Archipelago and Johnstone Strait. It seemed to me that I heard fishermen talking about catching more Atlantic salmon than appeared in the Department's annual reporting. So I wanted to ground-truth DFO's numbers, and I also wanted to look at the fish and learn what they got up to when they escaped from the farms.

The first day of salmon fishing in the waters around my home was completely socked in with fog and I didn't have radar on my boat, so I called a local water taxi and made arrangements to have the skipper pick me up and run me through the fleet in Johnstone Strait. When we plunged into the fog in Spring Pass, Dennis Richards didn't turn his radar on.

"You've got radar, right?" I asked.

"Yup."

"Could you turn it on?"

"Ask me if it works."

I'd spent the money and I didn't want to miss the opportunity, so I just had to hope for the best. Dennis was very experienced in these waters.

When we got onto the fishing grounds, I did a broadcast over the marine radio to the hundreds of boats busily setting and retrieving nets over several kilometres in both directions. Switching through each of the VHF channels used by the fishermen, I repeated, "Anybody with Atlantic salmon on board, could you come back to the *Blackfish Sound*, please?" (I used my own boat's name, so the crews would know whom to call as the fishing season continued.)

Silence.

I tried a couple more times. More silence. Then the skipper of the water taxi picked up the mic. "If you love the fish farms don't answer, but if you hate them talk to the lady with the pen, for Chrissake!"

The floodgates opened.

"I'm down at Izumi Rock. If you wanna come down and pick the goddamn things off my boat that would be alright," came the first call.

"I'm up at Blinkhorn with two for you," came a second call. I thanked Dennis for helping me break through, and for the next few hours we zig-zagged between boats. He drove as I took notes on everything the fishermen told me. Some of the guys threw the fish at me. They thought I was with DFO and they were furious at finding so many Atlantics in their nets. That night I did autopsies on all of them, collecting data on their size, state of maturity and what they were eating.

A few days later a pink salmon fishery opened in Tribune Channel and the boats caught dozens of Atlantic salmon. They didn't know what to do with them. Not only was there was no market for these fish, but Atlantic salmon were not on their licences. They did not want to throw them back—they wanted them out of the water completely—and so they were happy to fill my boat with them. When I picked the fish up, the fishermen said they had opened a few up to see what they were eating and found fish farm pellets still in their throats. This meant these fish had only been outside the pens for a matter of minutes.

They radioed the nearby Stolt farm at Sargeaunt Pass to tell them, along with a good deal of swearing, that they had a hole in their net and their fish were escaping. The company workers insisted there was no hole, but they put a diver down and, sure enough, they had a hole. As per the schedule, the fishery closed and then opened again seven days later; by then, the hole was sewed shut. Yet the fleet still caught up to 200 Atlantic salmon a day; the escapees hadn't gone far.

I picked up more fish off the boats, and when fishing closed I followed the boats to the packing plant in Sointula off Vancouver Island. As the workers cleaned the fish, I examined the discarded guts. Fish guts carry a surprising amount of information about the age, sex, diet and approximate state of health. One evening I was knee-deep in Atlantics in my boat. I had collected their measurements, examined their stomach contents and then didn't know what to do with them. I didn't want to throw them in the ocean, because they don't belong in the Pacific Ocean. I also didn't want to compost them and work them into my garden because of the drugs in them. I was so exhausted, I finally just left them in the boat while I got some sleep.

The next morning I went down to the dock to deal with the mess, dreading what I would find. The local raccoons liked to help themselves to anything they wanted from my boat, even my daughter's crayons. I was surprised to see that they had grabbed just one fish by the head, dragged it halfway out of the boat and then abandoned it. Apparently they found these farm salmon unappetizing. It's true they didn't smell like salmon, but like the farm pellets they ate; their flesh was so soft it could be scooped up into a ball like wet snow.

In the end, I called Stolt and they sent an employee to unload me. Poor guy was so sheepish. The companies did do something to lower the number of escapes after that fishing season. Every summer the fishermen keep me in mind and I generally get a couple of Atlantics from them, but nothing like in the year 2000.

That year the fleet reported catching 10,826 Atlantic salmon to me. I did autopsies on 775 of them. None of the eighty Atlantics caught on the first day of the escape from the Sargeaunt Pass farm had wild food in them. Eight days later, 2 percent of the Atlantics I autopsied had eaten wild fish. They also swallowed alder catkins and rounded bits of wood— anything that looked like a pellet. At that point, Stolt started buying the Atlantic salmon off the boats. The pay was better, so the fishermen took off their pink salmon nets and began targeting the Atlantics with larger-mesh nets. Soon no one was throwing Atlantics at me, except for fisherman Calvin Siider, who thought it was important that I look at as many of these farm fish as possible; he gave me his whole catch. That is how I learned that by the third week of freedom, 24 percent of the escaped farm fish I looked at had learned how to eat wild fish.

Learning to feed in the wild is one of the biggest hurdles that an exotic species faces on its way to becoming an invasive species and disrupting the natural order. The escaped Atlantic salmon were eating herring, larval fish, young salmon and shrimp. So much for DFO's assurances that an Atlantic salmon would not know how to catch wild food on our coast.

Ricky Laughlin from Sointula tied the end of his net right to the Sargeaunt Pass farm, where the escape had happened, and stretched it out at a ninety-degree angle from the farm, thinking that escaped fish might be hanging around trying to eat the pellets that drift out of the pens. He was right. Most interesting to me was that in addition to all the farm fish with small heads, large bodies and few-to-no spots that everyone else was catching, Ricky picked up two long, lean, green and heavily spotted Atlantics, one male and one female, that were very mature. Were they grabbing a snack at the farm before finding a river in which to spawn? Because these two fish looked so different than the others, it seemed possible the farm was attracting escapees from other farms. Four other pairs of mature Atlantic salmon hit the gill nets side-by-side.

All these fish had an average of twenty-six sea lice each and were so fat that when I dissected them, I found fatty frills attached to their organs, which were oddly adhered together. I had cleaned a lot of salmon on Billy's boat, *Twilight Rock*, and none of them had tiny hairs lacing all their organs together.

I could see where vaccine injections had gone in, causing the intestines to attach to the edge of the body cavity, and the yellow stain along their throats from the colorant put in the pellets to make their flesh look pink like a normal salmon. The tips of the farm fish tails were worn off— paddle-shaped instead of fan-shaped. Their dorsal fins were split and healed so many times from hitting the nets they were lumpy mounds of broken rays melted together.

I counted 40 percent more farm fish caught by the fleet than DFO did that summer. And mine is the only paper—"Description of Escaped Farmed Atlantic Salmon (*Salmo salar*), Captures and Their Characteristics in One Pacific Fishery Area in British Columbia, Canada in 2000"—that has been published on the fate of Atlantic salmon that escaped into the Pacific Ocean.

While DFO was telling us Atlantic salmon could never colonize BC's rivers, senior staff actually thought it was entirely possible. On February

19, 1991, nine years before I researched my paper, Ron Ginetz, chief of the Aquaculture Division, wrote a memo that was eventually forwarded to me. In it, he said, "In my view it is only a matter of time before we discover that Atlantics are gaining a foothold in B.C. . . . Do we prepare public/user groups for the possibility, and strategically plant the seed now, or do we downplay the idea and deal with the situation if and when it occurs?"

That summer commercial fishermen caught one million pink salmon in Tribune Channel. Another two million pinks entered the Kakweiken and the Glendale Rivers to spawn. This was the abundance that the Broughton Archipelago was capable of before the sea louse epidemics.

I was watching an ecosystem get sucked under. My efforts to stop it left skid marks across my life. I failed to grasp how big the interests protecting the salmon farms were. I still don't know who they really are. The industry is tiny when it comes to the number of people it employs, but as I pulled on it, I began to understand how deep and wide its roots went, extending to Ottawa, Norway, Washington State and down the west coast of two continents, into Chile.

At first I just tried to slow down the industry's growth—aiming to keep parts of the archipelago farm-free—and I was somewhat successful in that. A fish farmer I knew from before she took the job told me, "You have no idea the plans they have for Tribune Channel—wall-to-wall fish farms is the goal." In the end, this place where whales come to sleep, where millions of wild salmon migrate, only got hit with four farms because of the public pressure that arose from my science and reporting to the media. But I felt no sense of accomplishment. I had not protected these waters: four were enough to do damage to all the wild salmon that had to run the gauntlet past them.

In 1999, I got a surprising call on the Autotel—a precursor to the cell-phone for remote areas, not so fondly known in Echo Bay as the "auto hell." It looked like a phone, and sometimes acted like a phone, but I never got to say goodbye because it invariably dropped the call at some point. I got so frustrated with mine it bore the imprint of my teeth.

On the line was Harvey Andrusak, from the provincial Ministry of Environment, who was calling to tell me that he and his colleagues— whom I had copied in many of my letters to DFO—agreed with me that Atlantic salmon posed enormous threat to wild salmon.

I was stunned. The next day was calm enough for me to cross Blackfish Sound to Port McNeill, where I got in my car and drove down-island to Nanaimo to meet him, as he'd asked. There, Harvey introduced me to a group of men from the provincial Ministry of Environment whom I came to think of as the "river men." Their job was to keep the salmon, trout and steelhead in British Columbia's rivers and lakes alive. As a result, they were trying to stop the importation of millions of Atlantic salmon eggs into the province, warning their minister against allowing the salmon farmers to import these eggs. Each shipment that entered the country might be infected with a pathogen that could spread to wild salmon. In one of his letters of protest to DFO, the river men's boss, Dave Narver, had called it a game of Russian roulette.

Sitting on a desk in the corner of their office, I asked them why the Atlantic salmon were ever allowed in if so many experts didn't think it was safe. They told me that men in suits had showed up at the ministry for discussions that excluded them, where the higher-ups had decided that the industry would be allowed to use Atlantic salmon to stock BC fish farms. "We figured they were lawyers," Harvey said.

Years later, after I had mastered the art of obtaining internal government email conversations through the Access to Information Act, I saw how this conversation played out. In 2004, Dr. Laura Richards, who was DFO's Director General, Pacific Region, at the time, felt she had to allow the importation of Atlantic salmon eggs from an Icelandic hatchery even though they did not meet Canada's salmon egg import requirements.

Richards wrote in a department memo:

> Two BC salmon farming companies wish to import Atlantic
> salmon eggs from Stofnfiskur, an Icelandic company which is not
> certified under the Canadian Fish Health Protection Regulations
> (FHPR) . . . .
> - Failure to provide permission for egg importation
>   may trigger a trade challenge under the World Trade
>   Organization . . .
> - Additionally, DFO could also be viewed as causing a
>   competitive disadvantage of the aquaculture industry
>   by denying them access to alternate strains

These eggs were imported.

One year later the eggs were discovered to have an undescribed problem, which caused Stolt Sea Farm to ask DFO for permission to destroy
the young Atlantic salmon that had hatched from them. Stolt did destroy them, but the records showed that Stolt only got a portion of these
imported eggs; the rest went to another company for hatching. There is
no record of the fish that hatched from those eggs being destroyed.

The river men described how salmon farms were supposed to be
jointly managed by the province's Ministry of Environment and Ministry of Agriculture, but that was not how it was working. They told me
that the Agriculture guys did not inform the Environment guys of disease outbreaks until they were well under way. They also did not heed
advice from the Environment guys and worked closely with the industry. In fact, staff at Agriculture slid back and forth, employed first by
industry and then government, and vice versa.

In 1995, the river men had written a report on this for their minister,
called "The Salmon Farm Cover-up," but they told me it had never
reached him and it had vanished from the record.

They told me that if they said anything publicly, they could be fired.

They had reached out to me because they believed that I had more power to reach their minister than they did; they described the bureaucratic barrier between them and the minister as a hard ceiling. Nothing got through to the minister that the senior bureaucrats didn't approve.

Harvey encouraged me to keep up my research, to keep on writing letters and to meet with every politician involved. By now Rafe Mair, lawyer, political commentator, elected member of the legislative assembly (MLA) from 1975 to 1981, and colourful radio personality, was interviewing me regularly on his talk show, which greatly increased my reach. They asked me to keep doing that as well.

As I drove the old International Harvester SUV I'd inherited from Robin back from that meeting, through the Vancouver Island forests fed by salmon, to Port McNeill where my speedboat was waiting, I had a bad feeling. I was a field biologist. I didn't know how to brief a minister. It worried me that the people hired by government to protect our freshwater fisheries, which included wild salmon, were blocked by the government they worked for from fulfilling their responsibility to British Columbians. I had gone into the wilderness to learn about communication between animals. I was not particularly good at or interested in communicating with people. I wanted to drop this problem off on the right person's doorstep, like a baby in a basket, where it would be attended to and given the proper care. But no one was willing to take it. I was growing to hate the words *Keep it up*. This was not how I wanted to spend my life.

Doubt heaped upon doubt. If I was really a whale researcher, wasn't it time to leave Echo Bay, given that the whales I was studying were gone? Yes, I frequently encountered the mammal-eating orca whales, but they rarely vocalize, remaining in silent stealth mode to avoid alerting seals and porpoises, which fled at the sound of their calls. I wasn't interested in shifting my study to these whales.

But I couldn't leave. Echo Bay was my home. I loved it fiercely, as women all over this planet love the places in which they safely raise their children. I felt like I had already abandoned two miserable whales in a pool in California. Was I going to abandon the fight to restore this archipelago so their families could return? But this fight was exactly what had frightened me as a child, the kind that tore scientists from their research and pushed them into endless visits to talk to politicians and, eventually, to become activists. Was I going to abandon my whale research to fight an environmental battle to keep wild salmon from dying because of salmon farming?

The person who had to make this decision was different from the girl I had been; I had changed irrevocably when my husband drowned. I had experienced the shock that comes from losing someone I loved forever. I had learned, at the cellular level of grief, that beings can and do vanish forever. Now when I see tragedy, I feel it more acutely, more fully. It billows into those dark spaces of the subconscious and becomes a much bigger emotion than I was capable of before. After I lost Robin, everything I loved became more precious and I became more compassionate. I see this in other women too. The most empathetic have invariably suffered great loss.

I made myself a deal: I would fight to move the salmon farms off all major wild salmon migration routes in order to allow the archipelago to heal and return to some semblance of its recent past, in particular to protect the Ahta River in Tribune Channel, the last unlogged watershed in the Broughton. When I succeeded, I would turn my attention back to the whales.

Around this time, Billy Proctor was elected as the representative of the Regional District of Mount Waddington for Area A, which included the Broughton Archipelago and surrounding areas, and I was named his alternate. Every month we travelled to meetings of the Port McNeill resource board, which was tasked with providing advice on how the rich resources of the region, such as fish and forests, would be utilized. This was an exercise in frustration. It was clear the region was cutting more trees than the industry could sustain. Loggers would be out of a job at this rate, and salmon farms were considered the next great generator of employment, even though the jobs math never did add up. It did not take many people to run the increasingly mechanized farms and the jobs paid far less than loggers were making.

The board reviewed each new salmon farm tenure application. Also present at the meetings were representatives of the tourism and the commercial fishing industries. We found ourselves allies in trying to find ways to reduce the impact of salmon farms on wild salmon so that these jobs would not be lost. Tourism in the province is built on viewing whales and bears, both of which require salmon. Of course people from the salmon farming industry were at the sessions as well, and finally having the opportunity to sit with them in a structured setting and hear them talk, I learned a lot from them. I watched the table like I watched any grouping of mammals, and I noted alliances such as the one between the industry and the mayor's office.

The mayor owned a fuel tank farm that sold gas to the salmon farmers. This regular meeting would have been a good place to steer the industry into compliance with other businesses in the region to keep the economy diverse and resilient, but it didn't work that way. Years later the facilitator who had guided these meetings apologized to me for blocking my attempts to move the discussion towards solutions to protect wild salmon—for instance, moving the farms out of the most sensitive habitats and limiting the total number of farms in any one region. She was visiting my home in Echo Bay at the time, and said she had not realized how beautiful the archipelago was. But she did not offer to help us undo the damage.

Billy and I also attended the monthly meetings of the 1995 Salmon Aquaculture Review, which were held in a different town every thirty days. People told me this provincial government process was in response to my increasing outreach on the impact of salmon farms. In the end, the review made a number of good recommendations, including consulting local First Nations about where to site these farms and making farm data available to scientists. However, these recommendations were ignored. I also met several times with the then-premier of British Columbia, Glen Clark, and his NDP cabinet members.

By the mid-1990s my son was in high school in Port McNeill, boarding with friends. My little daughter now came with me on all my expeditions. She charmed everyone and was actually an easier baby on the road than at home. I'd met her dad, Eric Nelson, a rugged tugboat skipper and log salvager, when he'd radioed to ask if he could tie a couple of logs to my float. Eric could fix, build and invent anything in the wilderness. My relentless fight eventually wore him out, but for a few years we happily raised our daughter on the homestead we built together on the land I had bought from Billy.

The baby rode sandwiched between Billy and me in my pickup truck, and it was Billy's job to keep her from fussing. He spent a lot of time rolling organic cereal O's down her car seat to keep her amused as she caught them and threw them around the cab. I met professional environmentalists outside the back door of these meetings, nursing my baby upwind as they were defusing their stress with a cigarette. Catherine Stewart from Greenpeace, for instance, is one of the most commanding people I've ever met; in an effort to learn how to communicate the needs of the wild world to humans, I intently studied how she stood up to politicians and industry figures with unyielding grace and powerful delivery of the facts.

One thing I learned was that most politicians become actors. They lean into what you are saying, furrow their brows in concern, clasp your hand in appreciation for taking the time to meet with them, and then carry on as if the meeting never happened. One of the most ridiculous exchanges I had was with a minister who insisted there were no salmon farms on wild salmon migration routes. When I pulled out a map and showed him that the wild salmon would have to climb out of the water and walk through the forest to migrate out of the archipelago without exposure to the farms, he kept saying, "That is your opinion."

This man knew what the right thing to do was; he kept repeating that he had already done it. He told me that he had made sure that salmon farms were not on wild salmon migration routes, so they weren't, even if my map showed him that they were. I thought he was an idiot until I realized he was employing a technique designed to deflect concerned citizens. None of these politicians were actually idiots. They were just doing something else. I was recommending action to fix the problem; he and others like him were all about convincing me to give up and go away by refusing to see the obvious and repeating an alternate reality. There were times I honestly considered jumping up on the table and screaming to stop this nonsense just to jolt them out of spinning their wheels. I don't know how I didn't.

I subscribed to a European publication called *Salmon Farming*, which provided abstracts of all the scientific papers published on salmon farming each month, as well as headlines about the industry from newspapers all over the world. I realized that everywhere the industry went, there were people fighting fish farms. I read about politicians in Scotland who repeated the same lines the politicians used here. *This is the most regulated agricultural industry in the world. Salmon farms are good for the people in small coastal communities. Salmon farming is here to stay.* Meanwhile their own governments' scientists were warning that the disease, sea louse outbreaks and massive escapes of farm fish into the oceans were harming entire ecosystems.

After reading a couple of issues, I ordered all the back copies to dig into the industry's whole tarnished history, including the outcry echoing across the northern hemisphere from coastal people in Norway, Scotland, Ireland, the Faroe Islands, eastern Canada and Chile. The pattern was clear. In each new place, local people were the first to apply for the fish farm tenures, perhaps believing the farms *were* an opportunity for small coastal communities. When these inexperienced operators inevitably went bankrupt due to fish disease outbreaks, the big companies, generally Norwegian, bought their assets, gaining control of the precious tenures. Then the lobbying began. The standard tactics: Insert industry-friendly people at all levels where decisions were being made about the industry. Keep personnel sliding back and forth between industry and government, effectively making government a branch of the industry. Ridicule any scientist who speaks about the negative impact of the industry.

Remarkably, one government after the next lined up to be used this way. This was the hardest thing for me to understand. I got that the industry's goal was to make money, and that was all they had to think about. But what did government gain? Fish farming in BC was causing citizens to lose their livelihoods and homes. When these citizens went to their elected officials and asked, then begged and eventually raged at them simply for the chance to survive, those officials turned their backs on the people and served the industry. Meanwhile industry was on a trajectory to minimize employment through mechanization. This course of action destroyed small coastal communities and damaged the environment, yet it went smoothly (*Slick as snot*, as Billy would say) in every country these companies decided to use.

I got the opportunity to observe this process first-hand on many dispiriting occasions. Provincial politicians, like Gordon Wilson, who became the MLA for this area and then a cabinet minister, and who loves this coast, came to the archipelago to learn first-hand how damaging salmon farming was to his constituents and to the ecosystem, but did nothing to fix the situation. It was as if the people we elected to represent our region got into office and were suddenly living on the other side of a wall, influenced by unseen forces that caused them to ignore their own constituents, regulations, licensing and enforcement, and to forget compassion and integrity. It didn't matter which political party was elected. In government they all did the same thing, becoming foot soldiers in the destruction of wild salmon and the hundred species they feed.

I resolved that while I might not be able to convince government to stop handing out tenures to this wrecking ball of an industry, I could light up all the dark corners, revealing what happens to Pacific species exposed to the waste from a million Atlantic salmon that are forced to swim in circles.

I would never be a lobbyist, but I was a biologist.

6.

Salmon Coast Field Station

IN MAY 2001, a fishing lodge owner named Chris Bennett pulled up to my dock. He was not his usual cheerful self as he strode up the ramp, a bucket in hand.

"What are all these things all over these two salmon fry?" he said, holding the bucket up so I could see in. Fry are very young salmon. These little fish were bristling with short hair-like growths attached to their skin and they were not doing well. One was rolling over on its side, drifting downward, then rallying for a few seconds and trying to swim upright, only to start tilting again.

"These better not be sea lice," Chris said. "Fishermen are coming from Scotland to fish with me now, because they say that sea lice from salmon farms killed off their wild salmon."

Working as a deckhand, I had encountered sea lice on wild salmon, but these creatures were much smaller and a different shape. I had read a lot about sea lice in *Salmon Farming*, which also provided gruesome pictures of wild salmon covered in lice and farm salmon with so many lice grazing on their heads that their brains were exposed. The sea lice infestation in Scotland had driven local fishermen into the streets to protest against salmon farms.

I took a couple of pictures of Chris's dying fish and promised to look into it. No one around here seemed to ask DFO about these things anymore; they came straight to me. I forwarded the pictures to scientists who were authoring papers on sea lice in Norway and Scotland.

An expert from Norway was the first to respond. "Yes, those are juvenile sea lice. What do you want to know?"

"How do I study them?"

"Do you have salmon farms?"

"Yes."

"My suggestion to you is that you drop this. Your government won't be happy with you, and the industry won't be happy with you. You are going to have good years for lice and bad years and in the end you are not going to have wild salmon."

This was alarming on so many levels.

Then a Scottish scientist wrote, "It's sea lice. Can't you guys read over there in Canada!" He went on to write that of course there would be sea lice on the young wild salmon of British Columbia, since they were swimming past salmon farms. Young wild Atlantic salmon and sea trout, which he was studying, could tolerate about one louse per gram of weight of the fish. Any more than that and the fish would die. The fish in Chris's bucket weighed approximately 1.5 grams, and there were dozens of juvenile lice on them. They were dead fish swimming.

I emailed DFO about the sea lice. One of their biologists called me in response, asking me to collect some of the infected fish so they could see them. That was different, I thought: for once they weren't denying the problem and they actually wanted to look at the fish. I made a fine-mesh dip net out of copper tubing and the crinoline from one of my daughter's dresses. It wasn't hard to dip up five lice-encrusted fish with much older lice than the ones on the fry Chris had brought me. I packed them on ice, ran them to town in my boat and put them on a bus to DFO's Pacific Biological Station in Nanaimo all on my dime. A few days later a black DFO Zodiac pulled up to my float, and a woman in full uniform, including holstered pistols and very serious-looking government-issued black shoes, came to my door.

When I answered her knock, she said, "I am here to charge you with poaching. You caught five undersized salmon without a scientific licence."

Seriously, after twelve years of writing to DFO and being largely ignored, one of their biologists asks for samples over the phone so I have no record of the request, and they charge me with poaching! Clearly sea lice brought out the worst in the Department. In the end I only got a warning, but the Norwegian scientist was right. That was the start of the sea lice years.

A month later, DFO sent a large seine boat, *Odysseus*, to catch some of the lice-covered fish, perhaps in response to my images of lice-ravaged salmon appearing in newspapers and on the evening news. Unlike the other impacts of salmon farms, this one produced graphic images. Several environmental groups, including Living Oceans and the Georgia Strait Alliance, had stepped up to help me get this story out to the media. Now the Department could see that threatening me wasn't going to be enough, they had to been seen to be doing something. However, the infested young salmon were hugging the shoreline and inhabiting shallow bays. *Odysseus* was too big, with too deep a draft, and fishing with a net that was too massive, to scoop these schools away from the shore. The skipper radioed me to ask where he could try. In the end he got seven sample juvenile pink salmon from the Broughton and DFO announced I was wrong—there was no sea louse problem.

I immediately got a scientific licence to protect myself from going to jail for collecting fish, went out with my homemade net and examined 775 salmon, each approximately six centimetres long. I counted 8,207 lice on them. Seventy-five percent of these fish were infected at or above the known lethal limit for other species of salmon; one had sixty-nine lice. These tiny salmon had an average of five lice per gram of their body weight, five times more than the Scottish and Norwegian research reported Atlantic salmon could survive. If their research also applied to Pacific salmon, these fish were in trouble; no one had ever reported an outbreak like this in decades of research on the Pacific's young pink and chum salmon. I would go on to publish "Infestation of the sea louse *Lepeophtheirus salmonis* (Krøyer) on juvenile pink salmon *Oncorhynchus gorbuscha* (Walbaum) in British Columbia" in the *Canadian Field Naturalist* with Dr. Rob Williams, a colleague studying the impact of acoustic pollution on whales. He wanted to help and ran the statistics on my data.

Not all the farms in the Broughton were stocked that spring, as some had been harvested and not yet restocked. When I looked specifically at the young pink salmon caught near active farms, 98.4 percent were infected with an average of 12.3 lice. This suggested that only 2 percent of the wild pink salmon that passed the Broughton's salmon farms in 2001 would return. There was a considerable amount of scoffing from salmon biologists when a whale researcher dared to predict a salmon run. They warned me that predicting salmon returns was complicated, and I agreed—I didn't know anything about predicting wild salmon returns. But, though no one else in Canada had ever seen the lice numbers I recorded, scientists in Scotland and Norway were very familiar with sea louse outbreaks on young wild salmon near salmon farms. My calculations were based on their science.

The damage to the young Pacific salmon was visually catastrophic. These fish did not yet have a protective sheath of armour-like scales. The large female lice left tracks on the little fry where their appendages had punctured the fish as they gripped it. Some of the lice were grazing on the fishes' eyeballs. Other lice had dark red streaks down their translucent backs, the blood of the young salmon visible in their pulsing digestive tracts. These fish were no longer plump and glossy, but pockmarked with holes eaten into them, their bellies sucked in around their rib cage.

I made an appointment with the DFO senior scientist in charge of the sampling attempted by the *Odysseus*, Dr. Dick Beamish, to discuss the disparity between his results and mine. I knew the Department would make a public statement at some point soon. I suspected, given my experience, they would try to deflect my concern. Beamish was at a disadvantage, in that he had not seen the outbreak himself. I, however, had been aboard the *Odysseus* and saw that while the seven pinks they caught at the western edge of the archipelago were lice-free, the chum salmon they'd caught had so many lice hanging off them it looked like they were wrapped in shag carpeting. Did he know about them? Since a multitude of southern wild salmon runs migrate along the western edge of the archipelago, the seven pink salmon, caught just inside that geographic boundary, may not have swum past the farms.

I came to the meeting with Beamish carrying a few fish preserved in glass jars filled with alcohol so he could see the condition they were in, along with data and photos to allow him to draw his conclusions from a larger perspective. He thanked me for coming, but was condescending, making sure I knew that as far as he was concerned my observations meant nothing. As I left, he actually offered me a Beanie Baby, a child's toy he collected. It was humiliating. A few days later, he went ahead and announced there was no sea louse problem in the Broughton Archipelago. The salmon farming industry actually accused me of sticking the lice on the fish and taking pictures.

The next year, 2002, I armed myself with another scientific licence and a better net and learned how to identify all the life stages of a sea louse and to distinguish males from females.

For the first thirty days after they hatch, sea lice change their body size and shape every few days, so you can tell how long a louse has been on a fish. Beginning in mid-April I counted lice on sixty fish at six sites, once a week for ten weeks.

Where there were no farms, the young fish were perfect shimmering slips in sparkling shades of silver and iridescent blue. They grew rapidly as their internal programming drew them to migrate slowly to the west and north. As they passed the salmon farms at Glacier Falls, Burdwood and Wicklow, the little hair-like lice that I'd seen on Chris's fish appeared. These were the youngest lice, called copepodites. In a few hours they extruded a tiny filament and cemented it to the fish so they wouldn't fall off and became chalimus-stage lice. Thus tethered, they grew and, like a horse ground-staked in a field that eats the grass down to bare dirt, the lice ate through the fish's skin and into its flesh.

In the natural world (or the "real world," as Billy likes to say) so few salmon stay in the archipelago over the winter that there are not enough to host large sea louse populations. So come springtime, when young wild salmon leave the rivers and enter the ocean for the first time, there are not enough sea lice to harm them. However, in this new unnatural world, where schools of 600,000 to a million Atlantic salmon are swimming in circles in farms along the coast, sea lice breed on the crowded fish like never before and release billions of larval lice every spring into the young wild salmon migration routes.

I reached out to other researchers in northern BC who were studying pink and chum salmon in Prince Rupert, Rivers Inlet, Smith Inlet and Bella Bella—places on the BC coast with no salmon farms. They generously allowed me to examine the fish they had collected for other types of research, which allowed me, at no cost, to expand my study to cover two-thirds of the province's coastline.

I would publish "Sea lice (*Lepeophtheirus salmonis*) infection rates on juvenile pink (*Oncorhynchus gorbuscha*) and chum (*Oncorhynchus keta*) salmon in the nearshore marine environment of British Columbia, Canada" in 2004 in the *Canadian Journal of Fisheries and Aquatic Sciences*, with Dr. Rick Routledge, Aleria Ladwig and Corey Peet. The scientific team I could call on was growing. Dr. Routledge was a professor of statistics at Simon Fraser University; Corey Peet was a young scientist with an environmental organization that had been involved on this issue for a few years. Aleria Ladwig, the DFO representative for the Broughton area, got into serious trouble with the Department for being listed on this paper. We discovered that where there were no farms, there were almost no lice. The highest 2002 louse count outside the Broughton was a total of two lice on a sample of 566 fish. Meanwhile in the Broughton, 90 percent of young wild salmon were infected. Broughton fish had eight times more lice after they'd passed a fish farm and there were five times more lice on wild fish near farms stocked with farm fish that had been in the sea pens for over a year compared to fish that had been in the farms for less than a year. The numbers of copepodites spiked near the farms, suggesting the farms harboured the mother lice, which carry their eggs in string-like "tails."

As the little pink and chum salmon reached the first fish farms on their migratory path, many weighed just 0.3 grams. They weren't big enough to survive a single louse, and yet they were sprinkled with more lice at every farm they passed. I named a bay in Fife Sound the Bay of the Damned, because by the time the little salmon reached it, the lice had overwhelmed them. They hardly looked like fish, they were shrunken and blotched, pricked full of holes. Their gill covers were grazed away and they had lice on their eyeballs. They lay on the surface of the water waiting to die, and the kingfishers snapped them up.

As I approached a school of fish, I could tell if they had lice on them, because the newly infected fish were jumping, trying to dislodge the lice. Fish shivered as the lice crawled across their skin. The suffering was incalculable. Imagine having a parasite the size of a rat attached to you, gnawing away, and having no hands to remove it.

After counting them I couldn't leave the lice on them. At first the fish were scared of my tweezers, but after I removed one louse, the fish would stay still and let me get every one. I knew the fish were so full of holes that the ability of their skin to keep the salt out was shot, that viruses had an open door to their bodies and that there were billions more lice waiting for them at the next farm. But these moments of one-on-one first aid were therapeutic for us both, even if the relief was short-lived. When I asked the salmon farmers to let me count lice on their fish they refused. They were not the problem, supposedly, but they wouldn't let me confirm that.

The environmental groups did a good job telling the public that the wild salmon they loved so much were being eaten to death by sea lice from salmon farms. Dozens of newspapers printed my pictures. People were horrified. Every time the salmon farming industry applied for a new tenure, the application was sent for review to the First Nation whose territory it was in. While many nations had signed financial agreements with the companies and approved the tenures, the Broughton nations did neither. Yet Stolt Sea Farm was gifted with yet another tenure in Tribune Channel, called Humphrey Rock, by the province, against the wishes of the First Nations and despite the escalating public reaction to the sea louse outbreaks.

That spring of 2002 an unprecedented thing happened. Dr. Brian Riddell of DFO, who had been seconded to the Pacific Fisheries Resource Conservation Council, contacted me saying that he wanted to come up for a few days and look at the fish. I was so relieved that finally a salmon expert was going to assess the situation.

I took him into the bays where the fish formed big schools and Riddell stared intently at them. Leaning over the side of my boat, he muttered under his breath, "This isn't right, this is not right." He was a human encyclopedia on salmon. He understood how bad the infestation was.

That fall, 99 percent of the Broughton pink salmon that had migrated to sea the year before through the sea louse epidemic did not return. Pink salmon returns were good coastwide, except to the seven rivers of the Broughton where DFO counted returning salmon. This was even worse than the 98 percent drop my data had predicted. Brian Riddell called a meeting of DFO and provincial staff responsible for the salmon farms. There may have been representatives from fish farming there too, but I don't remember them. As I drove the two hours down to the meeting in Campbell River, I readied myself for the fight. My warnings had been ignored for over a decade, and now the industry appeared to be killing off massive amounts of wild fish. If I had been charged for poaching five young fish, what should happen to those responsible for destroying millions?

Riddell spoke first. He said sea lice from salmon farms appeared to be killing massive numbers of pink salmon in the Broughton Archipelago, and he recommended taking all the farms out of the area for one year to see what happened. I could not believe my ears. A thrill of hope shot through me. I held my breath waiting to hear what the provincial regulators would say in the face of the Department of Fisheries and Oceans' chief scientist responsible for salmon. Their pushback was feeble. The provincial reps countered that they would be willing to order that all farm salmon on the primary migration route of the Broughton pink salmon be removed for one year. I went on record to object that I didn't think this would work, because in six hours in the Broughton sea lice could drift ten kilometres, the distance the tides moved twice daily. I said all the farms needed to be removed.

However, Riddell was a better negotiator than me. He agreed with the regulators and then turned to me, asking me to pick the route. It would only be for one year, 2003, but it was the first victory in this fight in the thirteen years. I remember driving back with my windows rolled down and the music up high. As soon as I got home I created a map. The majority of wild salmon in the Broughton, even those from the Glendale River in Knight Inlet, migrated to sea via Tribune Channel, through the Burdwood Islands, and out Fife Sound. This should be the fallow route.

As usual, the province and the fish farm companies whittled away at the plan. First they nixed the easternmost third of the route, which left three salmon farms in operation and put the Glendale pink salmon at risk. Then they revised the plan so that the farms could either be empty *or* stocked with young fish, which my own research had shown were less damaging to the wild salmon than older fish. They also switched the name from the Sea Louse Action Plan to the Pink Salmon Action Plan.

I began counting sea lice on young wild salmon early in the spring of 2003 to measure the impact of the fallowing. By now I had upgraded to a beach seine instead of a dip net. The seine was 150 feet long and about 7 feet deep, one edge of the net lined with little floats and the other lined with lead weights, called the lead line. I nosed my boat up to the shore, jumped out, tied a line from the net piled up in my boat to a tree or boulder, got back in the boat and backed around in a large half-circle as the net played out. Then I jumped out of the boat again farther down the beach, walked along the beach to pull the net closed and then hauled the net in, mounding it on the rocky beach and leaving a pocket of the net in the water. I gently scooped up one hundred little fish from this pocket in the net at each site. This was my sample to examine for lice.

The beach seine allowed me to see all kinds of fish. Along with the salmon, I looked at herring, greenling, rock cod, sand lance, sculpins, pilchard and shiner perch. All the fish species were infected with lice. The voracious coho and chinook smolts, the "teenager" phase for salmon, much bigger than the baby pink and chum salmon fry, used the net to their advantage and grabbed the littler fish, swallowing them as fast as they could. When they were full they would grab another fish and swim around with it T-boned in their mouths.

The improvement in the condition of the young salmon in 2003 was unmistakable. The number of sea lice dropped from the average of seven lice per fish in 2002 to less than one. If these fish were to survive, this was the direction things had to go. This improvement showed that as salmon farms are removed sea lice infection of young wild salmon plummets.

When Dr. Dick Beamish, from DFO, submitted a paper on the increase in survival rate of the Broughton pink salmon during the one year that the salmon farms were fallow (in 2003 up 1,480 percent from 2002) to a scientific journal for publication, the journal sent a copy to me for review. It is standard practice for journals, before they accept scientific manuscripts for publication, to send them to other scientists in the same field. Such peer review is generally anonymous. I never know who is reviewing my work, and Beamish did not know I was reviewing his. He had completely omitted mention of the drastic measures put in place with the Pink Salmon Action Plan and its potential role in the unheard of rise in survival rate. Instead, the premise of his paper was that wild and farm salmon can coexist.

I recommended that his paper not be published without reporting the fallowing of salmon farms on the pink salmon migration route. When Beamish rejected my comment, I did not change my position. This went back and forth, until finally the editor asked whether I felt comfortable revealing my identity in order to resolve the situation. When I did Beamish immediately inserted a terse acknowledgement that some of the farms had been fallowed in 2003. If the paper had been published without recognition of the fallowing, its readers would have drawn a false conclusion that pink salmon were thriving among salmon farms. The opposite was true: pink salmon thrived when salmon farming on wild salmon migration routes was heavily reduced.

Many of us, including some DFO scientists, academics, Dr. Riddell and myself, requested that the fallowing experiment be repeated. If something happens once it could be a coincidence, but if the farms had been fallowed a second year and sea lice levels stayed low and wild salmon survival remained high, the evidence that salmon farms were driving Broughton salmon towards extinction would have been stronger. Not only were we turned down, but the province removed all reference to the Pink Salmon Action Plan from its website. The result did not support policy. Fallowing farms had worked too well, better than anyone expected. If people saw that wild salmon only thrived without salmon farms, the federal and provincial governments would have had to do something permanent about those farms.

Sea lice are a naturally occurring parasitic crustacean that has evolved to live on salmon. Female lice have two long tail-like structures that contain 250 to 500 eggs, stacked like hockey pucks, which remain attached to the female until they hatch. The newly hatched lice have no ability to hang on to a salmon; instead they have a helicopter-like attachment on their head that enables them to drift in the current. This ensures that the babies don't parasitize their mom's host fish and build up lice numbers that would be lethal to it.

After several days adrift, the larval lice moult into a new body and now they are ready to catch a salmon, the only fish they can complete their life cycle on. Though they are born with innate instructions to jump up really fast if a shadow passes over them, most young lice never find a salmon and die.

When they do find a salmon host, the lice moult within hours, and after extruding a tiny filament from their heads and cementing themselves to the fish, they can relax and graze on salmon mucus and grow and moult four more times as they increase in size. On the fifth moult, they disengage from the tether and adopt a suction-method of staying aboard the fish. Now they can move around on the fish, find mates and tuck into the least turbulent locations on the fish, just past the arc of the belly in the indent above the salmon's anal fin. There the lice keep moulting four more times as they grow. Eventually, they die when the salmon enters freshwater, which is lethal to sea lice.

In the wild, their difficult childhood keeps lice populations low. Sea lice don't seem to bother wild salmon, which appear to make more than enough mucus to feed a few lice and still protect themselves from disease. The problem caused by the salmon farms is the million or so salmon going around in circles that never migrate out to sea. Thus the lice keep breeding in the bays along the coast all winter, and in the spring their reproduction accelerates as water temperatures increase. Instead of entering an archipelago swept clean by the tides of winter, young wild salmon were migrating through clouds of lice at every operating farm.

Amy McConnell volunteered as my deckhand for my sea louse work. We became a well-oiled team, setting the beach seine net, collecting the fish in buckets, measuring and counting tens of thousands of lice and then setting the fish free. As I backed the boat away, releasing the 150-foot net into the water in a half-circle, Amy walked down the beach a short distance and caught the line I threw from the other end of the net. She then pulled in the net, corralling the fish in the bunt, while

I lifted the bottom of the net over submerged rocks and sunken logs. Some mornings my daughter slept in the bow of the boat, and we tried not to wake her—we called these "whisper sets."

This research showed that young wild salmon always and only get infected near salmon farms and that when the farms are empty, or even if the salmon in the farms are young and therefore have a lower accumulation of lice, the sea lice numbers on the wild salmon plummet.

I began to publish several papers a year on my sea lice research, and hoped that the appearance of these papers in international scientific journals would help the BC government understand that the sea lice pouring out of the salmon farms were driving wild salmon numbers down. But even at this pace, my research was not enough to bring the relief wild salmon needed to survive.

What could I do now? I'd watched so many young salmon die, losing their struggle to stay upright and alive. I had done talk shows and other media interviews, and met with fishing and tourism organizations, but it was not enough. I realized more people needed to see the suffering and loss and so I invited other scientists to the Broughton, offering to feed and house them while they were here. They came. Dinner was pretty much the same every night—brown rice cooked in coconut milk, kale from the garden and whatever else was at hand. My daughter, now six, dubbed this meal "glop." But it was all I could afford, and it was nutritious, inexpensive, stick-to-your-ribs food.

The teams of young scientists who stayed with us were hard-working and brilliant. They pursued more answers as to what the sea louse epidemic meant to the young wild salmon. With crews of volunteers, they travelled much farther than I did, sampling fish over a larger area. We published on the technique of counting lice without killing the fish, showing that we got the same results whether the fish were dead or alive and that fish could survive the procedure. After scooping approximately a hundred fish out of the seine net with a bucket, we deployed a tiny aquarium net to transfer each fish gently into a small plastic bag along with a little seawater. The fish could survive in the bag for a couple of minutes; during that time we examined them through the bag with a hand lens. We measured them by laying the bag, with the fish in it, on a piece of graph paper and counting off the squares. Then we released them into dark-coloured recovery buckets; we'd learned that these little salmon changed their colour to match the buckets. When we put them into white buckets, they lightened enough to make them easy targets for predators.

Of the scientists, two young women used a kids' inflatable swimming pool with a camera rigged overhead to discover that even if lice didn't kill a fish, a single louse exerted enough drag to put the fish in the high-risk "predator zone" at the back of the school. Another student rigged a model blue heron that tipped and hit the surface of the water. Every time this happened, all the fish darted away, but he saw that the fish that were infected with lice returned to this predator zone much faster than the healthy fish. He surmised that because the heavy grazing of the lice was draining the young fishes' resources, the infested fish became desperate for food and this drove them to take risks that would lead to increased capture by predators.

One young researcher caught cutthroat trout, put them in tanks and gave them a choice of eating a lousy or a lice-free fish. The trout preferred the lousy fish, and as they ate, the male lice jumped onto the trout. One cutthroat participated with such great enthusiasm, snapping up one lousy fry after the next, his researcher nicknamed him Wolf. Wolf sat perfectly still between trials to let the young man pick the lice off him. When the experiment was over, the scientist took Wolf back to the bay where he was captured and released him.

My home became known as Camp Sea Lice.

DFO finally had to accept that there really was an abnormally high number of lice in the Broughton, but they still weren't ready to make the logical conclusion that similar to everywhere salmon farming occurred, the farms were the reason. Around 2005, they began to lay the blame for the lice infestation on the prickly little fish, the stickleback. Researchers at Camp Sea Lice soon showed this could not be true: the high-relief stickleback scales have a jagged edge that caused the lice to lose their suction grip; also, stickleback simply did not produce enough slime to graze on. Lice could not complete their life cycle aboard a stickleback and thus were unable to reproduce. Furthermore, the young researchers discovered that stickleback actually tried to eat lice off salmon. They were not the problem.

The lengths that DFO went to exonerate the salmon farmers, despite everything that was known and everything we published, would have been funny if the consequences weren't so disturbing. In 2005, one DFO scientist, who I thought had seemed onside with the truth of the situation, told the media that he hadn't found all the lice I was talking about. He didn't mention that he had compared my 2002 data with his 2003 data (the fallow year). I knew that he knew my 2003 data was nearly identical to his. He retired shortly after he made those comments.

In 2004, the farms were restocked and the pink salmon populations continued to collapse. Bear tour guides said that the bears that had gathered at the Glendale River in August to fatten up on pink salmon were so hungry they were starting to eat each other. Tourists were traumatized. The lodge at Glendale began to lend boats to some of the Camp Sea Lice researchers, hoping we could deal with this growing threat to their industry. It might have been better if they had also hired lobbyists, like the fish farmers had.

As DFO reluctantly acknowledged that sea lice were real, the big question became, how many lice does it take to kill a young Pacific salmon? Maybe all these salmon infected with lice were fine. I needed that number so I could report on how many wild salmon the industry was killing. In 2005, I set up an experiment to find out. My partner, Eric, modified sixteen 50-gallon plastic barrels, fitting screens over the ends to allow seawater to flow through them and cutting a door flap in the top. I tied them along a U-shaped arrangement of floats and logs at my dock. I went out and caught young salmon and sorted them into the barrels according to how many lice they had. It was a massive undertaking. To get the right number of fish with the right number of lice on them, I had to examine 1,080 fish caught in the beach seine with my hand lens. Sixty fish went into each barrel. Three sets of four barrels per trial were stocked with fish with zero lice, four barrels had fish with one louse, four with three lice and four with four lice. Once the barrels were stocked, I fed all the fish the same amount every day and watched over them for thirty-five days. When local river otters became too interested, I set up a tent and my daughter and I camped by the fish. Ahta, a husky-lab cross was just a puppy then, and too terrified of the otters to chase them off, but she woke me by trying to dive under my sleeping bag every time she heard them and I scared the otters off.

I invited DFO scientists to view the experiment while it was running so that there wouldn't be any doubts or criticism later. Then, to strengthen the result, I ran the whole experiment two more times. I camped on the dock for over three months on otter patrol. The fish without lice grew impressively fast and went free at the end of each trial, but if just one louse remained attached long enough to moult into its adult stages, the fish died. I carefully preserved all the dead fish in case the Department wanted to examine them. I thought I had thoroughly guarded against anyone being able to dismiss these results. I published "Mortality rates for juvenile pink *Oncorhynchus gorbuscha* and chum *O. keta* salmon infested with sea lice *Lepeophtheirus salmonis* in the Broughton Archipelago" in the *Alaska Fishery Research Bulletin*.

The next year, a DFO scientist named Simon Jones did a similar experiment in a laboratory set-up. Before his study was over, I began hearing rumours that the fish in his trial were not dying of lice. I simply could not believe this. I had spent three months watching a total of 3,240 fish. The ones with even a single mature louse died. I made an appointment with Dr. Jones to view the fish in his experiment.

He took me into the lab with the fish tanks at four in the afternoon. It was pitch black inside.

"Simon, I can't see anything," I said.

"Yes, well, I can't turn the lights on. I am replicating the daylight hours in the Broughton," he explained.

"It is never dark in the archipelago at 4 p.m.," I said.

Dr. Jones did not respond and he did not turn on the lights. We stood awkwardly in the dark until I left.

What I should have done was go back the next day and the next and the day after that until he showed me the fish. But I didn't, and as a result I never saw these fish, which were allegedly thriving despite the lice or any pictures of them. When Jones published his finding that young pink salmon were quite resistant to sea lice, it was used to discredit mine. Marty Krkošek, the first young scientist to work out of my place in the Broughton, did the experiment yet again, using a different and more robust method with a larger number of fish. He too found that sea lice kill young wild salmon. Jones's result was an outlier, but DFO clung to it like a life raft in the rising sea of evidence that salmon farms were killing wild salmon.

Fortunately, from about 2003 to 2008, a lot of people demanded an end to death by sea lice for the runs of wild salmon in the Broughton. Images of young salmon wounded by the lice appeared on billboards in downtown Vancouver. We at Camp Sea Lice published our findings in one of the highest-impact journals in the world, *Science*. Environmental groups were drawn to help and they were relentless pressuring government. They were the first to make the point that the solution was to move this industry onto land so that the province could benefit from both wild salmon and aquaculture. The Living Oceans Society, Georgia Strait Alliance and Watershed Watch were leaders in this effort. Elected Chief Councillor Robert Chamberlin of the Kwikwasut'inuxw Haxwa'mis, one of the nations in the archipelago, a highly skilled statesman, became a force for wild salmon that government could not ignore. The nations of the Broughton delivered a clear message: they had zero tolerance for salmon farms.

In response to all this pressure, the province made the salmon farmers treat the fish in their pens with a drug called Slice to reduce the number of farm lice before the young wild salmon left the rivers in the spring. For a few years sea lice levels plummeted and the wild salmon bounced back. Everyone knew this was a temporary fix, because around the world sea lice were becoming resistant to drugs. As well, Slice was designed to prevent sea lice from forming a shell. It entered the ocean in farm fish feces and the crumbs of the medicated feed that blew out of the feeders. While I didn't do any research on this, many local animals that need to make a shell were likely attracted to the drug-laced feed, including prawns, crabs and shrimp. Prawn and shrimp fishermen were coming to me outraged at the decline in their catches near salmon farms.

These are the choices that burden society today. When we abandon natural systems honed over millennia of evolution and try to build new ones shaped by share price and global markets, we have to expect a high failure rate. As the American ecologist Frank Golley said, "Ecosystems are not only more complicated than we think, they are more complicated than we *can* think." Like a long slow fuse on a bomb, the impact of an action we take may seem manageable until suddenly it is not. If the politicians thought about the issue of sea lice at all, I am guessing they simply hoped the outcome would be delayed until they were no longer in office. Billy Proctor complained that the life cycle of a politician was shorter than a pink salmon's, so they never bore the consequences of their actions.

I knew Slice was bad and wrong for the archipelago, but I couldn't stand in the way of its application because the unique wild salmon DNA that fit Broughton rivers like a key to a lock was dying out. When it's gone, it's gone for good. The alternative was to keep fighting for the perfect solution, while allowing sea lice from salmon farms to drive wild salmon populations towards extinction. Slice might protect the young salmon from lice, but these salmon fed on zooplankton with shells that the drug was likely affecting. As long as the farms remained, it was a vicious circle with no good choices or outcomes.

———

In 2008, the filmmaker Twyla Roscovich asked if she could come live with me and make short films on my work. Twyla was a human hurricane who dominated every room she walked into. She was supersized in every way; even her feet were so big she never fit into women's shoes. She was a strikingly beautiful woman with a husky voice whom I first met when she was only eighteen and making a film on killer whales with the BBC. Her dad, whom she loved very much, was one of the early fish farmers, and she had spent much of her childhood on that farm. But she was able to look beyond her background to see the senseless monster that the industry had become. I saw in her the same filmmaking talent I'd seen in Robin, my late husband, and since more people needed to know about what salmon farming was doing to the coast of British Columbia, I said yes.

Together we made several short films, including one that was aired at the annual general meeting of Cermaq in Norway to make a plea to the shareholders that their company was crushing the life out of a place on the other side of the planet. Twyla filmed the sea lice and how we did the research and posted these films on her site, Calling from the Coast. She was never strident in her films; an innately gifted storyteller, she worked long hours to perfect the message. She deeply loved this coast, as I do, and she helped enormously in bringing this issue to people in a way that they could understand. The vast majority of us don't follow our minds, we follow our hearts. It's love that makes people stand up and react. The only places that are going to survive us are the places we love so fiercely that giving up is not an option, at whatever the cost.

When my daughter's father and I split in 2008 (and who could blame him, when all I did was sea lice science), I had to put my place up for sale, even though I didn't want to abandon the industrious young researchers of Camp Sea Lice, leaving them with no base to work from. Then a very unusual buyer named Sarah Haney appeared. She bought my homestead and asked if I would keep running it as a research station!

Sarah rolled her sleeves up and worked as the cook while crews arrived to install more solar panels, add a micro-hydro system that produced electricity from running water, and upgraded the dock and kitchen. We formed a society and Camp Sea Lice became the Salmon Coast Field Station; some of the original students joined the board of directors. Scott Rogers, who ran several years of sea lice sampling, stepped up to become the first onsite manager.

While I had vowed to never to start a research station, because I did not want to be surrounded by people that I needed to look after, I could see why others had taken this path. It is stressful trying to keep it funded and it won't last forever, but every year the station exists, we learn more about the impact of salmon farms and what wild salmon need in order to survive. If the farms were removed, we would need to act fast to salvage what is left. Knowing what is broken and how it was broken would speed that process. Without the work done at my field camp, the disappearance of the wild salmon of the Broughton would have been a mystery and nothing would have been done to try to save them.

The sea lice surveys I began in 2001 are still continuing. Long-term databases like this are as rare as they are valuable. *Sliding baseline* is a term used to describe the massive forgetting that is occurring world-wide. People such as Billy Proctor and the Elders of the Indigenous communities are the knowledge holders, reminding us of what was. I am becoming a holder of valuable knowledge too, even with my much shorter experience in the archipelago, because so much has changed in the thirty years I've lived here. Newcomer biologists don't know that this was once a wintering ground for the A5 whale families. In fact I fear the whales themselves might not know this anymore. Most of the matriarchs who were out in front picking the routes when they were chased away by the farms have died.

Our efforts and the use of Slice bought the salmon populations of the Broughton a fifteen-year life extension. But in 2015 the sea lice returned at lethal levels, perhaps due to the evolution of resistance to Slice in the lice, which (though the farmers denied this) happens everywhere salmon farmers operate in ocean pens.

By 2018, so few young salmon migrated out of the rivers of the Broughton that they were nearly invisible. When I began studying sea lice, there were so many young salmon they formed a near-continuous ribbon of tiny fish a couple of metres wide over the length of Tribune Channel. They filled entire bays. I lay on the roof of my boat on many days, drifting among them, because I loved watching them. To catch zooplankton, they coil into an S shape and then release, which causes them to dart forward. They often nudged the surface of the water in pursuit of prey, the bays of the archipelago so dimpled with their presence it looked like rain.

Now there are only small panicked schools. They know it is risky to be the last fish or the outside fish in the school, in the predator zone. But in the small groups of just a few dozen fish I observed in 2018 and 2019 there really is no safe zone. Only 0.1 percent of the pink salmon run returned to the Glendale River, Broughton's biggest river, in 2019. A local photographer, Rolf Hicker, posted photos of emaciated grizzly bears, starved for salmon, that went viral. It was no comfort at all that I had seen this coming.

7.

Norway, the Mother Country

AN EMAIL DATED May 2, 2006, from Georges Lemieux, the senior
trade commissioner with the Canadian embassy in Oslo, to international relations staff ended up in the inbox of Andrew Thomson, DFO's
Director of Aquaculture in British Columbia. In it Lemieux explained
that Cermaq's CEO, Geir Isaksen, was disappointed in Canada.
Cermaq wanted to see "more support from government in countering
myths and disinformation about the aquaculture industry," he wrote.
Lemieux explained that he had gone back to Isaksen to show him that
the Department had responded to Cermaq's concerns with a web page
titled "Myths and realities about salmon farming." This was a page on a
government-funded and -sponsored website that painted my science as
a myth.

The Norwegian CEO had replied that while this was a "good start,"
he wanted the Canadian government to do more—to "market" his industry to Canadians.

I figured it was time to go to Norway.

Flying into Oslo looked like flying over British Columbia, with the
same inlets or fjords and mountainous evergreen forests below me.
It was 2009, and I was with a delegation that included First Nation

chiefs Robert Chamberlin and Bobby Joseph, a filmmaker and political blogger named Damien Gillis, a BC tourism operator, and scientists and activists from Chile and Scotland. A concerned shareholder had invited us to speak at the annual general meetings for two of the three companies using the province of BC to grow salmon, Marine Harvest and Cermaq.

After two decades of dealing with their industry, I'd expected Norwegians to be oblivious to the subject of protecting the environment, but they were quite the opposite. People were actively conscious of their impact on the environment, riding bikes everywhere. Having lived off-grid since 1981, I loved that the plastic key card that opened my hotel room door had to be inserted into a slot in the wall to make the power come on. Every house in the world should have something like this so people can easily turn off everything that doesn't need to be on. Living off-grid, you learn not to waste power, never leaving useless lights or clocks running. If I forget to turn these little power-eaters off, my house batteries can lose 15 percent of their charge overnight.

However, when it came to protection of wild salmon, it was clear that Norwegians, as a whole, had made the choice to sacrifice wild fish for farmed. Where British Columbia had 120 salmon farms, there were over 900 in Norway. At the time a single farm salmon in Norway was almost as valuable as a barrel of oil and, later, they became more valuable than oil. Norway referred to salmon farming as its IKEA, as crucial to the country as IKEA was to Sweden.

Shortly after we arrived in the spring of 2009, I met with a group of Norwegian scientists who were researching the impact of salmon farms. This was the first time I had the opportunity to talk with scientists who completely understood the damage I was observing in the Broughton and who knew more than me. I had so many questions for them that when time ran out on the space they had rented for our meeting, we moved next door into a hotel lobby and talked for hours longer. They knew the sea lice were killing off the wild salmon and sea trout; in Norway, industry did not pretend this wasn't happening. They also suspected that farm-bred viruses were infecting their wild stocks, though this meeting was before they had discovered that piscine ortho-reovirus, a virus that I ended up chasing through British Columbia, was multiplying and mutating in hundreds of farms.

These scientists did not want to give up on wild salmon. They longed to have as many wild salmon as we still had left in BC. They described how only the young wild salmon they treated with anti-lice drugs before they left their rivers made it back to spawn. In their view, this confirmed that the sea lice on the farms were responsible for the collapse of wild salmon and sea trout. (Sea trout are related to salmon, but they generally stay in the estuary or fjord near the river where they were born, so they are exposed to salmon farm effluent throughout their lives.)

The Norwegian scientists told me their biggest problem with salmon farms was genetic pollution, something we don't face in British Columbia, except in the few chinook and steelhead farms on our coast. They described catching every salmon going up some rivers to spawn, tagging it, taking a tiny sample of its fins and putting it in a holding pool. Then they quickly ran tests on these samples to determine if the salmon were wild or had escaped from a farm. Only the wild salmon were allowed to continue upriver to spawn; the farm salmon were killed. These scientists were fighting to preserve the genetic adaptions that allowed salmon to thrive in each river.

The male escapees were aggressive, chased off the wild males and bred with wild females. Their babies were big, voracious feeders, qual-ities bred for by the industry. In the wild, these large hybrids outcom-peted the smaller wild fish for food, reducing the chances of survival of the wild fish. But when salmon with farm genetics left the rivers for the ocean they made poor choices; a large percentage did not make it back to spawn. Since escaped farm fish had starved out the young wild salmon and displaced the wild males, Norway's rivers were becoming increas-ingly empty of all salmon. Too late, big money was being spent to screen all the salmon entering Norwegian rivers and eradicate the farm salmon, but there was no getting ahead of the situation when farm salmon kept leaking out of the cages. These men had the wild salmon in Norway on life support. They knew they were losing the battle to save them, but they were not giving up.

The Vosso River held a legendary status in Norway. Before salmon farms, the Vosso salmon were the biggest Atlantic salmon in the world. To save them these scientists were catching them as juveniles before they left the river, putting them in large tubes that allowed water to flow through, and towing these tubes past the fish farms and far enough out to sea that they were safe. They towed them in order to get them by the farms as quickly as possible to prevent lice infestations, while still giving the young Vosso salmon a chance to memorize their way back to the river.

I told the Norwegians that I had tried to do a similar thing in 2008. The Kwikwasut'inuxw First Nation in the Broughton issued me a permit to catch and transfer young pink salmon in Bond Sound, coming from the Ahta River, and basically medevac them past the three farms owned by Marine Harvest (Mowi) and Cermaq to the open waters of Queen Charlotte Strait. I planned to use a fish boat, fill its hold with seawater and pump water from the ocean through the boat as it travelled past the farms to allow the fish to imprint on the route they would have to navigate on their return trip to spawn. But DFO sent an officer in a seaplane to intercept me in Tribune Channel, stopping me before I could go through with the plan.

I also went to meet Dr. Are Nylund at the University of Bergen. The salmon farming industry had gone after him hard, filing damaging ethics violation complaints and charges of fraud, first to the university and then to the national-level government Integrity Committee after Nylund and his co-authors reported that the most lethal known salmon virus, infectious salmon anemia virus or ISAV, had been introduced to Chile in farm salmon from a Norwegian hatchery. Nylund and his colleagues fought these charges. Their science was solid and eventually they were cleared, but the damage had been done to their careers. (Years after I met with Nylund, in June 2017, their experience was made public in an article printed in the Norwegian publication, *Harvest*, under the title "A Researcher's Nightmare.") Nylund had heard about my work and wanted to meet me. He told me to watch out; he was the second Norwegian scientist to do so.

I did not sleep well in Norway so much was coming to light. These companies had the audacity to blame tiny schools of stickleback for the lice problem in British Columbia, when scientists in their home country were towing wild salmon past farms as fast as possible trying to protect them from the farm lice. With impact of the industry so obvious in Norway, why was my government allowing these companies to damage Canadian ecosystems in the same way? Was industry scheming about how to take advantage of British Columbia in the head offices here in Norway or in Canada?

While the provincial government kept telling me they needed made-in-BC data before they would act, all the research they needed on the industry already existed here in Norway. To the scientists in Norway, it was entirely predictable that the industry was causing catastrophic damage to Pacific salmon. As my colleagues and I produced high-quality published science to reveal the dangers, the industry was silencing scientists around us and establishing more farm sites. All they had to do was make the public think that the harm resulting from fish farming was a subject of complex, honest, scientific debate. It wasn't. They fought peer-reviewed solid science with media lines crafted to seed doubt.

I learned that Norway's first salmon farmer was Norsk Hydro, a company that built dams on Norway's rivers. Geoff Meggs of the Fisherman's Union had once told me that he thought introducing salmon farming to BC was about weaning people off wild salmon so that the mighty Fraser River could be dammed and the power sold to the US. I hadn't believed him, but I had to reconsider his theory when I learned that a company that dams rivers to make electricity had started this whole industry.

———

Marine Harvest (now Mowi) was largely owned by a billionaire named John Fredriksen, nicknamed The Wolf for his predatory business practices. This is a Norwegian who became a citizen of Cyprus to avoid paying taxes at home, and whose main gig is tankers. Marine Harvest was just a small part of his empire. When I walked with the opposition delegation into the Marine Harvest AGM in Oslo, I was at last among the people who were profiting from the destruction of the waters I called home. I looked around, fascinated. These were well-dressed Europeans who mingled easily with each other. I was in a thrift-shop dress and I have never gotten the hang of makeup. I felt impossibly out of place.

I was seated next to a woman in a tight leopard-print jumpsuit. On the other side of me was a man wearing powder-blue cowboy boots. When the Chilean labour leader from our delegation told this crowd about the hardship caused by Marine Harvest to the poor coastal people of Chile, the woman in the leopard-print jumpsuit stood up and said, "If you people would just work with us, I think we would find that you love salmon as much as I do. I just love salmon."

I headed for the podium, suppressing my anxiety by thinking about the young salmon I'd picked the lice from. I kept my remarks brief, telling the shareholders how they were damaging British Columbia and also that they could fix this simply by moving their farms off the wild salmon migration routes of the coast. As I was heading back to my seat, the chairman of the board gave a little laugh and leaned into the microphone to say, "I hate to disappoint you but we are not going anywhere."

Chief Robert Chamberlin was next. He started his speech in Kwak'wala, then opened a small jewellery box and presented a pair of silver wolf earrings to the CEO of Marine Harvest, Åse Aulie Michelet. She thanked him. She may have thought these were a gift, but true to his culture, Bob was paying her to hear his words. It seemed that neither she nor anyone else in that room did.

On my last night in Norway, Michelet asked to speak to me in private at Marine Harvest's head office. We sat at a polished table in a room awash in the company's signature orange colours. She asked if I had enjoyed my time in Norway. I told her that I had been pleased to learn that Norwegian scientists shared my concerns about her industry and that I didn't think Marine Harvest was being honest about its impact in British Columbia.

She nodded and then got to her point. "What are you talking about when you told our media that none of our boats have licences on them?"

This was certainly not the issue I expected her to raise. Still, I told her that every boat carrying fish in Canada had to display a licence number large enough to be read at a distance, except for the boats moving farm salmon. She nervously pushed a plate of cookies towards me. Her biggest shareholder was a shipping magnate. He knew how to license ships.

"We are operating legally in Canada," she said.

I said it didn't look that way.

"What do you want?" she asked, with another gesture for me to take a cookie. Again I ignored the offering.

I have thought about her question a lot. Should I have said "a million dollars" just to see what would have happened? Instead I replied, "I want you to get your farms off wild salmon migration routes."

That was the end of the meeting.

A year later, Georg Fredrik Rieber-Mohn, the former attorney general of Norway who had been appointed in 1995 to devise a plan to protect Norway's wild salmon, published an editorial on the eve of the Norway vs. Canada hockey game at the 2010 Olympic Games in Vancouver. I'd met him in Norway, and in his editorial Rieber-Mohn referred to that meeting, saying that he'd experienced a sense of déjà vu while hearing me describe how Norwegian companies were causing harm to BC wild salmon due to their sea louse outbreaks.

Rieber-Mohn went on to write that sea lice from salmon farms had killed up to 90 percent of some Norwegian wild salmon runs and that his "wild salmon plan" had recommended prohibiting salmon farms in nine fjord systems, a ban that would have protected fifty of Norway's best salmon rivers. Apparently John Fredriksen, The Wolf, had agreed and had made a passionate plea for adopting the ban in 2007 as he stood on the River Alta, one of Norway's last great salmon rivers.

But, Rieber-Mohn wrote, intense lobbying by the salmon farming industry watered down the wild salmon plan in what he described as a "heavy defeat" that has led to the near extinction of wild salmon in many rivers in Norway. He ended his editorial with a plea to Canada: "If we don't seize the opportunity now to move salmon farms out of the way of wild salmon we will all be losers." This was an incredibly powerful statement by one of Norway's highest officials made when all eyes were on Norway and Canada in the Olympics. And still Canada and British Columbia opted not to listen.

Part II

A Year
of Activism

8.

Ground-Truthing

ON JANUARY 20, 2010, I received a tip that the Grieg Seafood farms in Nootka Sound, on the west side of Vancouver Island, were infested with sea lice that the drug Slice wouldn't touch. This was alarming news because I knew that rising drug resistance in sea lice on salmon farms was having catastrophic impact on wild salmon and sea trout in Scotland and Norway.

The research coming out of those countries provided a remarkable narrative of how sea lice eventually became resistant to every drug developed to kill them. There were drugs, like Slice, that stopped them from making a shell as they moulted, and neurotoxins that made them lose their grip on the fish and fall off. When salmon famers began using other species of fish to pick the lice off and eat them, the lice responded by becoming transparent so that the cleaner fish simply could not see them. If sea lice became drug-resistant in British Columbia, their populations would explode in the farms and they would not only disfigure the farm fish, there would be no protection left for the wild salmon. As it stood in 2010, DFO and industry were clinging to the tired media line that sea lice were under control, that they weren't convinced the lice were coming from the farms and that everything was fine.

Over the years I have received many tips from fish farmers. I have learned not to make a move until I hear the same report from several different and unrelated sources. This time, I wrote to Mia Parker, the communications person for Grieg Seafood, and got no answer. I wrote to the local First Nation fisheries and got no answer. Then several people who sounded like they were on scene began calling. They did not want to be identified, which is typical, but they provided eyewitness accounts and more details. They said that Grieg was culling their three-pound fish—seven pounds shy of harvest size—and moving others into fresher water, since freshwater kills sea lice.

I asked one of the people who called me if there was anyone concerned about wild salmon stocks in the Nootka Sound area who could step up and investigate this. The whistle-blower said no and went on to explain that representatives from Grieg had recently walked into the local watershed council meeting, where all issues affecting salmon are discussed, and dropped a fifty-thousand-dollar donation cheque on the table. This was an enormous sum for a group subsisting on bake sales and raffles to raise money to deal with wild salmon issues like stream habitat damage. The person who contacted me said that donations like this made it hard for people to admit that the salmon farms were doing damage. The industry was providing the first real money the watershed council had ever received.

Nootka wasn't the only place I ran into a situation where a group dedicated to protecting salmon was given money or equipment by one of the Norwegian fish farm companies and consequently refused to consider the impact their donor was having on the very fish they were trying to save. One of the many reasons I admire Billy Proctor is that when he was president of the Scott Cove hatchery near Echo Bay, he refused a donation from Stolt Sea Farm, saying that he would "rather pick shit with the chickens."

Next I wrote to the local point person for DFO, area supervisor John Lewis. He gave the well-worn response: the department was not in the driver's seat, I needed to talk to the province. This was not entirely accurate, given that DFO, not the province, was technically in charge of protecting wild fish, which includes protecting them from industrial effluent. The sea lice from salmon farms were an industrial biological pollutant flowing unchecked into the ocean. The people I contacted at the province did not answer; I was back in the vortex of disregard.

Then another informant contacted me to say that the farm fish from the infected pens were being trucked to Quadra Island, off the other side of Vancouver Island, for processing. Quadra is one of the Discovery Islands, which are the heart of the Fraser River salmon migration route. If drug-resistant sea lice were introduced there, the threat to Fraser River wild salmon stocks would be enormous. At this point, I had spent nine years observing the impact of sea lice on young wild salmon. I had extended this research into the Discovery Islands, where the young wild salmon were scarred and dying of lice, just like in the Broughton. First Nations and conservation groups used my science to pressure government into ensuring that the local fish farmers began treating their fish with Slice; this allowed a much larger percentage of the young migrating wild salmon to survive. Transporting drug resistant lice into the Discovery Islands put this hard-won progress at risk.

When I called the province again, this time about trucking infested fish into the Discovery Islands, Trevor Rhodes, director of the Aquaculture branch of the provincial Ministry of Agriculture, stated that the lice on the salmon from the Grieg farms had a "minimal chance of survival" on the truck ride across the island. If any of them were released with the effluent from the processing plant, they would be dead and therefore no threat to Vancouver Island rivers or the Fraser River. I didn't believe him. I had seen live lice moving around on the young salmon killed during the early years of my sea lice research. Researchers at the Salmon Coast Field Station were keeping lice alive for days on dead fish for use in experiments.

I asked my filmmaker friend Twyla Roscovich and Jody Eriksson, a fisherman and resident of the Discovery Islands, if they would dive the eighty feet down to the outfall pipe of the Walcan processing plant on Quadra where the Grieg lice-infested salmon were being processed and get me a sample. They were game. Twyla filmed the thick plume of blood spewing out of the facility's effluent pipe, carrying scales and bits of hearts and other organs. Jody placed a fine-mesh plankton net over the end and held it there for several minutes, then sealed the net and carried it to the surface. He put the contents into jars on ice and shipped them to me by bus. I looked at the contents under a microscope and saw adult lice and hundreds of larval sea lice. I watched through the lens of my microscope as the sea lice eggs hatched: they were definitely alive. Because I knew this was going to be a controversial finding, I took pictures and then sent them to an expert in zooplankton at the federal Institute of Ocean Sciences, a branch of DFO. She confirmed they were larval *Lepeophtheirus salmonis*, the salmon louse. Though we had the video and we had the lice, government and industry kept insisting there were no lice. In fact they said there was no effluent, that what we'd seen was just street runoff.

A few weeks later, Jody and Twyla made the dive again and found nothing coming out of the pipe. When they surfaced, they saw the plant's employees lined up watching them. So they went around the corner out of sight and, an hour later, dove in again, dragging themselves along the sea floor, hand-over-hand against the current, towards the plant. Sure enough, they found blood, guts and lice, likely drug-resistant, still flowing out of the pipe into the world's biggest wild salmon migration route.

I had asked the people who had alerted me to this lice situation to take some video and please go public, but as usual they wouldn't. Twyla convinced me we were going to have to go to the Grieg farm ourselves. So Jody trailered his speedboat, and we met up on a frosty January morning and headed for the west coast of Vancouver Island. We launched the boat into the calm waters of Nootka Sound and went in search of the farm fish packer, *Viking Star*. The online marine traffic website, MarineTraffic.com, showed it stationary at a Grieg farm in Esperanza Inlet, and so we headed that way.

Open to the Pacific Ocean, Nootka Sound is stunningly wild. We passed a raft of fifty sea otters bobbing in the gentle swell, holding paws to form a big slumber party. We passed two transient orca. We could feel the big ocean breathing under us in gentle swells, while the protective islands of this west coast paradise smoothed the waters.

The scene at the farm was shocking in contrast. Its generator throbbed a deep industrial undertone, the pumps on the *Viking Star* added another layer of noise, and the pneumatic hammer—used to kill each fish as it was pumped on deck from the pens before it was sluiced towards the ship's hold—punctuated the quiet day. Female lice were gripping the packer's black hull, their long egg strings hanging down. Jody leaned over the side of his boat and picked up a sea louse that was free-swimming; it had lost its grip on a salmon during the processing.

I dropped in a plankton net and we towed it around the farm for twenty minutes under the glares of the crew. I had done dozens of such plankton tows near farms; in twenty minutes, I generally caught one or two male lice and another couple of plankton-phase lice, which is the phase just after hatching, before they grow the equipment to latch onto a fish. Male lice jump off a fish if all the females on it are gravid with eggs; one mating allows a female to produce several batches of eggs and the males would rather take their chances free-swimming in the ocean look-ing for another fish, than stay on a fish where there was no foreseeable opportunity to reproduce. At this farm I counted 157 sea lice in my net after twenty minutes. Twyla filmed everything.

When we got back from this expedition, she edited together the footage from the farm, the effluent pipe and my microscope, showing that there was a serious sea louse problem in Nootka Sound and that these lice were entering the Discovery Islands alive, putting the Fraser River and wild salmon at grave risk. I then co-published a paper on this with scientists who had data they hadn't understood until now. Why were there so many lice on young wild salmon in the bay on Quadra Island when there were no farms nearby, only a farm-salmon process-ing plant? We published "Sea louse infestation in wild juvenile salmon and Pacific herring associated with fish farms off the east-central coast of Vancouver Island, British Columbia" in the *North American Journal of Fisheries Management*.

When municipal councillors representing the village of Tahsis, at the northern edge of Nootka Sound, saw Twyla's film they voted to have the salmon farms removed from the region's waters. Local fishermen and First Nations said their chum salmon run had collapsed in recent years. Of course it had: there was no way juvenile chum, which leave their rivers weighing less than a gram, could survive lice levels like this.

The solution was simple. Fine the company in the order of millions of dollars for exceeding sea louse limits and harming populations of wild salmon, and in that way, give the company the financial incentive to clean up or get out. But DFO and the province did nothing to stop the outbreak.

None of the science I did or the videos I commissioned made a difference to the wild salmon being eaten to death.

9.

Get Out Migration

BY THE SPRING of 2010, I'd been working on how to stop salmon farms from killing wild salmon continuously for two decades. At first I'd tried to alert people in authority about the dangers by writing thousands of pages of letters, but no one seemed to be in a position to stop or significantly reduce the impact of this industry. Then I responded to all the bureaucrats who told me that I had no evidence by publishing my observations in scientific journals, and turning my home into a research station where more scientists were publishing more findings on the impact of salmon farms. I'd raised funds for films so everyone could see the damage being done. But nothing changed, and the damage was ongoing.

People were always telling me to just sue the industry, and so I did that too. In 2006, I'd filed a charge against the company that was running the Burdwood farm for illegal release of sea lice under the Fisheries Act. Whoever drafted the Canadian Fisheries Act seemed aware there would be times when government might need help; the act encourages private citizens to file charges for violations. In this case, I combed through the act with a local lawyer, Jeff Jones, and we realized that it is illegal to release "fish" into Canadian waters. Sea lice are a crustacean, crustaceans are listed under the act as a "fish," and the lice were breeding inside the farms and pouring out. So we thought we had a legal argument to stop the lice outbreaks and we laid a charge.

A special prosecutor, William Smart, was assigned to assess the strength of my case. While in his opinion he recognized that the public interest was at stake, he recommended the charge be stayed and so it was not allowed to proceed. In 2010, I laid another charge under the Fisheries Act for Marine Harvest's illegal possession of "bycatch" in their boats—the herring and young wild salmon—and won.

However, that victory, and later ones, posed barely a speed bump to the industry. By 2010, I knew I had to do something completely different. As Einstein is supposed to have said, the definition of insanity is doing the same thing over and over and expecting different results. I kept up with the science and my ongoing legal challenges, but I realized I had to go at this a different way. I was in need of some fresh ideas.

On March 3, 2010, I hosted the first of a series of small dinner gatherings to which I invited the most creative critical thinkers in the area. The question I posed to them was this: Since nothing had worked and the farms were still killing wild salmon, what should I do now? As the wine and conversation flowed, I took notes. Ideas that sparked great enthusiasm around the dinner table faded in the glare of daylight. I wanted to do something meaningful and also impossible for government to ignore. Someone told me years ago that when the people of Harlem, New York, were desperate for support from the city, they threatened to flush their toilets simultaneously, which would have blown apart the sewer system, and got the attention they needed.

I don't know whether this story is an urban myth, but it was the kind of idea I was looking for—easy for lots of people to do and impossible for government to ignore. On March 5 I invited the artist Anissa Reed, whom I had recently met, to dinner, along with Don Staniford, a Scottish man who blamed me for derailing his life by motivating him to campaign against salmon farms in several countries.

I knew, from the constant outpouring of messages and small donations that kept my work afloat, that a lot of British Columbians wanted
wild salmon protected from salmon farms. Rumours abounded of epidemics in the farms. People could smell the rotting fish as they followed trucks down the highway, others reported barges off-loading the
foul-smelling morts in the middle of the night. Towns that had been told
that this industry would be good for them now saw that salmon farming
wasn't producing the promised jobs. The industry was all about mechanization. As commercial fisheries crashed, jobs vanished, not just the
fishing jobs but jobs in everything from truck sales to boat maintenance
and all the services prosperous people like to use. The rising wilderness
tourism industry offered far more opportunity to the people of the coast
than salmon farms. And whether the dozens of small tourism operators
offered fishing, whale watching, bear watching, kayak trips or cruising,
they needed abundant wild salmon.

The guiding operations taking people up the Glendale River in the
Broughton to view bears had grown into a multi-million-dollar business,
and they also had first-hand evidence of the collapse in the pink salmon
populations. They knew I was right—sea lice from salmon farms were
killing off wild salmon and the tourism industry felt abandoned by government. Many were angry.

What if the politicians harboured their own doubts about this
industry and just needed to realize how many people wanted the industry out of BC waters? Politicians are always trying to figure out what it
will take to get re-elected. Maybe what I needed to do was find a way
for everyone who opposed salmon farms to become visible so that they
could be counted.

Don, Anissa and I were a volatile mix, like the kids' science experiment where you put soap, water and vinegar together and they erupt
like a volcano. The three of us together lit a spark over dinner. I am not
sure who said we should walk the length of Vancouver Island to the BC
legislature, but the idea took. We jumped up from the table and timed
how long it took us to walk the kilometre to the dock where my boat was

tied, came back and began planning the trek on large sheets of paper I taped all over the table. We would walk the three-hundred-kilometre length of Vancouver Island from north to south.

Don said we should leave on Earth Day and arrive at the provincial legislature in Victoria on Mother's Day. We would invite people who thought salmon farms should be removed from the ocean to join us. Anissa dubbed it the Get Out Migration. We would migrate like the wild salmon in spring, and hope to build our numbers as we walked.

I wanted to remind people how important wild salmon are to this coast, that they are a power cord between the open ocean and the forests, collecting the energy of sunlight hitting the open ocean and carrying it up mountains. That they feed a hundred species, that everywhere they go life abounds. With great trepidation I chose to call this movement Salmon Are Sacred. I thought there would be pushback across unseen religious boundaries, but there wasn't. The name fit and people embraced it.

When I announced the Get Out Migration to my mailing list, and on Facebook, the response was electric. People asked if they could host us as we passed through their towns. The legendary hereditary chief Beau Dick, a world-renowned Kwakwaka'wakw carver from Alert Bay, called and said he would contact the other chiefs about a send-off for us at the Nimpkish River at the north end of the island on the first day of our journey. Denise Savoie, the federal member of Parliament for Victoria, said she would be there to receive us in the capital. Grand Chief Stewart Phillip, president of the Union of BC Indian Chiefs, endorsed the walk. Rune, who had toured us around Norway when we went to speak to the shareholders, called and said he would gather people and walk down part of the Vosso River in solidarity. Sometimes an idea is already alive in people, like a glowing ember that just needs someone to blow on it to start a fire.

I began to train, walking and running every day; I even taped my computer to a borrowed treadmill. I needed to be fit to cover the twenty kilometres a day to stay on schedule with all the events that Don and Anissa were organizing along the route.

I met with a representative from the RCMP so the police wouldn't be in the dark about our plans. Sergeant Mark Whitworth took me out on the highway to show me what we needed to do to keep people safe. "I have seen everything get hit," he said. "People just swerve towards whatever they look at and they are going to be looking at your group." That terrified me. What if someone got hurt?

One of the local fishermen, Dave Kaufman, who had let me board his vessel and go through his catch looking for flounder with the eye parasites, offered to carry all our gear from camp to camp on his flatbed truck. Leah Robinson and Marie Fournier, two women who patrolled Johnstone Strait to protect whales from boaters who tried to get too close, showed up offering to cook for the walkers each night. We didn't know if there would be ten or a hundred people joining us. These three made the whole effort possible.

I went out to Echo Bay with Twyla to symbolically begin the trek in the Viner River, in honour of the little salmon about to emerge from their spawning grounds and face death by lice at the nearby Cermaq salmon farm in the Burdwood Islands. I paddled a cedar-strip canoe my brother had made years ago, and my black wolf-like dog, Ahta, rode in the bow. Before salmon farms, the northern resident G-clan orca and the Alert Bay seine fleet came to fish chum salmon in the Viner every October. Tens of thousands of fish still went into the river to spawn, but the whales didn't come anymore and there was no fishery.

When I pulled up at the Kwikwasut'inuxw village, Gwayasdums, the people met me at the dock in full regalia and blessed my journey, sending me off with warm hugs and tears. Here they called me Gwayum'dzi, a name meaning whale that was given to me by the late Chief Alice Smith.

The night before the migration began, the town of Sointula on Malcolm Island, where I had come to live while my daughter attended high school in nearby Port McNeill, put on a beautiful potluck dinner in the community hall and gave me a giant key to the town cut in the shape of a salmon. A fishing community, the people of Sointula know the importance of salmon.

At seven on Earth Day morning the children of Sointula showed up at my door to accompany me to the ferry to Vancouver Island. I slipped a collar on my dog and said, "Want to go for a walk?" Surrounded by a school of youngsters, we made our way to the dock. I wasn't sure who from the community was going to make the trip, but Troy Bright, Bruce Burrows, Dave Parker, Leah Robinson, Marie Fournier and Kate Brauer were there. Anissa drove an RV we rented, loaded with signs for the walkers to carry; it became the media centre. A large group met us when we got off the ferry in Port McNeill and we walked together for the several kilometres to the Nimpkish River. When we got there, children danced in paper salmon headdresses. Chiefs and Elders stood beside the river that had sustained their ancestors to wish us well. Young Molina Dawson and her father, Clyde Dawson, from Ukwanalis (Kingcome Village) had decided to walk with us. Molina's mother would have too, but she was pregnant and close to giving birth. Chief Beau Dick filled two small leather medicine bags with items that he felt would keep us safe and tied one around Molina's neck and one around mine. I still carry it with me.

In the late afternoon we headed out again. Now there were twenty of us. We carried signs as we walked single file along Highway 19, south into the forested mountains of northern Vancouver Island. A woman dropped off her young daughter, who wanted to walk and picked her up several kilometres down the road. When we arrived at the first stopping place, Dave Kaufman was there with all the tents. He had built a lovely fire against the chilly spring evening.

The next day we walked another twenty kilometres. Jon Taylor from Sointula joined us, leapfrogging ahead to a spot where he would park and put his truck's tailgate down, laying out snacks and water. We loved seeing Jon along the way. Rod Marining, one of the founders of Greenpeace, and his partner, Chris Blake, joined us. They went ahead with a large sign warning drivers that there were people on the road. Don and Anissa were a blur, trying to find cell service to keep up the media coverage and organizing the daily events. I had the easy job. All I had to do was walk and talk.

Those first days in the mountains were some of the most enjoyable of my life. It was a soul-deep good feeling to be on foot with this small group, taking action for salmon. People waved and honked. Some cursed us. Others stopped to press money into our hands. Trapper Rick from the Thompson River found us and gave me a claw from a bear that had been killed and eaten by another bear that was starving for lack of salmon. The biologist in me noted that the side of the road was a well-used elk and bear trail; their tracks, which had been invisible to me all these years from my car, were pressed deep into the sandy soil. Occasionally, I saw audio cassettes on the side of the road in a snarl of tape, and even an eight-track reel in a similar state.

We took boats out to Quadra Island, where we were surrounded by a welcoming fleet of local boats. Inundated with salmon farms, this community was also seeing the impacts on wild fish first-hand and the loss of their way of life. Their boats were festooned with signs calling for the removal of the farms. Sea louse tattoos, magically produced by Anissa, appeared on people's faces. Two women swam the length of a farm, towing a sign that read *Fish farms are foolish*. Twyla went up in a helicopter and filmed it all from the air.

We were apprehensive as we drew closer to Campbell River, the heart of the industry in British Columbia. The RCMP had taken Don, Anissa and me aside to warn us that they'd heard rumours of a group that would stop us from continuing our walk. I tried to imagine what that would look like, but when we arrived in the middle of town, fifty people surrounded us in warm support. Then several hundred people swelled our numbers as we walked south through Courtenay a day later. A large traditional canoe picked some us of up and paddled us to Comox, while the rest walked alongside. People came out to meet us in regalia. That evening, after a feast celebrating the Get Out Migration, I asked Molina if she wanted to speak too, just before it was time for me to walk up onto the small stage overlooking the crowd. She was clearly terrified, but she said yes, and then leaned into the microphone and said, "I have eyes and ears, I know we need wild salmon."

The next day on the road, a white pickup truck came at me, driven by a woman screaming obscenities. Molina was walking beside me, and I pushed her out of the way. As the vehicle passed inches from me, I swung around, adrenaline streaking through me, with the intention of hitting the truck, but as I turned I was looking a little boy in the eye. He was strapped into a car seat in the truck, his face contorted in that moment before crying.

Afterwards, I sat in a friend's car as I tried to stop shaking, so relieved Molina was unharmed and grateful that Ahta had not been hit. Luke Rogers, who coordinated so much of the effort to keep the growing crowd safely on the side of the road, sat with me.

"I don't think people are ready for this. I think we should quit before someone gets hurt," I said.

"People might not be ready for us," he said, "but I am not ready to stop."

I looked at him. He seemed calm and he thought we should keep going.

"Okay," I said. I climbed out of the car, touched my dog for reassurance and started to walk.

In every town, people bear-hugged me, sometimes sobbing in my arms. For a person used to being in the wilderness, this was uncomfortable contact. It kept happening. These folks were unable to voice their sadness, so I don't know what triggered this release in them. I think they saw the faces of the people walking, flags and signs aloft, and felt something missing in their lives.

Don told me we were on the news daily. Our message was getting out and people knew where to find us. The salmon farming industry also made the news, saying they were donating to the Heart and Stroke Foundation in honour of our walk. An odd response that was drowned out.

Every morning I tied Ahta's leash around my waist and she became my partner, pulling me gently every step of the way. I kept checking her feet. Her pads were soon worn smooth but not worn through. At the campsites in the evenings, I didn't have the heart to tie her up and she pranced about greeting everyone, true to her wolf lineage. Wolves keep social order by making contact with all members of the pack.

A mother and daughter from Tofino, Cosy and Laterra Lawson, walked from the west side of Vancouver Island along narrow, winding Highway 4 to join us. They'd had a frightening encounter with an angry truck driver who forced them off the road on a very steep-sided section. Farm salmon travelled by truck along that road daily to the processing plants.

I had become afraid of every white pickup truck I saw. I'd given the licence number of the one that had come at me to Sergeant Whitworth, who had been tasked to stay with us the whole way. When he asked if I wanted to press charges, I said no, I just wanted to speak with the driver. Months later we did speak. She called while I was drifting in my boat and told me her husband was a salmon farmer. She had moved to accommodate his job and ended up isolated and struggling with being a single mom while he worked long shifts away from his family. She said she hadn't meant to get so close, but had drifted towards me while she stared at me in anger, just as the sergeant had predicted. Her little boy had become upset and asked why she had shouted at those people. She said she had felt shame even before the sound of her voice had died away.

I had imagined an entirely different scenario—that she must have been gloating over having almost hit Alexandra Morton. This was not really a paranoid thought; I'd been told there were dartboards with my face on them at some of the fish farms. I'd had crew boats swerve at me on the water too, one so threatening I picked up the radio mic and said I was going to issue a Mayday and name his company if he didn't back off. It hadn't been hard to make this incident on the highway into more than it was. I thanked the woman and told her I hoped it got better for her.

Every morning on our migration we gathered and repeated a pledge to be honourable in our actions, not to express anger and to take care of ourselves. Every nation whose territory we passed through continued to welcome us. Fred Speck, of the Gwawaenuk First Nation, one of the four tribes of the Musgamagw, came down from the Broughton and joined us, walking with a huge Indigenous sovereignty flag.

The journey was going well, but as we neared Victoria, I realized something critical was missing. While provincial members of the legislative assembly had come to join us for segments of the walk, they were from the New Democratic and Green Parties, not the Liberal government in power. We were making headlines in every town we walked through, as hundreds of people with signs and beautifully painted fish swelled our ranks, but we needed to do more.

In the evenings after the speeches and feasts, I went campfire to campfire and asked people whether we should remain camped on the provincial legislature's lawn until at least one salmon farm was removed from the coast. One of the groups among us was dead set against that. They were adamant we talk in terms of removing the entire industry, not just one farm—it had to be all or nothing. I was trying to keep this walk leaderless. I had seen what happens when groups get together and make one person the leader. That person can be turned in circles until they are going in the opposite direction.

This had happened with a coalition of environmental groups that I'd helped found. A big American funder had approached all the organizations that had risen up in response to the sea louse epidemic. The funder said that if we formed an alliance, entered talks with industry and hammered out a plan, they would fund us. It sounded right: get big to go up against these big companies. Marine Harvest volunteered to play ball with us. Enormous effort went into a plan to do research together. Marine Harvest said if the research showed sea lice from salmon farms were killing wild salmon, then the company would agree to transition their farms into closed tanks, where their effluent would be contained.

The first thing Marine Harvest did was ask for an end to an ad campaign that Living Oceans was running in California, where most BC farm salmon was sold, featuring a farm salmon steak on a Styrofoam tray, wrapped in plastic. The copy read *With All the Chemicals in Farm Salmon, You Might as Well Eat the Packaging.* The coalition agreed to pull the ad.

None of the parties to the coalition was supposed to put out public statements unless we all had signed off on them, but Marine Harvest repeatedly violated this term of the agreement. In pursuit of the larger aim, we just asked them not to do it again.

Then, behind closed doors, a couple of people entered negotiations with Marine Harvest on behalf of the coalition. Marine Harvest haggled over scientific practice until it got too complicated, and many scientists withdrew from the research that was the heart of the agreement. The negotiating team informed the coalition that Marine Harvest had agreed to fallow one of the two migration routes through the Broughton every other year if they could triple the size of the farms so that overall production levels would not be affected. (The negotiations had focused on the Broughton because of the sea louse research ongoing at my field station.) Allowing wild salmon to go to sea unharmed by sea lice every *other* year was like punching out every other tooth—salmon needed to go to sea every year. Smooth as oil spreading on water, Marine Harvest toyed with our leaders, letting them feel close to success, while using our agreement to convince government to permit larger farms.

The hairs on the back of my neck stood up. Sea lice is a numbers game; the more fish in a farm, the more sea lice. Everyone knew this. At first, when each farm was stocked with 125,000 fish, we didn't see the lice, but when they upped their stock to 600,000 to a million salmon per farm, the impact of lice on the young wild salmon became catastrophic. Marine Harvest was trying to use a coalition of some of British Columbia's most trusted environmental groups to secure the biggest farm sites in the world. The funder had brought us together with industry and turned us into something more dangerous than the industry on its own. I was terrified, perhaps because I was the one looking directly at the fish. This was their death sentence. My coalition colleagues told me not to worry because we could always cancel the farm expansions later.

I protested, asking the people at the table to name a time anything had ever been taken away from this industry. When they get what they want, they keep it. "Please, please," I said, "don't do this, Broughton salmon will not survive this." Much to my embarrassment I couldn't hold back the tears filling my eyes.

The others were immovable. I know the people negotiating with Marine Harvest on behalf of the coalition were looking at the long-term goal and had put a lot of thought into this path, but what I saw was a chess game that we were losing. There was nothing in the agreement to prevent Marine Harvest from walking away the moment they got a group of the province's leading environmentalists to endorse the tripling of their farms in the Broughton. I quit the coalition, went to a lawyer named Greg McDade, and asked him to find a way to get an injunction against this plan, which basically meant that I was taking legal action against my friends and allies. An awful situation.

When McDade reviewed the matter he realized it was illegal for the province to be regulating salmon farms at all, because the farms were in the ocean where the province had no jurisdiction. The only thing under provincial control was the anchors the farmers dropped on the sea floor. We went to court and won. Salmon farm regulation was transferred back to the federal government and so from that point on, no one in DFO could argue that they weren't the ones responsible for the industry's impact on wild salmon. Everyone thought the province was going to appeal the decision and try to keep control of the farms, but they didn't; they willingly handed this hot potato of an industry back to the feds. The tripling of the farms' size was halted because no one was yet in a position to make such a decision. In the end, the federal government hasn't done any better than the province, but at least the salmon of the Broughton survived another decade. After that experience I never joined another coalition and have refused to lead one.

Now, however, around the campfires of the Get Out Migration, I learned the weakness of *not* having a leader. How would we ever agree on next steps? Dealing with humans is complicated.

———

On the final morning, we left the town of Sidney on the Saanich Peninsula and headed for the legislature. John Caton, from a wilderness tourism lodge in Clayoquot Sound, arrived with four horses. He hitched two to a wagon driven by lodge staff. He and his daughter rode the other two and went out ahead of us. My son and daughter, my sister Woodleigh and her husband joined me.

As we walked the last twenty-five kilometres to the BC legislature, people abandoned their cars to walk with us. A crowd of thousands soon stretched as far as I could see, taking over an entire lane of the Patricia Bay Highway. Supporters had paddled three canoes across the Strait of Georgia from the Fraser River, where the impact of salmon farms was changing the lives of many people, and then they carried one of the canoes the entire way to downtown Victoria. A musician from Alert Bay played a trumpet, and bicycles were festooned with all things salmon. Many people from Sointula joined us for the last leg. I was deeply moved to see among us my dear friend, Bea Smith from Gwayasdums, who had blessed this journey at the start. Traffic cops stood at every intersection to guide us through. We choked the streets of downtown Victoria with a sea of people, migrating between the buildings, like the salmon migration along the submerged canyon that is Tribune Channel.

An Indigenous woman pressed a cedar headband with a feather onto my head and pinned a white blanket close around my neck. As she fastened it, she asked if I knew the significance of this. I said that I didn't, but there was no time to learn as we were swept forward onto the manicured lawn of the legislature. Security guards estimated the crowd size at five thousand to seven thousand people.

First Nations representatives, environmentalists, politicians, my friend Billy Proctor, Chiefs Chamberlin and Phillip, radio talk-show host Rafe Mair, NDP member of Parliament Fin Donnelly, and many others gave speeches. A three-hundred-person choir sang. But the politicians and bureaucrats in the great stone building looming above us gave no heed to our pleas to get salmon farms out of BC waters. The provincial Liberals had decided that their best course was to not react in any way to the Get Out Migration. So long as they did not come out to the crowd and commit to anything, they could pretend there was no problem. They knew we would all go home.

One good did result from our walk: we became known to each other and we realized how many of us opposed the industry. In 2010, this was the biggest environmental rally in the history of British Columbia.

The next day I collapsed in the back of my friend Jeff Jones's truck and slept for the entire trip back to Sointula, wedged between my daughter and my dog, who was snoring with her head on my lap. The day after that I headed out to the Broughton, nosed my boat up to a tiny white-shell beach in Spiller Pass, climbed out and sat quietly on the shore, my hands spread wide on the tiny bits of broken clam shell of the ancient village site, soaking up the presence of the place.

Well, I thought, *that didn't work. What now?*

10.

Compass Bearing

A WEEK LATER I was at the legislature again. This time I was meeting with a small group of opposition politicians, not about the Get Out Migration, but about the massive outbreak of sea lice I had documented in Nootka Sound. Opposition members came up as I walked through the high-arched, wood-panelled halls to congratulate me on the number of people who had showed up at their door at the end of the trek. These were nice, but empty, gestures. Back home in the Broughton, it was still sea louse season and young salmon were being eaten to death.

Dr. Mark Sheppard, the veterinarian for the BC Ministry of Agriculture in charge of farm salmon health, joined the meeting by phone. He claimed the massive lice outbreak on the Grieg salmon farms in Nootka Sound was *not* due to drug resistance. He said, instead, that dominant salmon in the pens would not let the subordinate farm salmon eat; the starving fish got infected because they were not getting the drug through the food pellets. *Okay,* I thought, *this man gets an A for creativity, but is* STUPID *written across my forehead?* The whistle-blowers who had reached out to me specifically said the drug was no longer working.

"Where is the evidence that dominant fish are the cause of the outbreak, and if it is the cause, why doesn't it happen in every farm?" I asked. He gave no answer.

This dominant fish theory was new. I wondered whether Dr. Sheppard had thought it up or had Hill & Knowlton, the public relations firm with seventy offices in thirty-seven countries that the BC Salmon Farmers Association had hired? Hill & Knowlton was known for its campaigns on behalf of the tobacco industry, for Exxon after the *Valdez* tanker ran aground and spilled eleven million gallons of oil into Prince William Sound, on behalf of the nuclear industry after the disaster at Three Mile Island, and for the Chinese government after the massacre of its citizens at Tiananmen Square. The firm was also known for spreading faked evidence that Iraqi soldiers had entered a hospital and dumped babies out of incubators onto the floor to die, which had helped the American public accept the Gulf War.

Sheppard went on to also blame the little sticklebacks—a theory disproven by researchers at my field station in 2007. And then he argued that the massive run of wild salmon the fall before had infected the farm salmon, ignoring entirely that all those wild salmon had entered freshwater to spawn, and so the lice on them had died, whereas the farm salmon bred lice to epidemic levels all winter. This line of reasoning always chilled me. It framed the wild fish as the problem. Were there people in power who believed that the collapse of wild salmon that was under way was the solution to the salmon farmers' problems?

I asked Dr. Sheppard whether he had tested the sea lice in the Grieg Seafood farms for drug resistance to at least rule it out. The company itself was responding in an extreme way, killing its own fish before they reached harvest weight and moving others into freshwater to kill the lice, actions representing losses in the millions of dollars. Wasn't Sheppard curious as to why?

"There is no protocol for testing resistance," he replied.

That was news to me. Testing for resistance is easy. It requires lice, the drug and a small stack of petri dishes. We were doing it at the field station in the Broughton. I wished I could see his face, rather than just hear his voice, which was becoming more and more heated as he lost the argument.

In the end, I told the politicians that some provincial government was going to be caught in the lie that it didn't know that salmon farms were killing off the wild salmon. I could only hope that this scandal broke before the last salmon sank to the sea floor encrusted in sea lice. They all agreed with me and walked me to the door. They were not the party in power so their agreement with me was, more importantly to them, disagreement with those in power. However, I reminded them that it was when the NDP were last in power that most of the salmon farm tenures had been granted in the Broughton, and that Billy and I had met with them repeatedly, practically begging them to leave one wild salmon migration route through the archipelago farm-free.

Ultimately the province held the power to give the ocean back to the wild salmon. They could simply not renew the tenures of the farms that were having the worst impact on the wild salmon migratory corridors. I know I had persuaded the MLAs in the room of the dangers, but there was a wide gulf between knowing this industry was damaging and doing something about it.

What next? Should I cross Canada in a caravan to Ottawa, occupy a fish farm, mobilize protest flashmobs? Maybe compete with the industry by outbidding them for tenures for the areas around their farms to grow wild fish? Run for government, start a political party—the Wild Salmon Party—with a platform that would bring us into ecological compliance? A friend offered to throw the I Ching for me. *Why not,* I thought. The result read: *Kill the king.* I felt like Frodo in *The Lord of the Rings.*

The Deepwater Horizon British Petroleum oil spill was under way in the Gulf of Mexico and no one knew how to stop it. This ongoing disaster heaped a sense of dread on my dwindling spirits. It made me scared to see that BP executives looked scared. Companies were creating global-scale disasters they had no idea how to fix. The news said this spill was so huge it could slow the Gulf Stream, which would impact the weather planet-wide. I checked the live feed of the submerged wellhead every morning, as it continued to bleed death into our world.

I was enormously relieved that the waters around me were not suffocating under a sheen of oil. But at the same time, I knew we were dealing with our own ongoing ecological disaster—the biggest industrial spill in the history of British Columbia. Tons of waste per day per farm, billions of larval lice per farm. When he testified later that year, at the 2010 Cohen Commission into the catastrophic decline of the Fraser River sockeye salmon run, a DFO virologist, Dr. Kyle Garver, stated that 65 billion infectious viral particles per hour were also flowing out of infected farms. It was only because this spill was invisible to most people that industry got away with it. These farms were pulsing with pathogens, and the strong ocean currents—the same currents that supported the diversity of life—were pumping them far and wide. Like toxic shock caused by septicemia in our bloodstream, these spills threatened life throughout entire inlets and passages. Politicians, meanwhile, squirmed uselessly under the thumb of industry.

As usual, I was broke. I opened an online store, hoping to generate some personal income from the sale of my books and T-shirts. I printed fish on the shirts and on large canvasses with a Japanese method called Gyotaku. To make ends meet, I have made such prints over the years, selling them at craft fairs and in a store I once ran with Billy Proctor's daughter Joanie in Echo Bay. (Currently I have an Etsy store called RainCoast Fishes.) But I have rarely been able to focus on making money. I lived on handouts, unexpected cheques in the mail from people telling me to please keep going. Both my children learned to support themselves early on.

As a result of supporters' generosity, I was able to mostly keep my mind turning over the problem of how to stop salmon farms from killing off the wild salmon. I figured, now, that there were three ways to stop the killing: government regulation, a huge class-action lawsuit against the industry, or a marketing campaign that persuaded the public to refuse to eat farm salmon until it came from an enclosed tank sitting safely on land away from the wild salmon migratory routes. All of these approaches seemed beyond my reach.

It grated on my nerves when people said, *Oh, you have done so much.* Fact: the farms in my home waters were growing and the wild salmon were dying. Yes, I had succeeded in revealing how the industry was impacting the wild salmon. I had slowed down what seemed at times to be the inevitable extinction of wild salmon in the Broughton and elsewhere. But extinction was still coming at the hands of this industry.

The coincidence of my being a biologist living in the Broughton when the salmon farms arrived and the fishermen coming to me with their observations of the damage is the only reason the BC sea louse epidemics became public knowledge. Had these outbreaks remained hidden, the industry would have known what was happening and maybe some in DFO would have been made aware, but neither of them would have done anything to save the Broughton salmon. The salmon would have died off in the early 2000s. The rights of the public and First Nations to wild salmon were nowhere on the radar of DFO, the provincial Ministry of Agriculture or the industry. Now, with rising drug resistance and disease outbreaks, the wild salmon were going to be just as dead in the near future. So I had not actually accomplished much.

The local conservation officer in the archipelago was a conscientious man, a stickler for details and regulations, good at his job. On his last tour of the region before he retired, he pulled up at my float. "I have something to tell you," he said when I came down to the dock to see him.

He described a conversation he'd had with the area manager for a Stolt Sea Farm site at the confluence of Knight Inlet and Tribune Channel, where all the salmon from the Glendale River and Knight Inlet rivers migrate. He said that the area manager had pointed at the schools of tiny pink and chum salmon outside the pens and told him, "You see all those little wild fish? Soon there won't be any." This suggested that the industry knew that the wild salmon exposed to their farms would go extinct.

I studied his face, trying to figure out why he was telling me this. Did he think I could fix it? Had he tried? "Did you report this to anyone in your ministry?" I asked.

He admitted he had not. He was not responsible for fish farms and so he didn't report on them. But he was reporting to me.

I had believed that people in the salmon farming industry were so focused on the fish in their pens that they never thought about wild salmon. But here I was faced with the realization that at least some of them, this one an ex-commercial fisherman, appeared to know they were participating in the extinction of wild salmon runs. And this conservation officer, a man of high integrity who was about to retire and so had little to lose, clearly cared and could have made a difference. Instead, he passed the information on to me, hoping I could do something with it.

People feel better when they tell me things like this. But I feel worse.

Imagine if this man had done everything he could to inform his minister and had gone public if he'd been ignored? The mounting concern over the impact of the industry would have been validated by a man in a position of public trust. Activism would not have become necessary. I suppose telling me was better than nothing, but I was caught in such a bind. On the one hand, people, including other scientists, were slandering me to destroy my credibility because I was talking about things no one else seemed to know about. On the other, concerned witnesses trusted me, felt I was the only one they could talk to and hoped that I would be able to fix the situation. The fact is we would have been able to fix it long ago if people working in the industry and government had felt safe enough to report what they saw to their higher-ups, the politicians and the public.

An experience described to me by a young man in a training program with the Ministry of Agriculture illustrated why they did not. He contacted me because he had evidence that young sockeye salmon were getting trapped in salmon farms in the Discovery Islands. If true, their presence in the farms suggested a number of violations: illegal bycatch,

fishing out of season, fishing without a licence, fishing with an unap-
proved gear type, and capture of fish too small to be legally retained.
During his training to become a provincial fish farm inspector, he
noticed that there were salmon in a farm that were clearly not Atlantic
salmon, the only species the company was licensed to stock. He took
pictures and reported the infraction to his superiors—the job that he
was training for.

Immediately, he was asked to surrender any prints he had made of
the images. Then, he said, senior staff started coming by his workspace
at the ministry multiple times daily to instruct him not to report the
trapped sockeye to the media or anyone else. At the end of the training program, he was informed that he was not going to be hired, even
though he had demonstrated both a keen interest and a sharp eye—
essential qualities for inspecting farms, for which he should have been
awarded a job.

After he was let go, he gave an electronic file of the pictures to me. I
took them to a lawyer. Because the farm in question had been harvested,
meaning the living evidence was now gone, and the pictures were low
resolution, the lawyer said we were too late to pursue charges.

One person who did try to stop this madness was Fin Donnelly, who
tabled Bill C518 in the House of Commons in Ottawa in March 2010
to transition the salmon farming industry into tanks on land. Fin had
swum the Fraser River several times to raise awareness of the state of
the wild salmon. He led children on rafts down the river every summer
to instill love and respect for the river in their hearts. The NDP were
not the ruling party in Ottawa, either, but even though his bill did not
pass, this was a significant step.

In 2009, I had been awarded an honorary doctorate of science from
Simon Fraser University for my sea lice research. That same year the
province of BC witnessed a profound collapse in the Fraser River
sockeye salmon. Only 1.5 million out of a forecasted 10.6 million fish

returned to the river, and many of these fish were found dead on the riverbanks just before they could spawn. Fisheries managers had no idea why this was happening, but they knew this is what populations look like in the moment before extinction.

The Pacific Salmon Commission, formed in 1937 to co-regulate Canadian and US fisheries on the salmon that flowed between the two countries, invited me to present the evidence that pathogens from salmon farms may have contributed to the unexpected collapse of the Fraser River sockeye. I presented my sea louse results on pink salmon, but I also presented my growing concern that viruses replicating in farm salmon populations might be an even bigger problem to migrating sockeye salmon than the lice, a view I supported with publicly available data on the IHN (infectious hematopoietic necrosis) virus outbreaks in salmon farms throughout southern British Columbia. I was also aware of what was going on in terms of die-offs in the Broughton. The salmon farms around my home in the archipelago can't hide large die-offs; my neighbours and I can see their mort barges moving back and forth to Vancouver Island transporting the dead fish. Flocks of crows escort these barges, pecking at the offal and maggots that bubble over onto deck. The industry reports that most of these losses are due to "environmental causes," such as low oxygen or algae blooms, but could I trust these explanations as reports surfaced on virus outbreaks?

The IHN virus naturally occurs in British Columbia and is common in wild sockeye salmon; the virus and the fish co-evolved and thus found balance. As humans learned through the COVID-19 outbreak, a virus can infect a host without making it sick; it has its biggest impact when other stressors weaken the immune system. When that happens to fish in the wild, predators move in, picking off sick fish as they begin to weaken and this prevents epidemics.

However, the immune system of the farmed Atlantic salmon had no experience with the IHN virus, and in the farm pens, the predators could not do their job to suppress outbreaks. When the farmers reported that the fish were dying of environmental stress, was it really a case of an environmental stress weakening an already infected fish to the point that it died of disease? The danger to wild fish is that when a virus spreads fish-to-fish in a farm, leading to the massive release of 65 billion infectious viral particles per hour into marine currents, as reported by Dr. Garver, the virus may be "natural" but there is nothing natural about the dose level wild salmon experience trying to migrate through a viral blizzard. There is a different risk of infection from standing on a football field with one person with a cold and being in an elevator with ten people sneezing in your face. The "distancing" required to slow an epidemic is simply not possible in a salmon farm.

In the early 2000s, Dr. Sonja Saksida, with the BC Centre for Aquatic Health Sciences lab in Campbell River, wrote a rare paper on the spread of this virus by way of the salmon farming industry. She reported that in August 2001, one salmon farm near Johnstone Strait became infected with IHN virus as sockeye salmon bound for the Fraser River migrated through the area. From there, the virus spread farm-to-farm. Over 50 percent of the BC industry became infected and twelve million Atlantic salmon died, shedding the virus from thirty-six salmon farms into the marine currents of the BC coast for over a year.

I wasn't doing research on viruses at the time, but in 2002 I'd organized a tour of this outbreak. Bill and Donna Mackay offered their forty-eight-passenger high-speed vessel *Naiad Explorer* to carry First Nations representatives, bureaucrats, scientists including Dr. Brian Riddell, and politicians such as Rod Visser (the MLA for the region), ex-minister of fisheries John Fraser and the provincial minister of agriculture, Stan Hagan. We went to the Sir Edmund salmon farm near the mouth of Kingcome Inlet in Dzawada'enuxw territory; the local herring were in the area preparing to spawn.

The stench of rotting fish was so thick no one wanted lunch. The workers were in the process of using a crane to pour a huge tote of dead fish into a metal bin that ran the length of the mort barge it was sitting on. As the decomposing fish fell into the bin we could see they were adult fish, amounting to millions of dollars in losses to the company. Congealed grease floated like lily pads on the water and bits of flesh and organs covered the bay. As Dr. Riddell leaned over the side of the boat he pointed and said, "It's—it's . . . it's an eyeball."

Below the infected blizzard of offal the silver glint of schools of adult herring were visible. As they opened their mouths to feed, the flaring of their gills flashed in the sunlight. I asked Stan Hagan, the minister in charge of this farm, if his department was doing any tests on these herring to see if the virus was transferring to them. He said that wild fish were not his responsibility.

In the ten thousand years since the glaciers receded from this coast, these herring were likely exposed to low levels of the IHN virus at some point during their life cycle, but they had never been soaked in a viral spill like this. In the absence of evidence, no one could convince me that this was not a threat to the survival of the herring.

Dr. Saksida's research showed that farms less than ten kilometres down-current from infected sites became infected. Young salmon being transported in vessels that pumped seawater through their tanks became infected if the vessel passed within forty kilometres of an infected farm. They also became infected when the boats passed farm salmon processing plants that were pumping effluent into the ocean. When these fish were placed in farms in the Broughton Archipelago and elsewhere, the virus began spreading farm-to-farm again. Thirteen sites in the Discovery Islands, six sites in the Broughton, all the sites off Port Hardy on the northeastern tip of Vancouver Island, and one farm on the central coast became infected. These farm salmon had been vaccinated against the IHN virus, but apparently it didn't work.

Government had the power to order a cull of the infected farms because IHN virus is a *reportable virus*, that special category no country wants. But when it orders a cull, government has to buy all the culled fish at market prices. Thirty-five farms, with a minimum of 600,000 fish each at a low-ball average value of twenty dollars per fish, meant that ordering a cull of all thirty-five infected farms could cost $420 million.

Government opted to just allow the virus to keep spreading. Only seven infected farms voluntarily culled their stock to protect their other farms nearby.

If the farm fish were infected over such a large area, the wild fish were also exposed. This outbreak, as well as an earlier epidemic from 1992 to 1996, was a flashing neon sign warning everyone that the pathogens breeding in salmon farms were capable of infecting fish over a large area beyond the farms. At the very least, Dr. Saksida's research should have caused the province to sterilize the farm salmon processing plant effluent to remove viruses before it was poured directly into the Fraser River sockeye migration route.

When I correlated the fish farm IHN outbreaks with the productivity of the Fraser River sockeye salmon run (a measure of the number of salmon that return for each adult of the parental generation), the data showed that the sockeye began to decline in synch with the first IHN virus outbreak. But this was only a correlation, not definitive proof of causation. Since the outbreaks began in 1992, the first year that salmon farms were situated on the Fraser sockeye migration route, I couldn't know if it was the virus that affected the run, something else about the farms or something unrelated to the farms. However, the fact that the dramatic collapse of the Fraser sockeye started when these sockeye were exposed to the farms and continued to accelerate as the farms grew larger seemed, at a minimum, cause for further investigation.

For the eighteen years the sockeye had been declining, salmon scientists had been turning over every other stone to find an explanation, avoiding the issue of salmon farms as people often choose to avoid bullies. One of Canada's most respected fishery scientists, Ransom Myers, did co-publish a paper reporting that wild salmon tip into irreversible decline everywhere salmon farms appear. Yet it seemed that even talking about the impact of salmon farms was taboo. Dr. Carl Walters, a well-known fishery scientist, yelled at me at one meeting: "Why do you have to go on and on about the impact of salmon farms?"

Because salmon farms were so closely correlated with the wild salmon declines. Because the sustained collapse was new. Because previous calculations used to predict wild salmon returns had stopped working, suggesting a large variable was not being measured. Salmon farms had become the elephant in the room. Look what happened to scientists around the world who spoke up about them. I was the only one who brought them up. If I stopped talking about the risk from salmon farms, no one would. So I took the yelling in stride and continued piecing the evidence together.

Though I had spent nine years publishing on the cataclysmic damage that sea lice from salmon farms cause to young wild salmon, not one Fraser River sockeye scientist dared wonder aloud what sea lice might be doing to the young sockeye squeezing past salmon farms in the narrow passages of the Discovery Islands. As much as the fish farmers were the problem, so were those in a position of authority who refused to even consider why the sockeye crash and the arrival of salmon farms began in the same year.

When the prime minister of the day, Stephen Harper, felt compelled to call a commission of inquiry into the 2009 collapse of the Fraser River sockeye, appointing Justice Bruce Cohen to lead it, an editorial in *the Province* read: "full marks to the Prime Minister for having the fortitude to order such an inquiry. In all likelihood, it will uncover some very nasty-looking warts in one of his government's departments."

Prophetic.

The Cohen Commission invited interest groups to apply to become part of the inquiry. If you were accepted, the commission would cover the cost of the lawyer of your choice to bring forward your group's information and views. The numbers of interested parties snowballed so quickly that the commission decided to pool interest groups together into coalitions: regional First Nations, fishermen, fish farmers and environmental groups.

No one but me wanted to bring the salmon farm evidence to this commission. So I became a coalition of one, among twenty-one groups with their ninety-five lawyers. I chose Greg McDade as my lawyer, the person I had gone to when Marine Harvest was intent on tripling its farm size.

My first instruction to McDade and his associate, Lisa Glowacki, was to request the BC Ministry of Agriculture's farm salmon health records, which had not been uploaded to the commission's database. Glowacki filed that request to the Cohen Commission on July 1, 2010. The BC Salmon Farmers Association pushed back, saying the records were too confusing for laypeople to understand. This wasn't the first time the association had played tug-of-war over these records.

Four years earlier, the Fisherman's Union's T. Buck Suzuki Foundation had applied through the province's Freedom of Information and Protection of Privacy Act for these same records. The Ministry of Agriculture refused to comply with the request on the basis that the fish farmers had supplied the information in confidence and that disclosure could subject them to various harms. When the matter eventually went to arbitration, the privacy commissioner ruled against the province, requiring the ministry to hand over the records on or before April 12, 2010. The privacy commissioner's decision document revealed that all three of the Norwegian-run companies, as well as Creative Salmon (a Japanese concern), stated that if the information on the health problems of farm salmon was made public, they would cease immediately to volunteer further health data to the ministry and would bar access to the farms to provincial inspectors. When the records were finally released to the Fisherman's Union, the fish farmers made good on their threat and kicked the provincial inspectors off their farms. While the records were at last in the union's hands, this was no help to me, as it refused to share them with me. I wondered at the time if this was because the Fisherman's Union was now reportedly accepting salmon farmers among their members.

Just three months later, the province was once again refusing to release the records, even though they had the ruling in hand that these records were public information. The fish farmers told the Cohen

Commission that if they had to release their disease records to the inquiry, the community enhancement hatcheries should have to release theirs as well. What did the industry know about those records? Were the enhancement hatcheries releasing infected fish into the marine environment? I made a note to follow up on this.

As the lawyers arm-wrestled over the farm salmon health records, I decided to try one of the other ideas I had been considering. In early August, I applied for three tenures in the Broughton right on top of three salmon farm tenures. Salmon farms are never granted exclusive occupancy but receive the lowest form of tenure, akin to the permits granted to companies to put antennas on mountaintops. Several companies can hold tenures for the same bit of land. They can't displace the other antennas, but they can put their own up on the same plot of land.

First I asked permission from the First Nations whose territory I was applying in, and they said yes. Then I filled out an application for three tenures to grow wild fish in the wild at these sites. The application went to the same office in the provincial government that had turned down my floathouse tenure request. The cost was $285 per application. That was a lot of money to me, but the trouble with being perpetually certain that one more big push will resolve this issue is that I always think I'm almost at the end of this road and can justify living on the edge of bankruptcy.

My reasoning was twofold. First, government would not lose the annual income from these tenures when the farms were removed. Second, I wanted to make the point that without a farm, these sites were not empty water. I picked three locations that created jobs and food because they supported so many wild fish.

I applied for Glacier Falls, Sir Edmund Bay and Whelis Bay. The scientific evidence collected by me and others directly implicated each of these farms in harm to the salmon runs of the Ahta, Wakeman and Embly Rivers, respectively. I also knew from my own observations of juvenile salmon migration and those of my fishermen neighbours that these three locations made an enormous amount of wild fish, including prawns, salmon and other species. My applications caused gears to grind within the provincial ministry of Crown Lands. They didn't know what to do. In the end they just kept the money and stopped corresponding with me.

Around this time, the *Globe and Mail* columnist Margaret Wente called me the "best known fish farm fighter, a folk hero and media darling." She then claimed that I and other environmental groups had received tens of millions of dollars in funding from huge US charitable trusts. Like all good character attacks do, it had a kernel of truth. I had been part of the coalition that had been given a million in funding to make a deal with the fish farmers, but I had left this group when the deal became a threat to the wild salmon. Perhaps there were tens of millions going elsewhere, but I was using my line of credit to pay for the dentist. Her claim was also a danger to me: the angriest fish farmers I have encountered all think I am getting rich from threatening their jobs. Instead, I was growing older with no savings account, no safety net.

On July 10, 2010, Don Staniford came for a visit. He and his girl-friend, Elena Edwards, also an activist, were planning a week-long, 150-kilometre paddle for wild salmon down the lower Fraser River, from the town of Hope to Vancouver, to raise awareness of the impact of salmon farms on Fraser River salmon. They aimed to arrive on October 25, the opening day of the Cohen Commission hearings in Vancouver. And they wanted me and my "folk hero" status on the pad-dle. Since I knew how big a threat the salmon farms were to the salmon of the Fraser River, I said I would do it. They asked Anissa too and, bam, we were a team again. I borrowed a canoe to start building pad-dling muscles.

David Wooldridge of Ridge Wilderness Adventures lent us ten voya-geur canoes, each of which could seat ten people. We sent out an invite and people responded. Nicole Mackay, of Mackay Whale Watching in Port McNeill, stepped up to help. She knew about keeping people safe on the water, understood the risk of canoes full of people on a river as huge as the Fraser, and worked to assign experienced people to each boat. Even so, the memory of my husband drowning triggered bouts of panic in me until Darwin and Sue Baerg from Fraser River Raft Expeditions offered to escort us and be our chase boat throughout the whole trip. They knew the river like I knew the Broughton, and taking people out on this river and keeping them safe was their life. I could breathe again.

Elena, Anissa and others took on the nightmare task of where a hundred people would stay every night as the flotilla progressed down the river, along with how to feed us. The Squamish Nation donated time on their rotating billboard on the Burrard Street Bridge in downtown Vancouver to advertise the paddle: it read *Calling the Wild Salmon People*. When it came to saving salmon, people wanted to help.

I packed my car, whistled for Ahta and hugged my daughter farewell again. As I was riding on the ferry to Vancouver, Greg McDade called to tell me we might be denied the farm salmon disease records at the Cohen Commission. Standing on the deck of the ferry looking out at the Salish Sea, I realized that I now had the kind of specific goal that had been missing in the Get Out Migration down Vancouver Island. I would use the paddle and all the media it drew to ensure that people knew that the release of the farm salmon disease records was crucial. Don, Elena and Anissa agreed. We were going to use this effort to make sure BC farm salmon disease records became public information.

11.

Mission for Salmon

THE FRASER RIVER is 1,375 kilometres long. With a network of thirty-four rivers pouring into it, the Fraser drains one-quarter of the land mass of the province of British Columbia—more than 21 million hectares. This massive watershed contains lakes, swamps and countless streams that were once the spawning grounds and nursery of the largest run of salmon in the world. And the river passes through the city of Vancouver before it fans out across a broad estuary, into the Salish Sea.

Before the Paddle for Wild Salmon started, Don, Anissa and I took a road trip up the river to its headwaters to speak with the salmon people of the Fraser's watershed. I wanted to meet the people watching over the places where tens of millions of salmon used to come to bury their eggs, both newcomers and the nations who had been here for thousands of years. I wanted to hear why they thought the salmon were vanishing and to tell them of the risks their salmon faced as they swam through the millions of sea lice and billions of infectious virus particles flowing from each Atlantic salmon farm.

Don Staniford is one of those people who somehow finds the right persons to connect with so that important conversations happen. For instance, when we pulled up to what looked like a random gas station, four hundred kilometres up the Fraser River, Don told me there was someone there who wanted to do a radio interview with me. This was Secwépemc territory, near Chase, BC. The person waiting to talk to me was Neskie Manuel, who pulled out a small audio recorder and asked me how I thought salmon farms were affecting Fraser River salmon. Members of the Manuel family—including Neskie's father, the late Arthur Manuel, one of Canada's strongest and most outspoken Indigenous authors and leaders, and his sister, activist Kanahus Freedom Manuel—are on the front lines in defence of the rights for all Indigenous Peoples.

From there we drove north to Prince George, where we picked up Paul Kennedy, host of the CBC Radio show *Ideas*. Paul wanted to join us for part of our journey and interview me on the side of the river. The only hotel that was open when we got to Vanderhoof wouldn't take dogs, so I slept in the car with Ahta and Anissa's dog, Jade. (I can sleep anywhere.)

We were 1,500 kilometres from the ocean by now, and yet there were salmon here. We met with Sharolise Baker, the Stellat'en fisheries manager. She said that the fishermen of her community were telling her that the salmon were becoming too soft for traditional methods of preserving them. They also wanted to know why they were finding so many sockeye salmon dead on the riverbanks, still full of the precious eggs they had travelled upriver to lay in a pebble nest. Why were their fish changing? People were worried.

This was Stellat'en and Saik'uz territory. These nations were fiercely protective of their salmon and were fighting the aluminum corporation Alcan after the BC government had gifted Alcan with the flow of the Nechako River, one of the big Fraser sockeye spawning grounds, to provide electricity for their smelter. In 1995, these nations stopped the expansion of this project, which would have taken most of the water out of the river. The people I met told me that DFO's opinion was that the sockeye would be fine despite the water diversion. Apparently, the Department was not just a handmaiden to the salmon farmers; it smoothed the way for other industries as well. Perhaps that was DFO's unspoken role and why it never made sense to me. It was running interference for industries—whether mining, logging, smelters or salmon farming—making it appear that precautions were being taken when in fact I knew from growing experience that they were not.

The nations guarded the spawning grounds, as taught by their ancestors, a duty passed down for generations. Now they used a counting fence and cameras that allow twenty-four-hour surveillance to accurately count how many salmon entered the spawning grounds. They compared that total against the number of juvenile salmon they observed leaving the grounds in spring to calculate how many should return. While Fraser River sockeye returns used to be predictable, they had grown increasingly less so over the past eighteen years.

What the nations didn't know was that the young salmon leaving their river would swim through the pathogen-rich excrement from millions of Atlantic salmon and that the new softness of the flesh of their fish could be due to exposure to pathogens from that farmed species. Learning from these nations, I began to think about what could be done to provide answers to their questions about the changes in their fish. At one meeting a young man standing in the back of the room, wearing an expression of deep-seated rage, said, "You are telling me that fish farms might be killing our fish."

Yes, that was exactly what I was saying.

On the evening of our stay they held a blanket dance. A large blanket was laid out on the floor. People danced around it, throwing money into it. Clueless, Anissa, Don and I got up, circled the blanket and also threw money into it. It was embarrassing to learn minutes later that the money was for us to help with expenses.

I felt the weight of their hopes, and hoped I wouldn't let them down, but I was also grateful for the strength of their support. More than once people drew parallels between the threat of European viruses spreading from the Atlantic salmon farms and the smallpox virus brought to the province by Europeans that had killed well over half of their ancestors. I heard repeatedly, *They killed us and now they are killing our food like they did to the people of the plains when they killed the buffalo.*

When we arrived at Fort St. James, we met Betsy Leon, who was eighty-seven and still fishing the river. She noticed an angry red bug bite on my leg and treated it with a poultice of vinegar and nettles that worked immediately. In Tachi, we met Kirby Johnnie, the local fisheries manager. As requested by his Elders, he took us out to the river. His care, love and knowledge for this river, full of miniature sockeye called kokanee, was revealed in every graceful gesture. These fish had adapted to remain in freshwater and never go to sea. To do this they had to shrink themselves to fit a life in the river.

We were too late for the early Stuart run—these were the sockeye that swam the entire length of the river—but I saw the dried head of one lying on the riverbank. Its face was small and delicate, curved like an Arabian horse, not at all like the stout, deep-bodied look of the sockeye that spawned in the Adams River much farther downriver. It was remarkable that all these fish were called sockeye, because the sockeye from every tributary of the river looked different. The fish had adapted themselves to the river. Their unique DNA was their key to survival; as the river changed, so would they.

When salmon enter a river to spawn, they stop feeding. They swim uphill, sometimes powering right up waterfalls or through frothing cauldrons caused by millions of gallons of water boiling through narrow canyon walls. The fish rely on the energy they had collected over their life at sea to fuel them day after day, as they powered their way a thousand kilometres and more upriver. There was no food for them in the river.

In addition to the energy demands of the migration, the males undergo dramatic changes as they travel. Their bodies blush with red and green. Some species glow in shades of purple and stripes appear on their bodies where there were no stripes before. Some species of salmon grow enormous humps and hooked noses, while others sprout long curved fangs. Their investment in this stunning regalia ensures the best possible future for their offspring, because these changes in appearance speak to the females. They say something like, *Hey baby, I went out to the ocean, took a spin around the Pacific gyre, swam up this river and I brought all this wealth home to you!*

When you watch spawning salmon, it is hard to see how the female decides which male she will mate with, but she is looking the guys over, head to tail. She is making a critical decision for the future of her species by picking the male she feels will make her babies the strongest. Salmon have exceptional diversity stored in their genetic code; as their rivers change, becoming faster, slower, colder, warmer or more silted, the female's choice hones the next generation to evolve rapidly in synch with the river.

Run of the River, a book by a senior correspondent with the *Vancouver Sun*, Mark Hume, tells the story of trying to put salmon back into a river that had lost its fish. It's an impossible task for humans because the salmon and their river are one organism. A salmon is only half a creature; it can't survive without its river. This explains why a hundred years of work by salmon hatcheries has not been able to restore *wild* self-sustaining runs of salmon. If you take away the mysterious signals between the males and the females, you have stolen their most important tool for survival. You might as well cut off their tails.

Our next stop was Takla Landing, nearing the headwaters of the Fraser River. We were warned that the "dirt" road in was hard on tires, so we parked Anissa's van behind and piled into my car. Indeed, the road was a bed of jagged rock fragments, but two hours later we were just in time for dinner at the village's little hotel. As I walked Ahta after the long drive, a black fox came boldly at us until the local dogs put the run to it. Ahta was unsettled; nothing about this place was familiar, not the smells or the animals. So she stuck close. Good dog.

At a meeting with Elders the next day we learned that here, so close to the Fraser's headwaters, the people were still very much on the land. They still maintained their family fishing spots on the river, handed down generation to generation over the centuries.

Margo French, the Takla fisheries manager, took us in her extra-durable truck, bouncing and lurching 210 kilometres further upriver.

We followed the shore of Takla Lake into the headwaters of Driftwood Creek, the highest reach where so-called Fraser River sockeye spawn. The water tasted like snow.

Margo set out food to share on the tailgate of the truck: canned groundhog (woodchuck), wind-dried salmon, bear grease and apple-sauce. She described how the chiefs traditionally watched the river and did not allow fishing until they felt enough fish had made it into the river to spawn. I had assumed that before modern industrial fishing, people simply didn't have the tools to harm salmon runs. But I learned this was not true. Looking at the tiny streams that poured into Takla Lake, I realized that it would have been easy to kill all the fish in each stream. The people who lived here for thousands of years had learned to make sure the needs of the fish came first, so that future generations would always be fed.

Although the Takla Nation continued to guard the spawning grounds of these salmon, fewer fish were showing up year after year. Margo was deeply troubled when I showed her pictures of the young Fraser River sockeye salmon I had caught near salmon farms. Unlike the pink and chum salmon of the Broughton, the young sockeye do not linger around the farms but rocket past to get out into the open ocean. Still, they were infected with sea lice. If the sockeye were picking up the lice from the farms, they were also exposed to the bacteria and viruses. Indeed, one year the young sockeye in the Discovery Islands had open sores so deep I could see their bones.

Margo was a woman as rough as the land she was part of. But through her, Kirby Johnnie and Sharolise Baker, First Nation fisheries managers along the Fraser River, I was exposed to Indigenous sockeye knowledge. I knew from talking to Billy Proctor that nothing compared to convers-ing with the people who lived with the fish. Billy's knowledge was at least a hundred years deep, based on his own experience and that of the old-timers he'd talked to while growing up. Indigenous knowledge was thousands of years old, and while it had been fragmented by the heavy suppression of their culture, a lot of the knowledge had been protected.

I began to think that if I was to become DFO's director of wild salmon, I would travel to every community living with salmon and absorb not only the essential baseline knowledge required to understand what the system was capable of, but also the ancient instructions on how to live with salmon. The fish had proven that they are able to adapt to us, but only if we follow their laws. The knowledge I was exposed to on this voyage was the key to living by salmon laws.

From Takla Landing we turned around and headed downriver to Williams Lake. Chris Blake told us about the twelve-thousand-square-kilometre Quesnel Lake watershed, where an average of 500 millimetres of rain a year kept fifteen-hundred-year-old cedar trees alive. It took the sockeye twenty days to get here from Vancouver. Twenty days of no food, swimming against the river, as the eggs were ripening in the females and the males were manufacturing their regalia!

One year later, I would come back here to witness the aftermath of the collapse of an earthen dam built by Vancouver-based Imperial Metals that held a toxic cocktail of mining waste. The company also was paid to truck human sewage up from Vancouver to dump into the tailings pond. When the dam broke, people on the far side of Quesnel Lake were hit with a toxic wind from the spill. After it blew past, trees were missing leaves on the branches that faced the lake, while the leaves facing away from the industrial spill were still green.

Hazeltine Creek had become a broad smear of brown sludge that made my throat burn. I ached with anger and sadness to see the tracks of elk, bears and cranes who must have been wondering where their creek was. Bits of splintered wood from the shattered trees were black-edged where they made contact with the sludge. I realized they were burned. The feet of the animals that had left tracks through this wasteland must have burned too. Did they try to lick them clean? Did that kill them?

I took samples of the sludge that had reached the lake, where it formed an enormous underwater mountain, as soft as talcum powder.

Any small current caused the toxic material to lift into the water column and begin its journey of death down the river.

A first responder told me that when he put his arm into the water to set a rope around one of the hundreds of trees that had been swept into the lake, in order to tow it to shore, his skin began to burn and turned bright red. He was afraid to talk to anyone about it.

As a child I did not believe in "evil." I thought it was something religions thought up to scare us into compliance. But at Quesnel Lake I saw that evil is real. To threaten life on such a catastrophic level, forever, is evil. Kanahus Manuel, Neskie's sister, would spend years battling Imperial Metals to get them to clean this mess up and stop mining in salmon watersheds. The succession of Liberal and NDP governments of British Columbia have not even fined Imperial Metals for this spill, which still affects the river. The lack of political reaction to the damage caused by salmon farming is not an isolated blunder; it's part of a fatal continuum.

Next we drove down to Adams Lake. I was excited to visit the spawning grounds of the magnificent Adams River sockeye, which I had fished off the west coast of Vancouver Island when I worked for Billy Proctor. They were everyone's iconic image of a Fraser River sockeye, brilliant red, with a green head and tail—the largest sockeye in British Columbia.

A park had been built at the grounds complete with parking attendants, a gift shop and trails along the river. The fish, used to humans, went about the business of spawning without fear as we watched. The words of German, Japanese and French tourists mingled with the rushing noise of salmon splashing as they fought for mates and dug their nests.

Male salmon guarded nesting sites, slashing at other males that tried to move in. As they fought their backs exploded out of the shallow water like scarlet flames. The females were on their sides beating at the pebbles to form a shallow depression. They constantly assessed the excavation, hovering over it to measure it with their anal fin. Then they went back to work until it was perfect. The male guarded the female digging on his turf and, at the right moment, sidled up alongside her to release his sperm. Salmon eggs can only be fertilized for the few moments after they leave the mother's body, because shortly after an egg contacts freshwater, its outer edge forms a watertight barrier. The male has to release his sperm at the same second as the female releases her eggs in a river alive with the distraction of thousands of other fish involved in the many stages of the same process.

Among the big males, I spotted an occasional much smaller male, called a jack. These jacks, a year younger, used a different strategy. Sneaking in at the last second, they released their sperm into the cloud from the older male. In doing so they provided the wealth of genetic material from two otherwise separate generations. This meant that two different males could fertilize the hundreds of eggs from one female.

I loved watching the children around me absorb the wildness of the fish and the river. Some of the adults did not appear to know how to express the emotion they were feeling. Most stood still and simply watched. Many kept telling neighbours to look, even though we were all looking at same scene. Others, however, seemed to want the fish to pay attention to *them*. They threw rocks or tried to jab the fish with sticks. No one from BC Parks was there to tell them not to do this, though the gift shop was well staffed. BC Parks personnel, did however tell us to cover up the stickers all over Anissa's Volkswagen van that read *Calling the Wild Salmon People*, *Salmon Are Sacred* and *Stop Fish Farms*, or we would be asked to leave the park. We didn't have a blanket big enough so they made Anissa move the van behind the RVs, where the tourists could not see it.

In Lumby, Priscilla Judd, a musician and a local streamkeeper, took us to Shuswap Falls. The Wilsey Dam was built on the Shuswap River seventy years ago, blocking salmon from reaching the upper river. The promised fish ladder has never been built. As we stood there, a single sockeye threw itself against the wall of the dam, brilliant red against the slick black of the wet wall. He knew he was supposed to return to the spawning grounds of his ancestors. How he knew is a mystery. *If we just let salmon guide us, we could live successfully together*, I thought.

Priscilla held a potluck dinner for us that night and, once again, I scribbled notes as I listened to people who knew the fish and generally knew what the fish in that region needed. When DFO had refused to post signs prohibiting jet skiers from running over top of the huge chinook salmon trying to spawn in the Shuswap River, locals made signs reading *NO JET BOATING* and put them up. The jet skiers complied, which protected the untold millions of chinook salmon eggs laid safely into the gravel, benefitting people along the entire coast of British Columbia and the orca that depend on chinook to survive. It baffled me why DFO would refuse to do this, but I was learning that people all along the Fraser River were kick-ass, edgy, independent doers. I liked them a lot.

The *Calgary Herald* called. They were dedicating a section of the paper to Dr. Jane Goodall and were looking for the "Janes of Canada." They wanted to talk to me, and that meant a lot.

We were approaching the town of Hope—the end of our road trip—and the launch of the week-long paddle loomed. Don was in charge of media coverage, and he and Anissa tried to persuade me that before the paddle started, I should raft through the Hell's Gate rapids, holding a *Salmon Are Sacred* sign aloft. They said it would make a great picture to kick off the trip.

Tourists do this all the time, but my years on the water had taught me fear. As one of my friends, Nicole Mackay, says, "I don't play in rough water." My attitude exactly. Don and Anissa insisted I needed to do this, throwing in the fact that an unfortunate cow once rode the rapids and survived. I was glad for the cow, but I really, really did not want to do this.

In the end I gave in and climbed into the second of two rafts. At first the trip was lovely, as we floated downriver on a huge, comfortable inflatable. Then the river began to narrow between high banks and the water moved faster in a series of large rollers. *I got this*, I told myself. *This boat is well designed for the rough water.*

Then we came around a bend and I could see where the river fell away into a huge hole at the bottom of a steep drop. Boiling white waves towered over us, knocking us around. Just before we dropped into the most frightening watery violence I have ever seen, the outboard that was keeping our raft from taking the waves broadside quit. The guide stood and began pulling on the cord to restart it. "Shit, shit, shit," he repeated, pulling hard and fast.

I was gripping the side of the boat with one hand, holding onto the damn sign in the other, looking at how I could unlash the oar beside me to provide some sort of steering. The front of the boat reared up, folded in two and then hurled the stern into the air. The engine sputtered to life. I squeezed my eyes shut and, as we fell into hell, I held up the sign. Would it even be visible in the chaos of water?

Don and Anissa missed the shot.

We set out on our paddle from Hope, BC, on the frosty morning of October 20, 2010. National Chief Shawn Atleo drummed ninety of us into the large voyageur canoes and several smaller ones, and we slipped out onto the peaceful rushing river. It was 160 kilometres to Vancouver. Chief Marilyn Baptiste of the Xeni Gwet'in Nation was among us. She'd won a tough fight to save Teztan Biny (Fish Lake) from Taseko Mines' proposal to locate one of the biggest copper and gold mines in the province there. An hour after we started paddling, the BC Salmon Farmers Association put out a press release under the headline: "BC's salmon farms: well-managed and sustainable."

As the sun rose, a warm wind picked up. Sockeye were leaping around us. Our first stop was Cheam, where the formidable First

Nation Matriarch June Quipp took me aside and said, "I have been watching you." I froze. Then she hugged me and provided food for the whole flotilla.

We arrived in Skwah territory as the sun was setting, turning the river red-golden. The moon rose behind the silhouetted drummers on the riverbank welcoming us. Skwah Elder Eddie Gardner was there. He was one of the thousands of people who'd showed up at the Get Out Migration, making the trip from his home in Chilliwack. He went on to lead sixty farm salmon boycott events at Walmart, Costco, Save-on-Foods, Real Canadian Superstore and Safeway.

Eddie, relentless but deeply kind, spoke to us around a fire that night, making it clearer than I ever could how important this work was. We had to get the farm salmon disease records, he told people, so that we could learn why the salmon in the Fraser River were changing, and why they were vanishing. *Thank you, Eddie.*

The next day the canoe I was in hit a gravel bar. In an instant, the boat swung sideways and tipped dangerously. Our skipper, Will, who had been raised on the river, rapid-fire instructed us not to set foot outside the boat; the current was so strong we would have been swept away. Though the chase boat spotted us immediately, Will had us sorted and gliding downstream again within moments. River water is so different from ocean water.

As we approached Matsqui, ninety kilometres from the ocean, young Aaron Williams of the Squamish Nation called all the boats together. Ninety people, holding on to each other's canoes, rafted together in the middle of the river. He explained to us in his deep raspy voice that we couldn't behave the way we'd done the night before: we needed to learn some manners.

"I am embarrassed to be seen with you!" he said in a booming Big House voice. "Treat your paddles like your wife, husband or child. Don't just walk away from your canoe at the end of the day like a child. Take your paddle with you and treat it with respect. Make sure your canoe is perfectly clean before you leave it for the night.

"Second," he went on, "when we approach a village, you are going to raise your paddle and remain still until you are invited to land. If that invitation comes, you are going to turn the canoe around and back into the beach, signalling that we do not intend to raid the village!"

It had been a long time since ninety people in canoes had travelled nation-to-nation on a quest along the river.

Before getting into our canoes at Matsqui the next morning, we were smudged with sage smoke. When we arrived at Katzie, thirty-five kilometres downriver, Chief Willie Pierre received us. Standing alone on the riverbank, he drummed and sang a hauntingly beautiful song. We remained silent and motionless, our ninety paddles raised. When he realized that we were waiting for his invitation, his eyes brimmed with emotion. The clearing where we camped that night was strewn with old rusting equipment, but the food was nourishing and the fire warmed us. There was singing, laughter and discussions about how to stop those who saw killing off the wild salmon as simply the price of doing business.

Don, Elena, Anissa and I intentionally faded into the background as this paddle became an Indigenous-led voyage; chiefs and elders set our schedule and they told us where we were going every evening after the paddling to various gatherings. Grand Chief Stewart Phillip and his wife, Joan Phillip, paddled with us. Fin Donnelly, the MP who had introduced Bill C518 to the Canadian Parliament in Ottawa to move salmon farms into tanks on land, joined us. The provincial MLA, Michael Sather, got into one of the canoes, and the mayor of Vancouver, Gregor Robinson, paddled with us on the last day. As we entered Musqueam territory, the last stop before we reached the ocean, their First Nation fisheries powerboat came out and escorted us.

Twenty more people arrived in canoes that night in Musqueam, including Chief Darren Blaney of the Homalco First Nation, located on the mainland across from Campbell River, in his dugout canoe. In the band hall at Musqueam, we stood in a circle and listened to band members talk about losing wild salmon. I was learning from the people whom salmon had nourished for ten thousand years. Someone that night asked me if I was tired. As I thought for a second, I realized I had no idea. I had been swept into something ancient, human, spiritual, wet and cold—a river. In that moment I could not feel myself as separate from it.

The next morning we would leave the river and enter the ocean to round the point from the Fraser River into Vancouver. There was a stiff breeze. We asked the littlest children with us to go by land for this leg of the voyage, since we would have to turn broadside to the waves to navigate around Point Grey. Some of the river people were nervous but now I felt confident. Ocean water was familiar. We assembled like a pod of whales, and 110 people in canoes headed for the Cohen Commission into the decline of the Fraser River sockeye.

The ocean was gentler than anticipated and carried us easily around the headland. When we landed at Jericho Beach, Chief Bobby Joseph hugged me so warmly that for a second I felt like I belonged. This man has travelled the world, met with the pope in Rome and done everything he could to bring reconciliation and respect to the Indigenous Peoples of Canada. Bobby Joe, as he is called, is beloved. As a full media contingent watched, he and the other chiefs said it was critical that the Cohen Commission produce the farm salmon disease records. Their fish were being exposed to viruses and sea lice, and they wanted to know what was going on in the farms.

The next morning it was raining so hard we could barely tell when the sun rose. For the last time we picked up our paddles, which had been lying beside us every night, and took our positions in the canoes. There were dark grey thunderheads over the city of Vancouver and the water was silver. One hundred and ten paddles pulled the canoes towards the city.

We arrived at Vanier Beach to a sea of umbrellas. Margo French had come all the way from Takla Landing to greet us. Protocol was observed. Hereditary Chief Ian Campbell stood in front of the crowd, the feathers of his regalia rippling in the wind. Chief Robert Chamberlin stood alongside him in the sea of people; it felt good to see his familiar face.

I thanked my canoe, took my paddle with me and asked a young man standing in the parking lot if he knew the way to the Burrard Street Bridge. He said, "Yes, for sure."

I asked, "Could you lead us there?"

He said yes, and he did.

The rain poured down on us as we took over one lane of the Burrard Street Bridge, the crowd stretching the entire length of the bridge. When we got to the downtown office building on West Georgia Street where the hearings were to be held, a small group of us, including Chief Chamberlin, Fin Donnelly, and the chief of the Musqueam Nation, whose territory we were standing on, entered the hearings. As we filed in, Justice Bruce Cohen kept his attention on the witness who was testifying. A map of the Fraser River was up on the screen. That image meant so much more to me now. Together our group held open an elk hide that supporters had signed as we travelled the river, in support of protecting wild salmon. The hide was so wet from the rain that it was slippery and elastic. Water pooled on the carpet at our feet, as though we had brought the river with us.

Finally, when the speaker concluded, Commissioner Cohen turned to look at us. We dipped our heads in unison to acknowledge his attention and then turned and left without saying a word, carrying our soggy hide with us.

In the coverage of the opening of the inquiry, we appeared on the front page of every newspaper, along with our message: the people of the river and the coast want the BC government salmon farm disease records to be made public. The inquiry did order the province to hand over the records. Mission accomplished.

And it changed my life. Unexpectedly I was about to become a virus hunter.

12.

The Cohen Commission

IN RESPONSE TO the Cohen Commission's instructions to DFO to provide all documents that might pertain to the decline of the Fraser River sockeye, over three million pages of internal government documents were filed. These documents were assembled into a database to which each approved participant in the inquiry was given tightly restricted and confidential access. To release a document from this database, the participant's lawyer had to request that it be made into an exhibit during their allotted time in front of Justice Cohen and Cohen had to accept it into evidence. The lawyers were paid by the commission for their time, but participants, such as me, were not.

As I began combing through the documents, some of them tens of pages long, I borrowed the treadmill again, taped my laptop computer to it and spent nine months staring at the screen. The commission database was painfully slow to search and my internet connectivity was equally slow; the file downloads would grind away interminably.

As a whale researcher in Echo Bay writing letters to government, I only saw DFO's impenetrable slippery facade. But now I was on the other side of that wall. I began following trails that led deep into the fortress that DFO has become. I saw the responses to many issues I had raised with the Department. For example, when I had reported oily gas bubbles rising to the surface close to Cermaq's Cecil Island salmon

farm in the Broughton in July 2008, a senior aquaculture biologist was
sent to investigate. Eventually, she wrote me with these results: "During
the three visits we collectively undertook, there were no further bubbles
seen, nor any information we could find to explain your observations."

However, in the Cohen database, I found an email in which she
described what she had actually found: "In another sampling location, at
the edge of the feed shed, near where the community member [i.e., me]
had reported bubbles at the surface, our grab became entangled and we
pulled up a mort lift pipe full of dead fish . . . . We were unable to explain
how it got to that location, especially full of fish. The pipes are normally
inside the pens and they suck morts up from the bottom of the pens . . . .
It's possible the pipe was dropped off the system by mistake." Right, a
pipe full of dead fish had been lifted out of the pen, over the walkway,
and dropped "by mistake." What had really happened?

The time I'd spent watching animals closely had sharpened my obser-
vational skills. People give up important information in their body language. Government lawyers glance at industry lawyers as interrogation
by a judge moves in a direction they are uncomfortable with. Scientists
clench their lips and visibly swallow the things they mustn't say. Federal
employees blink compulsively during certain questions. As nervous people attempt to skirt an issue, they define the boundaries of what they are
trying to hide like chalk at a crime scene.

The enormous fuss that industry and government kicked up to prevent the provincial farm salmon health records from becoming public
was a prominent chalk outline. Even as the industry followed through
on its threat to ban government fish inspectors from taking samples of
farm salmon after the health records were released to the Fisherman's
Union, I found that the companies continued to send farm salmon samples to the same ministry's Animal Health Centre for diagnostic work.
The industry didn't trust government, but they trusted this government
lab. Was this lab responsible to the companies or government?

One month into reviewing the Cohen documents, I found hundreds of the Animal Health Centre diagnostic reports provided to the

companies, many of them done after the government inspectors had been barred from the farms. I printed the neatly typed reports, signed by provincial fish pathologist, Dr. Gary Marty. His reports went back to 2006, when he had been hired. The date, company and submitting industry veterinarians were identified, as well as the health concern of the fish, though usually the farm site in question was not listed. Dr. Marty provided extensive detail in each report on the lesions found in the organ samples submitted to the lab and noted what he thought might have caused the cell damage he observed.

The company veterinarians had asked Dr. Marty about a wide range of symptoms in the farm salmon: cloudy eyes, bloody eyes, blood in the brain, bloat, green livers, open sores, lesions, meningitis, hemorrhages, and scores of other issues. In response, Marty provided detailed descriptions of the abnormalities visible under the microscope. When he described specific cellular damage, he referenced published scientific papers to support his opinions. I looked up those papers, read them and learned about the pathogens that were worrying the salmon farmers in British Columbia.

In addition to these reports to the companies, I found Dr. Marty's quarterly health audits of the farms from before the industry brought them to an end. This was Cohen file BCP002864, an Excel file with 2,278 lines of entries. I reviewed and graphed these data to find the patterns.

What jumped out at me first were Dr. Marty's 1,100 reports of the classic lesions associated with ISAV infections in BC farmed salmon. ISAV, or infectious salmon anemia virus, is an internationally reportable virus, meaning the world is trying to prevent it from spreading. Infected countries have to report outbreaks of the virus to the World Organisation for Animal Health, OIE. The virus is a member of the influenza family, and influenza viruses in farm animals are a worry. Think avian and swine flu. Influenza viruses have no "proofreading" gene. The typos in genetic sequences of the virus are not corrected as the virus replicates, which means they mutate easily. This makes them particularly dangerous in feedlots, where the opportunity to mutate is accelerated.

No animal in a feedlot is going to live out its natural lifespan, and so, under those conditions, there is no benefit to a virus to live lightly on its host. It would be a losing strategy for viruses in a farm to bet on a long-term opportunity to replicate and spread. Instead, they adapt to replicate as fast as possible, before the animal or fish is harvested or culled. If the virus kills its host, no problem, it has already spread through the farm population. Higher replication rates equal higher virulence. Crowding animals in the absence of predators is a recipe for plagues.

When the Norwegian salmon farming industry accidentally introduced ISAV to their farms in Chile, the companies ignored the appearance of the virus. They foolishly hoped it would behave differently in Chile than it had Norway, where it was considered one of the top three most dangerous fish viruses. In 2007, one company grew worried about a small, unexplained spike in mortalities in its Chilean farms, and sent samples to the North American ISAV reference lab for the World Organisation for Animal Health at the University of Prince Edward Island. ISAV was not only confirmed, it proved to be a new strain, dubbed HPR7b (the HPR stands for "highly polymorphic region"), and it spread through Chile like fire on gasoline. The salmon farming industry reported they had never seen a virus spread so fast.

Chile doesn't have any naturally occurring wild salmon to infect, but the ISAV epidemic caused two billion dollars in damage to the Chilean salmon farming industry, which, as in British Columbia, was largely Norwegian-owned. When the government of Chile threatened to sue Norway for contaminating their waters, Norway turned the tables and threatened to sue Chile for laws so lax that they allowed the Norwegian companies to make the mistake of importing ISAV infected stock. This was the volatile situation that Dr. Are Nylund and his associates got caught up in when they traced HPR7b in Chile to the salmon hatchery in Norway and were investigated as a result for "unethical behaviour."

Viruses not only have "fingerprints" in their genetic sequence, but they have molecular clocks that allow scientists to estimate the date of arrival of foreign viruses in a new region.

Two years into the Chilean outbreak, in January 2009, the international salmon farming news service *IntraFish* wrote: "How long can BC avoid ISA? British Columbia is the only major salmon growing area in the world that hasn't been impacted by ISA. How long will that last?"

Given this troubling history of ISAV's unstoppable spread through salmon farms, I didn't understand why Dr. Marty kept reporting "classic lesions associated with ISAV infections" in BC farm salmon. Why didn't he resolve whether or not it *was* ISA and either stop raising the question, or pull the alarm bell to begin the process of eradicating it before it went viral.

In July 2009, the record showed that Marine Harvest suddenly began sending samples to Dr. Marty specifically asking for ISAV testing. They ordered thirty-two tests in one year, up from two such requests total in the previous four years. At the same time, the BC industry abruptly stopped importing Atlantic salmon eggs, something they had told government regulators that they couldn't possibly do. Then, on April 16, 2010, the three Norwegian companies signed a memorandum of understanding to co-manage viral diseases between themselves, with no government involvement. Had something scared them?

Since Dr. Marty was only a pathologist, his reports were passed up a level to the veterinarian, Dr. Mark Sheppard, the person who had assured me that sea lice in Nootka Sound were not becoming drug-resistant, to make the actual diagnosis. I searched the Cohen database for any records from Dr. Sheppard on ISAV. I found one he had signed, an August 1, 2007, briefing note to the minister of agriculture, labelled "confidential." It was on the risk to the province from the ISA virus in Atlantic salmon farms. The BC government was keeping an eye on the situation in Chile, perhaps because the same companies were operating in both places. Dr. Sheppard wrote that they had been doing ISAV surveillance but, he told the minister, "there is no importation of live

Atlantic salmon or eggs to BC" and so if ISAV showed up in British Columbia the most likely source would be "migrating wild fishes."

In point of fact, thirty million live Atlantic salmon eggs had been imported into British Columbia from five different countries, and Dr. Sheppard was the man in charge of the health of the fish these eggs produced. Since he was one of only three or four people in the province who had access to Dr. Marty's records, presumably he was aware that the pathologist was reporting ISA-like lesions in farm salmon every month. I could find no record of whether anyone in government had ever followed up on these alarming reports by sending samples to the ISAV international reference lab. I flagged this document for Greg McDade; he would call Dr. Sheppard as a witness and ask him to explain himself to the commission.

As I continued to search the commission documents, I found the federal Atlantic salmon egg importation certificates. I saw that a signature was required to import the eggs into the province, guaranteeing that the eggs were free of several viruses; ISAV was not on the list. Then I found an internal DFO conversation triggered by an email I'd sent in 2009 asking if the Department was screening imported Atlantic salmon eggs for ISAV. The response I received at the time was confident: "all introductions of eggs into BC are closely tracked by the federal–provincial Introductions and Transfers Committee. As has been communicated to you previously, eggs are screened for *all known viral agents* prior to shipment to BC." It was signed by the DFO director of science, Pacific Region, Dr. Laura Richards.

However, internal emails revealed a much less confident DFO. The Ottawa-based director of science, Sharon Ford, wrote, "would it be possible to call the hatchery (in Iceland) [which had already shipped eight million Atlantic salmon eggs to British Columbia] and ask what they did import for the last couple of years? Are there import restrictions? . . . Is there testing for ISA in the country?"

Andrew Thomson, the regional director of Fisheries Management, wrote: "I have already asked Laura (R.) the specific questions about the presence of ISA in Iceland and how confident we are in the position that ISA does not occur in eggs. No response yet."

Ed Porter, manager of Aquaculture Policy and Regulatory Initiatives, added, "There is a small possibility that ISAV could be transmitted with reproductive fluids . . . . However, surface disinfection of eggs, which is routinely carried out . . . provides assurance that ISAV will not be transmitted."

Then Thomson asked if Canada was actually requiring egg "surface disinfection." Porter answered, "Disinfection isn't a regulatory requirement by FHPR [Fish Health Protection Regulations], but strongly suggested."

To that, Stephen Stephen, director of Biotechnology, replied, "The I&T [Introductions and Transfer] committees can make this a requirement for import and set any other conditions . . . . That being said I'm not sure that this is happening in every case."

None of what Dr. Richards had told me appeared to be true. DFO had no idea how many Atlantic salmon eggs had come into the province, a check for "all known viral agents" was not occurring, and disinfection of the eggs was not even required.

Until the documents were accepted as exhibits in the upcoming commission hearings, I could only discuss these discoveries with my lawyers. However, when my friend and colleague Dr. Rick Routledge, a professor of statistics at Simon Fraser University who I had published several sea louse papers with, lamented that he had done everything he could think of to figure out why Rivers Inlet sockeye on the central coast of British Columbia were declining, I offered a suggestion. "What about testing for ISAV?" I said.

My research prior to 2010 had been focused on the Broughton Archipelago. Now, as part of the Cohen Commission, I needed to mine the commission database in a crash course on what was going on with the Fraser River sockeye salmon. Reading through the document cache,

I learned that year after year since the early 1990s, more Fraser River sockeye were dying in the river just before spawning. DFO's salmon biologists were stumped as to why. Generally when wild fish die, no one finds their bodies, and so there is little evidence to be gathered. But in this case, sockeye salmon were lying dead along the thousands of kilometres of tributaries to the Fraser River. Called pre-spawn mortality, this was nothing new, but what *was* new was that it previously had been tied to high water temperatures. The warmer the water, the more fish died. Now astronomical numbers of sockeye were dying in water of any temperature.

Between 1995 and 2010, up to 95 percent of the late run Fraser sockeye were dying of pre-spawn mortality. Internal DFO documents reported that 100 percent of the once abundant Cultus Lake sockeye died in 1999, 2000 and 2001. By 2008, the mysterious die-off was described as "system wide," meaning the entire Fraser River. In 2006, DFO biologist Timber Whitehouse had written to DFO's Laura Richards and Brian Riddell, to inform them that "pre-spawn mortality for females exceeds 85%." The scientists knew these populations could not survive this level of mortality, and so the search was on for the cause of death. I read the shared ideas and observations between scientists from DFO and elsewhere.

"Definitely something out of the ordinary," reported someone named D. Willis about sockeye in the Upper Pitt River that were dying as they were netted in a beach seine (which is designed not to kill fish).

Some of the fish bled profusely when handled; others appeared to have bacterial kidney disease, but lab tests failed to find the bacteria.

"I think it is well worth not overlooking the possibility of a viral agent," wrote Dr. David Speare to Mike Bradford at the University of Prince Edward Island.

In a DFO memo, Dr. Christine MacWilliams wrote that "despite finding everything but the kitchen sink, there's no smoking gun."

"This raises the spectre of a novel pathogen," concluded David Patterson.

"The mystery deepens," wrote Dr. Speare.

While the Fraser River sockeye was one of Canada's most important fisheries, funding from DFO to solve this mystery of mass mortality was stingy. From an internal DFO email thread in May 2009: "A year class of Nadina sockeye have all died prespawning and all we have [to test] are the 11 gill arches and they are virtually useless . . . . we no longer have the necessary resources to send a field crew out . . . . Our system to try and solve these problems or at least learn from them appears to be very broken."

Despite these biologists' clear sense of urgency, they seemed unable to identify any known environmental factor, parasite, bacteria or virus that was responsible for these millions of dead sockeye salmon. Commercial fisheries were closed and livelihoods threatened; even if an abundance of sockeye was detected approaching the coast in early summer by the DFO test boats, no one knew if any would survive to spawn and produce the next generation. By drastically cutting fishing quotas, DFO managers were successful in getting viable salmon to the spawning grounds, but they died there before spawning. The numbers of Fraser River sockeye kept tumbling like a boulder down a mountainside.

Two months into exploring the commission database, I came across a PowerPoint presentation, dated September 27, 2008, by Dr. Kristi Miller of the Molecular Genetics Lab at DFO's Pacific Biological Station in Nanaimo. It was titled "Epidemic of a novel, cancer-causing viral disease may be associated with wild salmon declines in BC." The cover photo was of a brain tumour in a sockeye salmon. I hit download.

The document described preliminary data Miller and her lab gathered through a new technique that suggested that an unknown virus was causing tumours in the optic lobes of the Fraser sockeye and killing them. I searched the database for every document with Dr. Miller's name on it.

In 2007, she had been tasked to join the search for what was killing off the Fraser River sockeye. The documents revealed that Miller was pioneering the ability to "read" the immune system of salmon. By looking at which genes were up- or down-regulated in their expression in the fish, Miller could figure out what the fish were experiencing. Different genes respond to different stressors. Her field of research, called genomic profiling, was new for fish, but quite a bit of work had been done on identifying these patterns in terrestrial animals.

DFO expected that Miller would find that the sockeye died because they were weakened by a lack of food in the open ocean. However, the dying and living fish showed starkly different immune system patterns. Like a road sign on the highway this data revealed which direction the investigation should go. In the fish that died, a unique set of immune system switches had been left on. In terrestrial animals a similar pattern signals that the animal was fighting a retrovirus or leukemia. Why had no one talked about Dr. Miller's work at the scientific meetings I'd attended on the 2009 collapse of the sockeye? Why was I asked to present on the evidence that pathogens in sockeye were killing them to the Pacific Salmon Commission when this lab's work had been going on for three years?

Miller had only been able to find two fish viruses in the scientific literature that might produce a leukemia-like immune response, and only one of them occurred in salmon. Called salmon leukemia virus, it had been discovered by DFO scientists in the early 1990s in the same research station in which Miller's lab was located.

Putting the Cohen documents aside, I downloaded all the papers I could find published by DFO on salmon leukemia virus. The story unfolded. In the 1990s, most fish farmers were trying to grow chinook salmon from eggs robbed from local and distant rivers, such as Robertson Creek and the Yukon River. It was not going well. Marine anemia, as the farmers called it, began killing off entire farms. The industry seemed doomed and the DFO scientist, Dr. Michael Kent, director of the Pacific Biological Station in Nanaimo, began researching the cause. He announced his discovery of a retrovirus he called salmon leukemia virus in the journal *Cancer Research* in 1992, describing how it could be transmitted from farmed chinook to sockeye. Tumour growth in the optic lobe of the salmon brain was one of the features of this disease.

Dr. Kent and others described how the virus travelled with the industry from Sechelt Inlet, where it had first appeared, into the farms in the Discovery Islands and the Broughton Archipelago. As the industry spread, so did the virus, depopulating entire farms. I felt a sickening pull in my gut, realizing that the salmon leukemia outbreak was at its peak when the fish farmers in Echo Bay told us they had been throwing pellets into empty pens after all the fish had died. This was when we lost all the wild chinook that used to overwinter in the archipelago, the winter springs. According to these DFO documents, millions of farm salmon were shedding salmon leukemia virus into the Broughton. People in DFO knew this was happening when I was writing to the Department about the loss of wild salmon and the Department was writing me back to say there was no evidence of such a loss. They had the evidence all along. This was also precisely when the decline of the Fraser River sockeye began.

I turned back to Dr. Miller's research documents. She reported that there was one run of Fraser River sockeye, the Harrison sockeye that did not carry the leukemia signature in its immune system. Flipping back to a series of graphs among the Cohen Commission documents, I saw that while the other runs of sockeye in the Fraser River were in decline, the number of Harrison sockeye had increased during the same time period.

Turning back to the internet I found a paper by DFO reporting that during the years 1996 to 2007, Harrison River sockeye DNA was never detected on the primary sockeye migration route through the Discovery Islands. It was only found on the other side of Vancouver Island. The paper surmised that Harrison sockeye were migrating in the opposite direction from the rest of the Fraser sockeye, heading around the southern end of Vancouver Island instead, which meant they were not exposed to the salmon farms. Why didn't everyone working on the sockeye collapse know this? It felt like Miller had been reduced to casting messages in a bottle into the ocean of commission documents.

The Miller lab had drawn up a three-year plan to verify the presence of the virus in Fraser River sockeye, its effect and source. Kent and others working on the salmon leukemia virus in the 1990s had never published its genetic sequence, which made it much harder to trace. Miller had strong circumstantial evidence; the next step was to test the farm salmon to see if their immune systems were exhibiting the same pattern. This is when things started to go badly for Miller.

Dr. Gary Marty, the BC Ministry of Agriculture pathologist who was steadily reporting lesions that he associated with salmon leukemia virus in both the chinook farms that remained in the Discovery Islands and in Atlantic farm salmon, was very critical of Dr. Miller's hypothesis that the Fraser sockeye might be dying of this virus. To begin with, he wanted to convince the department that the growths Miller was documenting in the sockeye brains were bruising due to "blunt trauma," not tumours. I wondered why DFO didn't send the brains to a cancer specialist who could resolve that debate.

Then Miller got her research on the unique immune response in the sockeye accepted for publication in *Science*. Reporters were eager to speak to her because this was huge—the first scientific evidence as to what was happening to the Fraser River sockeye. I read the emails from reporters all over the world requesting interviews; I saw that Prime Minister Harper's office decided not to allow Miller to speak to them. As a result, the press got it all wrong. The headlines were all variations of "Fraser River Sockeye Die of Weak Genetics." As Dr. Craig Stephens, who studied the salmon leukemia virus epidemic in the 1990s, wrote in his PhD thesis, "The evidence supporting the hypothesis that marine anemia is a spreading infectious neoplastic [tumour-causing] disease could have profound regulatory effects on the salmon farming industry." DFO had chosen to allow "profound" effects on wild salmon returns, instead of the salmon farming industry, and had done nothing to stop the virus from pouring out of the farms.

This was not the end of the story. One year after the 2009 collapse of the Fraser River sockeye, the fish surprised everyone by returning in huge numbers. I first saw them in August 2010, off Lady Ellen Point near Port McNeill, while I was out fishing. Hundreds were visible on the surface at any one time as they rose and dove—"finning," as the fishermen called it. I went out day after day just to be near them, to see them, to feel their presence. It was adorable to see the diminutive harbour porpoise swimming among them. The fish were too big for the porpoise to eat, so their association was a mystery.

The salmon farmers put out the word that this run was proof that their industry was not damaging the wild salmon. But I remembered the "exceptional survival" of pink salmon in 2003 in the Broughton, the one year when the salmon farms on their migration route was fallowed, and wondered what had really happened.

I went back to the commission documents to see if I could determine what had been going on in the salmon farms when this generation of Fraser sockeye headed out to sea as juveniles in 2008. (Most sockeye spend a year in a lake before heading out to the open ocean, where they live for two years before returning to spawn.) According to file CC1001187, Marine Harvest had removed the last chinook salmon farm, Conville Bay, from the Fraser River sockeye migration route in 2007. This meant that the first Fraser River sockeye to go to sea without exposure to chinook salmon farms that had been shedding a leukemia virus since 1991 were the fish that returned in 2010. Miller's lab didn't find the leukemia virus signature in the 2010 Fraser sockeye run. The sockeye stopped dying on the riverbanks.

I pushed my chair away from the kitchen table where I had been working, jumped on my stationary bike and tried to burn up the rage, sadness and sense of helplessness these revelations caused me. Government wouldn't believe me about sea lice, which you can see with the naked eye; no one was going to believe that DFO had let a virus that causes leukemia in salmon to pour out of salmon farms and just watched the wild salmon go down.

Back at the computer, buried in the reports that Dr. Marty was providing to the salmon farming industry, I also found Case #08-3362, from

September 19, 2008, reporting the discovery of the pattern of inflammation described by scientists in Norway as heart and skeletal muscle inflammation (HSMI). I entered the instance in the database I was assembling on these reports. I was so incensed by the other information I was finding, it didn't mean anything to me at the time. But it would.

While few of the Cohen Commission hearings were well attended, the fish farm hearings, held in August 2011, drew large audiences. Many of the people who'd joined the Get Out Migration and the Paddle for Wild Salmon, and many who wished they had, showed up not only to the hearings, but also to the street demonstrations that took place every day in front of the building where the hearings were being held, on one of downtown Vancouver's busiest streets. People wore masks made of photos of the federal minister of fisheries' face and stretched crime-scene tape in front of the building. Huge graphs depicting the sockeye collapse were displayed, and people wore headbands with large papier mâché tumours stuck to them.

On the second day of the fish farm impact hearings, Greg McDade questioned Dr. Michael Kent, the man who had headed the DFO Pacific Biological Station in Nanaimo in the 1990s, and had discovered and named the salmon leukemia virus.

Dr. Kent's research papers had reported that all of the sockeye they experimentally infected with salmon leukemia virus became sick with the disease and one-quarter of them died during the experiment. Kent, who now taught at a university in Oregon, had been hired by the Cohen Commission to write a technical report titled "Infectious diseases and potential impacts on survival of Fraser River sockeye salmon." In that report, he rated the risk posed by salmon leukemia virus to Fraser River sockeye as "low," despite his own findings.

McDade asked him, "Have you talked [in your report] about the risk of transfer of farm disease to wild salmon?"

Kent responded, "No."

"Did you look at the fish farm health database?" McDade asked.

"I scanned them this morning."

"Did you have [access to] the farm disease database when you wrote your report?"

"No."

Had Kent reviewed the provincial farm salmon health records, he would have noted that the organ damage considered salmon leukemia's signature was still being reported in both farmed Atlantic and chinook salmon by Dr. Marty and that rates of this disease had spiked in 2007. That year half of the farmed chinook still being raised in the Discovery Islands had the lesions that DFO scientists reported were caused by salmon leukemia virus. The Fraser River sockeye that swam past those diseased fish farms as juveniles in 2007 were the ones that never returned in 2009, triggering the Cohen Commission's inquiry into their disappearance.

Under questioning, Dr. Kent revealed that he no longer supported his own published papers describing the existence of the retrovirus in salmon farms that he had named salmon leukemia virus. He testified he now believed that what he had described in the 1990s was a "syndrome" of unknown cause. Dr. Marty agreed with him in his testimony, and so did Dr. Sheppard, who called the occurrence of whatever it was "natural" in chinook.

When McDade asked Dr. Sheppard about his briefing to the minister of agriculture stating that *no* Atlantic salmon eggs had been imported to British Columbia, Sheppard's response was that "these briefings are drafted and then go places after me . . . this one was done in a fairly rushed manner . . . I would probably tend to word [it] more accurately now."

McDade asked Dr. Kent, "If ISA virus appeared in salmon farms would you blame the wild fish?"

"Yes," Kent said.

———

When Dr. Miller arrived at the inquiry to testify, large men in black suits wearing earpieces flanked her. She came in by a back door, avoiding the crowd out front. On the stand she spoke with astonishing directness for a government scientist. She testified that it appeared that a virus was heavily affecting the Fraser sockeye. "It could be the smoking gun," said Miller, "but we have work to do."

Dr. Miller told the commission that it was difficult to get people in DFO to understand the meaning of the genomic signature that she had found in the sockeye. The Conservation Coalition's lawyer, Tim Leadem, asked Miller why she was not allowed to present her findings at the Simon Fraser University think tank of scientists who had gathered to examine what clues might exist to explain the 2009 sockeye crash. She replied, "The worry was it would automatically be associated with aquaculture."

"Looking back," Leadem said, "have you been under pressure?"

She replied, "Oh, very definitely, yes."

Krista Robertson, the lawyer representing the Musgamagw Dzawada'enuxw from the Broughton, asked Miller about commission document CAN166765, Miller's request to DFO to analyze the immune systems of farm salmon on the sockeye migration route to learn if they were carrying the same genomic profile as the dying sockeye. If she could establish that a virus in farm fish was the cause, an easy fix was in reach. Instead of grappling with an oceanic change in food, predators or temperature, saving the Fraser River sockeye would simply be a matter of extinguishing a virus in a few dozen salmon farms.

Dr. Miller testified that in response to her request she was denied access to the salmon farms and that her funding to continue working with the Fraser sockeye was cut off. The virus that left its lethal signature in the immune system of the vanishing sockeye would remain a mystery. Since the scientist who discovered salmon leukemia virus in the 1990s never published its genetic sequence, the virus that appeared to have killed millions of Fraser River sockeye could never be matched to the virus infecting the farm salmon, just like a fingerprint match cannot be run unless that person's fingerprint already exists in the database. This had the makings of a perfect crime.

On September 7, 2011, I was called to testify. In one of the greatest honours of my life, Chiefs Bobby Joseph and Robert Chamberlin escorted me with drummers along Georgia Street and into the hearing room. I had prepared a large binder, with tabs marking the key evidence I'd extracted from the commission database. I wanted to make sure that Justice Bruce Cohen saw the evidence from Dr. Miller's lab. I'd prepared a sixty-page report I titled "What is happening to the Fraser sockeye?" to enter as evidence; from it, Greg McDade and I could drill down on facts we believed Justice Cohen needed to hear. But as soon as McDade mentioned my report, the lawyers for the federal government and the province sprang to their feet to object. They argued I was there to provide spoken testimony, not written, and that a report prepared by me was "not factual evidence."

Specifically, Alan Blair, a lawyer for the BC Salmon Farmers Association, pointed to the sentence in my report that would introduce into evidence Dr. Miller's paper, "Epidemic of a novel, cancer-causing viral disease may be associated with wild salmon decline in BC."

Greg McDade argued that I had followed Justice Cohen's instructions to comb through the database and bring forward the information that shed light on why the sockeye were vanishing. Cohen, who used my honorary doctorate as a reason to address me as Dr. Morton, did accept my report into evidence, but not until some weeks after I'd testified. As per the rules of the inquiry, any document that had not yet been accepted as evidence could not be made public. Since my report referred to over one hundred documents, my lawyer and I spent much of my short time on the stand identifying each one and requesting that it be allowed into evidence.

Every time I tried to bring forward documentation of salmon leukemia virus, one or more of the lawyers for the province, Ottawa and industry would say, "Mr. Commissioner, I rise to object again."

The obfuscating tactics directed at Dr. Miller were now being directed at me, as I tried to bring her work into the daylight. Wild salmon were so important that Canada was spending $27 million on this inquiry, yet the scientific evidence of what had happened to them was being skilfully suppressed. On the stand, I almost broke down into tears of frustration and anger. At the lunch break, as people came forward to pat me on the back, I took my son's arm and said, "I need to get out of here." I was not going to cry in public.

Back on the stand after the lunch break, I pulled down an imaginary fencing mask and carried on.

Steven Kelliher, the lawyer for the pro–salmon farm Aboriginal Aquaculture Association, asked me to explain why other scientists had agreed in the end that wild stocks can coexist with fish farms. Why was I the only one who said they couldn't? I started to explain that because I did not work for government, a university, or a First Nation, I was independent and could . . .

He cut me off. "You are pure, are you? You're the only one that isn't corrupted by business, by government, by a university: is that correct?"

I thought about colleagues who had taken the stand before me and who had caved under questioning from this man when he had attacked them for trying to take salmon farms away from poor Indigenous communities. They hadn't had the benefit of watching his tactics for several days like I had. He was predictable.

"Perhaps I am." I stared back at him. Human economic considerations did not change whether wild salmon could survive the disease and the sea lice that poured out of salmon farms.

The next day, the questioning devolved into a personal attack on me. But there was a light moment when Mitch Taylor, a lawyer for the federal government, put an Anissa Reed cartoon up on the commission screen marked exhibit 1839. It depicted Justice Cohen in his robes leaning over his podium to stare at the government employees who were testifying. He was saying, "Let's take a short break. It appears your pants might be on fire." I had posted the cartoon on my blog.

Taylor asked, "Now, this, Ms. Morton, deals with the evidence that the veterinarians gave on August 31, doesn't it?"

"Yes," I replied. "That's correct."

"And this is a cartoon of what appears to be the Commissioner speaking to those four witnesses. The words that the Commissioner says, in the cartoon, that is, *pants on fire*, what does that mean?"

"Well, I'm going to leave that to you. It just . . ."

He cut me off as the audience started to snort and giggle. "Well, you're familiar with the saying—"

"The reason . . ."

He cut me off once more and continued himself. "Liar, liar, pants on fire?"

Several people rushed for the door, exploding in laughter before it had completely closed behind them.

"The reason that I posted this," I said, "is because Dr. Gary Marty is reporting symptoms of a disease that's of enormous significance to this Commission, and—"

Taylor cut me off again. "Okay, let me ask you this . . ."

I needed to finish this. "Yet Dr. Sheppard does not acknowledge that the disease exists."

Taylor said, "Yeah that's all fine, we've heard that, but let me ask you this: Do you agree with me that that cartoon is disparaging of those witnesses' evidence? Yes?"

"I felt it was a representation without saying the words."

"Are you saying they lied?"

"How can you look at the symptoms of a disease, have somebody like Gary Marty report those symptoms—"

"My—my . . ."

"—as being the clinical signs of marine anaemia, which a DFO scientist thinks the majority of Fraser sockeye are being killed and weakened by, and the vets above him, Peter McKenzie of [the fish farm company] Mainstream, and Dr. Mark Sheppard, simply don't recognize that that disease exists? That—"

"Ms. Morton—"

"—cannot stand."

"Ms. Morton . . . this is not—not an opportunity for you to make a speech."

"Well, then—"

"And I ask, again—"

I cut him off this time. "—don't ask me questions."

Scott Renyard, an independent filmmaker who took it on himself to video the entire Cohen Commission hearings, edited my testimony into the film *The Unofficial Trial of Alexandra Morton*, which made the rounds at film festivals and is now available on The Green Channel.

It would be another year before Justice Bruce Cohen would finish his report on the 133 days of testimony he'd heard and the 2,147 exhibits entered into evidence, but long before its report came out, the Cohen Commission redirected my life. After everything I learned and witnessed there, on top of the ten years of hearing the government deny the impact of sea lice from salmon farms, I had zero confidence in what DFO, as a department, was saying about viruses. I realized I needed to figure out how to assess the virus situation myself.

But first I needed to go to the Maritimes.

13.

Fear and Silence

IN OCTOBER 2011, Dalhousie University flew me to Halifax to deliver the fifth Ransom A. Myers Lecture. The late Ransom Myers was a scientist who'd left a job at DFO, with its good pay, pension and security, because the Department refused to use his science to reverse the commercial extinction of the North Atlantic cod. His data showed clearly that DFO was allowing cod to be captured before they had reached spawning age and that, as a result, the population was declining every year. When he finally confronted senior management, they told him not to talk about this anymore. He quit seven minutes after they hushed him. The cod did collapse and the cod fishery was closed, causing widespread hardship throughout the Atlantic provinces. Was it a coincidence that the Hibernia oil wells were approved to start drilling on the Grand Banks, once one of the most productive fishing grounds in the history of this planet? Myers himself moved on to become one of the most highly respected fisheries scientists at Dalhousie University.

In 2007, Ransom had visited me in Echo Bay, and I had toured him around the archipelago in my boat. He was a remarkable man. Some people don't know how to see things on the water. In the busy terrestrial environment our eyes go from one object to the next, but on the water you have to learn to slide your eyes over the often featureless space around you so you're ready to see things that appear and disappear quickly. Ransom saw everything. He was full of questions, insight and compassion. He warned me that because I lived so isolated a life with my children, I needed to figure out how to keep up with the outside world. While I never felt isolated in the archipelago, it was a reminder to make sure my children were equipped to live in the world beyond Echo Bay.

He had come to see me because he and one of his students, Jennifer Ford, were about to publish their meta-analysis of wild salmon population trends across the planet. They'd found that wild salmon tipped into exceptional decline everywhere in the world that salmon farms operate. Alaska and Russia were the only places where wild salmon exist without threat from salmon farms and, as a result, had the last abundant wild salmon populations in the world. I was so relieved that a scientist this honest, confident and respected was going to wade into this fight. He was also extremely blunt. "DFO is a criminal organization," he told me as we drifted on a perfect fall day. Despite everything I had experienced from the Department, he startled me with this statement. At last I realized that my failure to convince DFO to stop allowing salmon farms to kill wild salmon wasn't my fault.

Shortly after his visit Ransom was diagnosed with a brain tumour; he died a few months later. A huge loss.

Around the time of my Dalhousie lecture, Anissa Reed was working with me to raise public awareness that when you buy farm salmon, you are putting money into an industry that is causing enormous harm to our oceans. One of the companies operating in British Columbia, Grieg Seafood, was running an ad showing farm salmon sashimi, which is easily identifiable by the thick white layers of fat running through it, under the heading *Another Wild Salmon Saved*. Marine Harvest was funding children's sports, hatcheries and churches, all things that gave the impression that it cared about community. Anissa and I decided to tour the Atlantic provinces to see what people in Nova Scotia and New Brunswick thought about the salmon farms in their waters.

Just as in British Columbia, the industry in eastern Canada had begun with mom-and-pop operations. New Brunswick residents tolerated the arrival of salmon feedlots in the bays their towns were built around because their neighbours were the operators. When infectious salmon anemia, ISA, began killing off the stock of entire salmon farms and sea lice spiralled out of control, the local owners lost their investment. And in a pattern with which I was familiar, Cooke Aquaculture, an eastern Canadian company, began buying up the industry.

The people we talked to said they felt like they had let a predator into their communities. They were also afraid. No one wanted to speak with us on camera; fishermen said if they did, their boats might be damaged. They said security guards working for the industry patrolled the docks where both the salmon farming and fishing industries tied their boats and the fishermen did not like those guards recording the names of everyone who came and went. They worried that if something ever happened to the industry vessels they might get blamed.

In 2010, when a bay in Nova Scotia filled with floating chunks of dead farm salmon, the stench was unbearable, but everyone looked the other way. They did not want to "make trouble." Most of the people in the fishing communities blamed the salmon farms for killing off the inshore lobster fishery with their delousing drugs and waste, but they were afraid to say so on camera. The fear seemed worse here than in BC.

I was surprised to hear that the salmon farming industry in New Brunswick was actually shrinking. It had peaked at 37,000 tons a few years earlier, but in 2011, when we did our tour, it was 27,000 tons. The locals thought the farms' production was suffering from their own waste, disease and lice.

When I bought two farm salmon from a market to examine them, I counted approximately thirty sea lice on each fish. I couldn't believe it. In British Columbia the lice are removed from the fish before they are displayed in markets. Most of the lice I found were buried under the gill flap, where they aren't easily washed off during cleaning. I knew what this many lice on farm salmon meant to young wild salmon trying to migrate to the Atlantic Ocean. Anissa posted pictures of the fish on Facebook, where they got thousands of likes and hundreds of shares. The media called the store the next day and it pulled the rest of the fish. They were not used to such scrutiny here.

The wild Atlantic salmon from the inner Bay of Fundy are a unique genetic stock. They never stray far from their home, an area so rich these wild salmon did not need to travel out into the North Atlantic to feed. Unfortunately, this now meant they were heavily exposed to salmon farms for their entire lives. As soon as farms arrived, the inner Bay of Fundy Atlantic salmon populations collapsed, in the same extinction trend we'd seen in the Fraser River sockeye, from 45,000 to less than 200. In 2003, they'd been listed as endangered. Here DFO publicly recognized that aquaculture was one of the top threats to these salmon, but it did nothing. Since the salmon from the outer Bay of Fundy migrated out to sea towards Greenland, they were less exposed to salmon farms and their decline was not nearly so steep.

Though most people in eastern Canada wanted to remain anonymous, they were eager to talk. They said big aquaculture pressured local mayors to lobby government on its behalf. If the mayors refused, the companies threatened to build their own docks and not pay municipal fees.

The lobster fishery had been greatly affected. The fishermen keep their catch in pounds in the ocean until they are sold. A young fisherman told me that they expect a 2 percent "shrink" of their catch while it's being held in a pound, meaning that an average of 2 percent of the lobsters die. When a salmon farm was put near a pound, the shrink increased to 15 to 30 percent. This was similar to what prawn fishermen endured in the Broughton. If a farm went into a prawning ground, the prawns vanished over a large area near the farm. Fishermen on both coasts blamed drugs like Slice for the mortality rate. Sea lice, lobster and prawns are all crustaceans; what kills one of them is likely to kill them all.

The young fisherman said, "My great-great-grandfather started fishing here in 1726 and we been fishing ever since. But I think I'm the last generation gonna fish here. I am tired of fighting the salmon farms and their chemicals." Then he turned and walked away, so upset he couldn't continue to talk about it.

"It's a big spider web and we're trapped in it," said another fisherman, who also wouldn't tell me his name.

"Feels like we are playing with a bunch of cheaters," said a local over a delicious lobster chowder. He said that before salmon farms were introduced in West Bay, Nova Scotia, a rural community in Inverness County, DFO research reported twelve to fourteen lobster per square metre on the sea floor. After just one farm salmon production cycle, all the lobster were gone. Then the Harper government closed the DFO lobster research lab and ended government research into Canada's most lucrative local fishery. No data, no problem.

"DFO tells us the lobster are gonna have to find another place to spawn," said Frank, who didn't want me to use his last name. "But you gotta understand, lobster are real fussy about where they can spawn. No one else could get away with this. It doesn't make sense to us why government is so in love with farms. What's in it for them?" Many of the fishermen we talked with told us that Cooke Aquaculture was taking the bulk of the herring quota to make into farm salmon food.

Gloria Gilbert, a concerned citizen, said, "There used to be an Irish moss [a highly valued nutritional seaweed] and a mussel harvest here, but that stopped when the farm went in. During a three-year period when there were no fish in the pens for whatever reason, these things started to come back. The eel grass came back too. But now the farm is back and things are disappearing again."

A common target of complaints was the provincial NDP politician, Darrell Dexter, who'd promised during his election campaign to respect the wishes of communities that did not want salmon farms. When he was elected premier, his government gave Cooke Aquaculture $25 million in funding to develop an even bigger industry in the communities that had voted him into office on his promise to remove the farms. His government was kicked out after one term, but the farms remained.

Everyone on the boat tour of the farms Anissa and I took along the coast of Nova Scotia shook their heads.

We came off the sea and warmed up with a bowl of corn chowder. As we savoured the meal, a small crowd asked us familiar questions: *How do you think we can stop this? What do you do when politicians make promises and then turn on you? Why don't locals count?*

I answered that I only knew of three ways to stop the salmon-farming industry from destroying marine environments:

- Educate consumers who care about our oceans so they stop buying the product until the industry moves into closed, land-based tanks
- Take government and industry to court to stop them from breaking the law
- Convince politicians they might not get re-elected if they keep issuing the licences the industry requires to operate

Today, I would add a fourth: peaceful, unrelenting activism. Do science, legal action, education, activism—then repeat, as often as you have to. None of these courses of action are easy. They all require money and endurance.

Anissa and I took the ninety-minute ferry ride into the Bay of Fundy to the island of Grand Manan on the border between Canada and the United States. A fish farmer on board recognized me, and came over to say, "You know fishermen could get a job on the farms, but they're lazy and don't want to work all year." What was I to say to that?

At the dock on Grand Manan, a fisherman, Allan Green, met us and offered to show us around the island he loved. Allan had fished since he was a child and had bought his own boat when he was seventeen. "When I was a boy all you had to do was get up in the morning to get a job," Allan said.

He was one of the few people we encountered who was not afraid to put his name to his comments about the impact of salmon farming. He had worked for the industry and knew a lot about how it got started in Grand Manan. He said a Norwegian corporation called Stolt had arrived on the island in the mid-1990s and had begun buying up the family salmon farms that were failing to make money. (Stolt did the same thing in BC and later sold its interests to Marine Harvest, which changed its name to Mowi in 2019.)

Allan said the rumours about disease outbreaks caused by the ISA virus and by bacterial kidney disease (BKD) were present from the start. ISA virus is an Atlantic salmon virus; no one was sure if it came from the farms or came from the wild salmon, but it multiplied in the farms. No one was studying the impact of this influenza virus on wild salmon exposed to the farms. When Stolt abandoned Grand Manan, Cooke Aquaculture took over.

We stopped to chat with a small group of fishermen working on their gear by the docks. As I stared out at a salmon farm anchored just off-shore, one of them said, "This was prime lobster ground, but lobster don't come here anymore."

A fisherman painting his trap floats brilliant orange added, "Two weeks into the season about five years ago the lobster were exceptionally high. I was getting twelve counters [legal-sized lobsters] to a trap and a lot of bobs [immature lobster that are thrown back]." It takes seven years for a lobster to grow into a counter.

"Well, a fish farm wellboat showed up on that farm there," he said, pointing to where I was looking, just beyond the harbour. "They was treating the farm for lice. Next day when I pulled my traps, half the lobster were curled up, stiff, their tails and claws tucked in tight. If you pulled on them, they just snapped back into that position. I learned this was what they looked like just before they died, because when I went out the next day all my traps were empty. Never seen or heard of anything like that before." Then he turned to Anissa, telling her, "You can't take my picture. Things happen when people speak up about what goes on near salmon farms." He was talking about vandalism of fishing boats.

The cheapest, least stressful, delousing treatment is soaking the feed with Slice. When the lice develop resistance to this form of treatment, the wellboats show up. They suck the farm salmon up out of the pens, bathe them in delousing drugs and pump them back into the pens. That chemical bath is dumped into the ocean. The fish farmers say the drug is all used up when the bath is dumped, but the fishermen said that whenever the wellboat shows up the lobster vanish.

I heard the same things over and over. *Industry showed up and we lost our livelihood. Don't take my picture. Bad things happen if you talk.*

Allan Green had invited me to speak to the community on Grand Manan at the island's museum that evening. When Anissa and I arrived, the place was dark. No sign of life. I assumed I had the wrong address, but I checked the emailed invitation and we were in the right spot. I thought the talk must have been cancelled. Given how many times I heard *bad things happen to people who talk* on this trip, I was relieved. But then we noticed there were a few cars in the parking lot, so Anissa and I walked around the dark building, pulled gently on all the doors and found a side door that was unlocked.

When we entered, everyone gathered inside turned and looked at us in complete silence. If I hadn't seen Allan there, I would have assumed we had walked in on a secret meeting and run for the car. But thirty islanders had come to hear me and we all stood there awkwardly for a while. When I realized no one was going to introduce me, I just began to speak, telling them what had happened to the fishing community where I lived when salmon farms arrived. It helps to know you are not alone in this fight and to have your experience corroborated by others.

Here in eastern Canada, in 2011, the Norwegians did not yet dominate the industry (although they would as soon as the pressure on them increased in British Columbia). The locals were more concerned about the fate of their lobster, not wild salmon. But they also expressed more fear than the people on the west coast did, and there were a lot more young fishermen here than I encountered at home. Otherwise, we were in a very similar situation: the damage to the environment, the loss to local economies, the way government danced to the industry's tune.

Leaving the island the next day at dawn, I thought about what one mother had said to me after my talk. "We don't want our children to have to leave and go work in the oilpatch in Alberta," she said. "But government ruined our way of life so a couple of companies could get rich." She wouldn't go on camera or share her name.

A couple of days later, I gave my Ransom Myers lecture at Dalhousie University. Drawing on what I'd seen in British Columbia, I talked about the social disruption, politics and the risk from placing a feedlot into a wild environment, and received a standing ovation. Other scientists who attended told me they were very concerned about the changes they were observing as a result of the salmon farming industry on the east coast of Canada. They described the industry as out of control and out of compliance with the rich ecology of the region. That was an assessment I knew by heart.

Part III

Virus Hunting

14.

A Reportable Virus

SOON AFTER I got back to British Columbia, I received a call one night from my friend, Dr. Rick Routledge, who was researching the sockeye in Oweekeno Lake, in Rivers Inlet on the central BC coast, just north of the Broughton Archipelago. Rick couldn't figure out why they were vanishing. Nothing that he measured in their environment added up to the profound collapse of this important run of salmon, once 1.5 million strong, but now down to 1 percent of those numbers despite a decade of no commercial fishing. As I had suggested a few months earlier, he had sent samples of the sockeye for testing for the ISA virus to the World Organisation for Animal Health North American reference lab on Prince Edward Island. Two of the forty-eight samples came back "weak positives—ISAV EUROPEAN GENOTYPE."

I immediately took pieces of the fish that Rick had sent to Prince Edward Island and couriered them to Dr. Nylund at the University of Bergen; Nylund was one of the scientists who'd tracked ISAV from Norway to Chile. He got the same result as the Canadian reference lab: weak positives.

Since ISAV is a reportable virus, the reference lab informed the Canadian Food Inspection Agency of the test results. The CFIA took the samples from the lab and sent them to DFO's reference lab in Moncton, New Brunswick, to run tests too. This lab produced the same weak positive results. These samples were in poor condition because they had been stored in a household freezer by Routledge prior to testing, not at minus eighty degrees Celsius, the temperature considered optimal for preservation of viruses in tissue. This meant the lab couldn't determine whether the results were "weak" due to the condition of the samples, a minimal level of virus in the fish, or because this was a new variant of ISAV for which the test was a poor match. (Molecular tests search for a specific piece of genetic sequence; if that sequence varies slightly from what the test was designed to recognize the result can be inconsistent, or "weak.")

At the same time in late 2011, fishermen were reporting dead salmon in the lower Fraser River again, and so Anissa and I headed there. The World Organisation for Animal Health reference lab had sent me instructions on how to take virus samples; I was outfitted with sterile tools, latex gloves, sterile plastic bags and 1.5 millilitre plastic vials full of RNA*later*, a solution that would preserve virus genetic sequences intact.

Standing on the shore, we saw dead chinook and other salmon drifting downriver out of reach. As we were thinking about swimming after them, a couple pulled up to the beach in their speedboat. They recognized me and offered to help us retrieve them. They had heard of our paddle down the Fraser and were very concerned about the declining salmon in the Fraser. Among the fish we took samples from were pink and chinook salmon that were an odd shade of yellow.

When these samples also produced an ISAV positive result, the lab notified the CFIA as per regulations, and because the samples came from the Fraser River, the food inspection agency notified the Cohen Commission. The results went directly to the commission lawyers, who passed them on to Greg McDade. I was surprised that my results had been redirected to the Cohen Commission and that my lawyer was the one telling me that they were positive. When the news sank in, I was devastated. Even-tempered as always, Greg asked me, "What did you expect?"

When I got off the phone with him, I called a colleague in the US who ran a reference lab for another reportable fish virus. "What would you say if I told you ISAV had been detected in BC?" I asked.

"You'd better be talking hypothetically," he replied. When I described the results and where they had come from, he just said, "No, no, no."

By the time these results came in, the Cohen Commission had wrapped up its 133 days of public hearings and was in the process of writing its recommendations. But Justice Bruce Cohen recognized the unprecedented level of risk that these results represented to the Fraser River sockeye salmon and decided to hold three more days of hearings on ISAV just before Christmas 2011. All of the labs involved were asked to testify and to provide any related documents, including Dr. Miller's lab.

This is how Canadians learned about a draft research paper co-authored by Simon Jones and Garth Traxler, both with DFO, and scientists at the North American ISAV reference lab where I had sent my samples. In 2002 and 2003 they had screened farmed and wild salmon in British Columbia for the ISA virus. They had detected segments of the virus's genetic sequence in chinook, pink, sockeye and Atlantic salmon. The ISAV segment detected in the chinook was 99.7 percent identical to Norwegian ISAV isolate #810/9/99 registered in the virus database, GenBank. The scientists did not find whole "live" virus, only segments, which was similar to what we had found, but they found those segments repeatedly. The paper also reported that testing of the Cultus Lake sockeye, the most endangered salmon stock in the Fraser River, detected the virus in all of the fish they sampled. Was this why the Department's sixteen-year Cultus Lake sockeye recovery plan was not working?

This explosive draft research paper, so important to the mandate of the commission, had not been disclosed by the DFO scientists, Jones and Traxler, even though they had been specifically instructed by the Cohen Commission to produce *all* documentation on diseases that could potentially impact the Fraser salmon run. It was the North American ISAV reference lab I was working with that provided the draft paper.

Also among the DFO documents submitted for these three extra days of hearings were "weak positive" results on Rick Routledge's Rivers Inlet samples from both Dr. Kristi Miller's lab and DFO's New Brunswick reference lab. In a November 4, 2011, email, Nelle Gagne of the DFO reference lab wrote to a lab colleague, "I am not convinced it [the results] should be reported to our friends in Ottawa, guess why!"

I found an October 25, 2011, email from Dr. Gary Marty, the provincial pathologist who had reported 1,100 instances of "classic lesions associated with ISAV infections," stating that in 2009, when Marine Harvest began requesting ISA virus tests, he switched tests and began using an ISAV test that was "designed by a master's student . . ." Now, his was the only lab not finding ISAV positives. He did not explain why he used a different test than everyone else.

Exhibit 2052 was a report by a post-doctoral fellow in Kristi Miller's lab on the state of the immune system of a Fraser River sockeye salmon that had produced one of the weak positive results. He wrote that it was clear from the configuration of the fish's immune system that it had been fighting a virus in the influenza family, which is the virus family ISAV belongs to. Immune systems are a planet-wide language shared by the cells of all animals; the immune system of humans and salmon fight influenza by up- and downregulating the same genes. However, DFO rejected all these results except Dr. Marty's and ordered Dr. Miller to stop the testing. I also saw an email in these new filings from the Canadian Food Inspection Agency, instructing hatcheries not to give me samples to test. The CFIA had taken responsibility for the virus away from the Department of Fisheries and Oceans because it was a reportable pathogen.

Also among the documents was an internal CFIA staff email chain that made it clear they viewed the situation as a public relations war: winning meant keeping the public in the dark about the apparent presence of the ISA virus in British Columbia. They thought they had it all under control, that they had "won" the PR war. In this November 9, 2011, email chain, CFIA's Dr. Cornelius Kiley stated, "Concentrate on the headlines—that's often all the people read or remember." Staffer Joseph

Beres followed up, "One battle is won, now we have to nail the surveillance piece, and we will win the war, also."

Dr. Kim Klotins of the CFIA testified at the hearing that if ISAV was confirmed, exports of BC farm salmon would cease.

Commission lawyer Brock Martland questioned Dr. Klotins. "Is it an adversarial thing?" Martland asked. "Is the CFIA going into this out of a concern for trade partners and other interests with a view to, however we get there, to announcing there is no ISAV?"

Klotins responded, "We may get a little exuberant internally."

That's one word for it. As far as the Canadian Food Inspection Agency was concerned, trade appeared more important than taking precautionary measures to stop a contagion. I later learned that the Agency took extraordinary action. In an internal email sent to staff on May 30, 2012, Alfred Bungay, national manager, Aquatic Animal Health, DFO Ottawa, reported that the CFIA had lowered the permit requirements for Atlantic salmon eggs shortly after the ISA virus hearings. He called it a "stream of commerce policy" and mentioned that the lower requirements would be in place for one year. "That is to say if a shipment arrives at the border without a CFIA permit or it does not meet all of the requirements the CFIA may still allow the shipment to enter Canada."

Then the CFIA constructed a testing surveillance scheme in which technicians preserved samples of salmon organs for testing in a fixative. But the fixative they used rendered the virus undetectable by the only test Canada accepts as confirmation of ISAV infection. In other words, they rendered the virus non-infective, which meant it would never be "cultured." Once that was done, the agency announced to the world that there was no ISAV in British Columbia. I guess that's what Beres meant by nailing the surveillance piece to win the war.

In early 2012, I began sampling wild salmon from all parts of British Columbia. Since the salmon farmers would not let me test the fish in their pens, I went shopping and bought farm salmon from markets. I sent the samples I was collecting to the lab where I'd sent my first samples, and it repeatedly detected low levels of fragments of the ISA virus. This result is what you'd expect if the fish was an asymptomatic carrier—carrying the virus but not dying of it. As well, the farm salmon I bought had been cleaned, which meant that all their internal organs had been removed; I was only able to test their gills and flesh—not optimal for this research. When sequenced, the genetic fragments consistently matched known European ISAV strains.

When I made the results public, the CFIA claimed to the media that my results were not repeatable, casting doubt on my methods. However, the agency never would explain what tests it was using when trying to confirm my results and just kept insisting that the ISA virus is not in British Columbia. But if these genetic sequences were not ISAV, *what were they?* Viruses do strange things, including swapping out genetic sequences with other viruses that are close by. Tests from a top lab were consistently picking up something that appeared to be in the influenza family and that should have been a concern to someone.

On top of the government's flat denial of my results, someone started a rumour that I was spiking the samples I sent for testing with European virus. To be able to do that, I would have had to travel to Norway and smuggle the virus home. Really?

I kept sending samples to the lab. In December 2012, I sampled a fish that produced a strong positive result for the HPR0 strain of ISAV. HPR0 doesn't kill salmon and is considered the original wild "mother" virus that existed before salmon farming. HPR0 had gone unnoticed in Norway until it began mutating in the salmon that the Norwegian industry was breeding towards domestication. The new strains had dropped part of HPR0's genetic sequence, and these deleted strains (as they became known) were killers. For years, the salmon farming industry didn't cull salmon infected with the more benign HPR0 strain, until they began to realize that HPR0 was as dangerous as the deleted strains because it produced such virulent children. In 2018, the World Organisation for Animal Health added it to the animal pathogen watch list.

The BC fish testing positive was from a company that identified where each fish it sold had been raised, down to the name of the farm in Nootka Sound. This meant that the CFIA could go to that farm and take its own samples. They could take better samples than I could, because at the farm they could sample the whole fish, including the organs where the virus is known to accumulate. I wrote the Agency suggesting they do just that, so we could get the bottom of why their lab could not find the virus. As far as I know, they did not take my suggestion. They did not follow up on tests revealing an internationally reportable virus from a known farm.

After learning so much from the internal DFO communications supplied to the Cohen Commission, I began to file my own access to information requests. I made one such request to find out how the CFIA had responded to my HPR0-positive test results. I learned that the Agency immediately withdrew all their ISAV samples from the federal labs they had been using for surveillance and, amid great internal debate as to whether it was allowed under protocol, sent them to Dr. Gary Marty at the BC Animal Health Centre in Abbotsford, BC. The CFIA's Dr. Maria Perrone wrote that she was surprised that such a move was even being considered. Dr. Joanne Constantine, also with the CFIA, warned that no outside country would accept ISAV testing by a non-CFIA lab such as Dr. Marty's. Staffers voiced concerns that moving the testing would be viewed as a biased decision, but the CFIA's Andrea Osborn shut those concerns down: "We have to move forward, even if it's imperfect." She did not explain why the Agency felt this move had to be made, or why she thought it was a move forward.

Even with all this going on, I couldn't understand why CFIA could not replicate the results I was getting from an actual reference lab for ISAV. This had to be a technical problem that should have been easy to resolve: take two samples from the same fish, send them to two different labs, have them run the same test, look at the results and go from there. On July 8, 2013, I wrote to a CFIA spokesperson, Elena Koutsavakis, who was quoted in a Canadian Press article saying they were "obligated to confirm the test results at another lab." When I pressed for which lab, I was directed to correspond with Dr. Gary Kruger, Area Program Specialist, Western Operations, CFIA.

So I did. Dr. Kruger wrote back to say that the Agency had a policy not to retest my samples. He explained that after the CFIA took possession of them, they soaked them in ethanol, which made them unsuitable to retest. Over the course of several emails, he went on to explain that the CFIA was "not interested" in running molecular tests on my samples "because such testing will be of no value to the CFIA at this time."

What the hell was going on? After years of issuing statements claiming that the test results from the lab I was using were irreproducible and therefore wrong, the CFIA, through Dr. Kruger, was telling me that the agency *never* ran any tests on my samples at all. To top this off, Kruger told me that, as a concerned member of the public, I should "contact the CFIA so that we can collect and submit samples to the appropriate laboratories if necessary."

This was a Mad Hatter's tea party. Three years of effort and we had gone in a complete circle.

At this point I commissioned Twyla Roscovich to do a film on what could only be described as the ISAV cover-up. I released her seventy-minute documentary, *Salmon Confidential*, on social media where over two million people viewed it. In January 2016, five years after our discovery of the virus's genetic fragments in BC farm salmon, doctors Fred Kibenge and Molly Kibenge, Rick Routledge, Tokinori Iwamoto, Yingwei Wang and myself published our ISAV results in *Virology Journal*, in a paper called "Discovery of variant infectious salmon anaemia virus (ISAV) of European genotype in British Columbia, Canada."

Dr. Gary Marty and the DFO's Nelle Gagne tried to persuade the journal to retract our paper after publication, but the journal refused. Despite the documentary and the paper, which had been accepted and published by a reputable journal, the Canadian government and its trade partners ignored the findings.

From documents I obtained through access to information, I learned one more thing. In 2011, the CFIA had hired a team to investigate my first sets of ISAV results. From a table in that team's report, it appears they got positive results from the same samples as my lab. They have never admitted that they had confirmed my earliest results and then opened the Canadian border in a year-long import-anything-you-want free-for-all for the fish farms.

In 2012, Rick Routledge and I won the Simon Fraser University Sterling Prize in Support of Controversy for this work. But as a direct result of the CFIA's denial of my science, other scientists and funders started distancing themselves from us. Environmental groups didn't know whether to believe me anymore. I was no longer invited to meetings, and most politicians refused to acknowledge my letters.

A loner by nature, I did not fight back hard enough. At first, I didn't see where this was going—that I was being branded as someone to ignore. The more hypocrisy and denial I uncovered in science and government, the more uncertain people became about whether to believe me. The series of events *was* unbelievable, I agreed, but it was happening. To no avail, I wrote to all 182 member nations of the World Organisation for Animal Health, urging them, if they were serious about stopping the spread of the ISA virus, to examine the facts. My research colleagues in academic institutions suffered far more than I did, as I existed outside the system, and we eventually had to stop testing for ISAV. However, before we quit, we noticed that ISAV-positive results had dwindled significantly in the Atlantic farm salmon I was buying from the markets. Something had changed, and it wasn't us or the tests we were using. Perhaps the farms were responding to our results and screening their fish, but who knows?

At this point, when I met someone and they asked me what I did, I began my answer with, "I fight bad guys." People laughed nervously, but I was serious. I still am.

15.

Lock Her Up

THERE ARE MOMENTS when a threat creeps up on you so quietly, it triggers no alarm, like the long low swell of a tsunami far out to sea. But don't turn your back on it because it will sweep you away when it makes landfall.

In May 2012, Vincent Gogolek, the executive director of the non-profit BC Freedom of Information and Privacy Association, contacted me to warn me about the proposed Animal Health Act, Bill 37, that had been tabled by the province's agriculture minister, Don McRae. The act would make it illegal for me and others to report on viruses in farm salmon. Gogolek wrote, "The definitions are very broad and the penalties are being specially set at well beyond the level of other offences. The intention is clearly to prevent any release of information regarding disease outbreaks and to severely punish anyone who does release that information."

In a November 10, 2011, press release with the headline "Test Results Indicate No Confirmed Cases of ISA," Minister McRae had already refuted my findings, and had stated: "Since Premier [Christy] Clark is currently on a trade mission to China, I have personally asked her to reassure our valued trading partners that now as always BC can be relied upon as a supplier of safe, sustainable seafood." A few months later, on March 27, 2012, McRae stood in the BC legislature to warn that Asian and US legislators were threatening to close their doors to BC farm salmon, following positive tests for salmon flu virus. "It just reminds me, as well," he said, "that you do not want to give a nation a reason to close the border to a B.C. product without having all the facts." His bill, if passed, would guarantee me two years in jail and a $75,000 fine if I was found to have reported any further virus results in BC farm salmon. At that moment I had over six hundred samples of farm salmon, wild salmon, eulachon and steelhead in labs for testing.

The *Province* newspaper wrote: "The minister said he's having his staff look at options to deal with the perception that the new act will restrict free speech by citizens and journalists. One option would be shelving the bill until after the summer recess, he said. McRae didn't appear to favour that option, saying an outbreak this summer could occur without the new act's protective limits on free speech." Indeed rumours were circulating that salmon in farms on the west coast of Vancouver Island were dying of IHN virus again, another internationally reportable pathogen.

On May 3, 2012, the provincial privacy commissioner, Elizabeth Denham, wrote to Minister McRae to warn him that his bill was "extreme" and "would override the Freedom of Information and Protection of Privacy Act." She also got the real priorities straight: "This is a matter of deep concern considering the importance of disease management."

Twenty years earlier, senior government officials such as DFO's director general of the Pacific Region and staff with the provincial Ministry of Environment had warned that introduction of an exotic virus was "guaranteed" if the salmon farming industry was allowed to import Atlantic salmon eggs. The threat of international trade penalties was used to silence them. Now the BC minister of agriculture was trying to arrange a prison sentence for me to stop my science, because my work was indicating that those early warnings appeared to be on target. Would the bill pass? I wondered. If it did, how long would it take to come into effect? Did I need to remove all references to test results from my blog before the vote, in case it passed and was enacted immediately? Should I find someone out of province, beyond the reach of Bill 37, to receive the upcoming lab results? Who was going to accept this risk? Was I ready to go to jail over this? Would my daughter have to finish high school without me? Who would look after my dog for two years?

Was the BC Liberal government in so deep with the salmon farming industry that it couldn't see that this was an oppressive move? Was democracy as threatened by the presence of this virus as the wild fish?

Who are these fish farmers *really*?

I travelled to Victoria and took a seat in the public viewing area of the legislature to witness the vote. If the government was going to pass a law that would send me to jail for two years and plunge me into deep debt, I was going to witness the landfall of this tsunami. I had never met Premier Clark, but she and I had a moment where our eyes locked; the smile didn't leave her face. That day, Bill 37 was never called to a vote, but it continued to linger on the order papers, like a trap ready to be used another time.

My daughter texted me, "Are you going to jail, Mom?"

"Not this time," I texted back, along with a smiley face.

Maybe I was a little proud that the BC government thought it would take the threat of a large fine *and* a prison sentence to silence me.

In October 2012, the Cohen Commission released its 1,191-page final report on how Canada should respond to the collapse of the Fraser River sockeye salmon. In it were seventy-five recommendations, eleven of which were directed at the salmon farms. Justice Cohen had absorbed the evidence and he wrote that the "potential harm posed to Fraser River sockeye from salmon farms is serious or irreversible." He admonished DFO for doing little or no research to assess the impact of salmon farms on migrating sockeye, warned of the Department's "divided loyalties," and suggested that management of the industry be taken away from it. He advised against placing salmon farms on wild salmon migration routes and recommended that the salmon farms in the Discovery Islands should cease to operate by September 2020 unless the federal minister of fisheries could be certain that the farms posed less than minimal risk to the sockeye *and* could provide the science to back that assessment up. He recommended the creation of a position in DFO at a senior management level dedicated solely to preserving wild salmon.

In the years since, very few of these recommendations have been followed, and the website hosting all the transcripts, exhibits and the final report has been shut down. I could perform no such erasure in my own mind. For me there was no going back to a time when I didn't realize the sheer amount of disease flowing from salmon farms.

16.

Damage to the Heart

ON AUGUST 29, 2008, Dr. Peter McKenzie of Mainstream (the company that later became Cermaq) submitted four fresh tissue samples of Atlantic salmon to Dr. Gary Marty's lab. The company asked the lab to run molecular virus tests (virology) and to study the samples through a microscope for signs of cellular damage caused by disease (histology). Dr. Marty labelled it "Case: 08-3362."

The testing revealed the first evidence of heart and skeletal muscle inflammation disease outside of Norway. HSMI was a mystery illness spreading fast through the salmon farming industry in Norway. Millions of farm salmon were becoming listless, barely moving and refusing to eat. Not knowing whether their condition was caused by environment, diet or a pathogen, the farmers had no way to halt the disease's spread. There was also no way to screen imported eggs for it. In 2010, a team of virus sleuths in Norway and the United States reported that the cause of HSMI appeared to be piscine reovirus (PRV, later named piscine orthoreovirus), which used the red blood cells in fish to make copies of itself. As the virus filled those cells, it leaked out, inflaming and weakening the salmon's heart and skeletal muscles.

In Case 08-3362 Dr. Marty wrote, "This pattern of inflammation has also been described with Heart and Skeletal Muscle Inflammation in Atlantic salmon raised in Europe, but this disease has not been identified in BC salmon." As the disease was highly contagious and weakened infected fish to the point that they became catatonic, every Atlantic salmon showing signs of it should have been removed from contact with wild salmon. Norwegian researchers were concerned that the disease might be more harmful to wild salmon than to farm salmon. It would make them extremely weak and thus vulnerable to predation and unable to swim up a river.

My neighbour and friend Billy Proctor once found half of a stone fire-starting tool on a beach where an ancient village had stood in the Broughton. Ten years later he found the other half on the same beach. The pieces fit together perfectly and became a significant find. Something similar would happen with Case 08-3362. At first it was only an isolated mention of a new salmon disease. Eight years later, I found the rest of the pieces that would reveal the significance of this case to the survival of wild salmon in British Columbia.

I'd found Dr. Marty's report on Case 08-3362 among the fish health records downloaded to the Cohen Commission. When I began hunting viruses in the markets, rivers and marine waters of British Columbia, I added testing for PRV to the short list of viruses I requested the lab to screen for.

The storm we'd caused with our ISAV results had bonded the people at the lab on Prince Edward Island, Dr. Rick Routledge and me. We were now a team. I did much of the fieldwork, the virologists in the lab ran the tests and produced the results, and Rick crunched the statistics that made sense of what we found; we co-wrote and published the results. As I became the target of what I can only call a smear campaign, funding and collaborators fell away, but there were always just enough funds to continue so long as none of us were paid for our work. I was able to just about cover the expenses to travel to the remote reaches of the province, courier samples across the country and run the tests.

Viruses are a long way down the evolutionary ladder from the whales I began my scientific career studying. I received a steady stream of criticism from scientists, industry representatives and politicians that I should not be studying viruses, because I am not a virologist. True, but I am a field scientist. I can find the fish, take the samples and send them to the research lab where virologists take the next steps.

We were able to keep going thanks to two funders that stuck with us and crowd fundraisers that I posted on social media. We stretched those funds and remained uniquely free to explore the questions we deemed important.

Nearly all salmon disease research looks solely at farm fish. That's where the money is. So while many teams of people were studying farm fish disease worldwide, almost none were looking at wild fish health. This was similar to the situation I'd encountered with sea lice. There was no research on the impact of the lice on wild fish in British Columbia until Camp Sea Lice and then the Salmon Coast Field Station were created.

Like us, DFO staff scientist Dr. Kristi Miller was very interested in the health of wild salmon; her cutting-edge technique of studying genomic immune response patterns has enormous potential to yield insights into the fish. But Dr. Miller was ruthlessly micromanaged by her bosses and political masters. She was told which fish she could test, which pathogens were off limits and what tests she could use. Then, when she tried to speak about the results, she was muzzled for many years. Her testimony at the Cohen Commission made it obvious to me that, in order to break the ice that was impeding research into the role of pathogens in wild salmon survival, wild salmon needed someone to do this research who was beyond the grip of the government and industry handlers. The team I was a part of became the small icebreaker that would eventually allow movement by the larger ships—research teams with universities and from the Pacific Salmon Foundation.

We decided to do a study that would compare infection rates in wild salmon that were exposed to salmon farms against those that were unexposed, similar to the work I had done on sea lice infections in wild salmon. This meant sampling wild salmon throughout British Columbia, both from the coast and from some of the biggest rivers, as well as farm salmon from markets. We concentrated on a few viruses, including ISAV and PRV. I was interested, first, in what percentage of farm salmon were infected and, second, in what percentage of the wild salmon were being infected as they passed the farms. British Columbia is a big province; the sampling took two years. I searched the scientific literature for similar studies, but no one had published, in any country, on whether wild salmon that swam near fish farms were more infected with PRV and ISAV than wild salmon that never went near farms. This was an obvious study, essential to our understanding of the impact of salmon farms on wild salmon. I felt the absence of such work in the scientific literature revealed the long arm of the salmon farming industry. Without this knowledge, the industry and others could repeat that there was *no evidence* of impact on wild fish.

My 2010 trip up the Fraser River had given me a head start: I knew where to find the salmon I wanted to sample. When the First Nations fishery teams who had been so generous with their knowledge in 2010 didn't answer my first round of emails about my sampling program, I sent another email saying I hoped to meet up with them on the river. No answer to that one either. When I ran into one First Nations team on a riverbank, they told me that if they talked to me, DFO would withdraw all their funding, so they'd lose their jobs. I understood. We wished each other luck and went our separate ways. I did wonder how many other people were being pressured to thwart research into viruses associated with the salmon farming industry. I know I was an intense object of DFO and industry interest because of the results of my access to information requests. I had seen, for example, correspondence among DFO staff discussing whether they could prohibit me from testing dead salmon: Was I breaking any laws by sampling dead fish in the rivers? Apparently I was not.

I relied on Jody Eriksson and Farlyn Campbell to sample the more northern areas of BC. Jody and Far were as independent and resourceful as it gets. Both of them had been raised off-grid in a tiny community in the Discovery Islands; with no school nearby, they'd absorbed a wealth of knowledge by other means. Neither of them knew what *impossible* meant. When they headed upcoast on my shoestring research budget, hitching rides into remote river valleys on helicopters and boats, people they encountered loved them so much they sent me the money to keep the pair going.

I also collected samples from the beach seines we used in the ongoing annual sea lice research, and I covered the lower Fraser River myself to sample spawning salmon. During commercial fishing openings, fishermen let me sample their catch if I was quick about it.

I also bought hundreds of farm salmon, checking the best-before date for the freshest I could find. People would look at the pile of farm salmon in my cart and ask whether I was catering an event and how I was going to cook them. "Oh, I am not going to eat these," I would answer, leaving them bewildered. I didn't want to alert the stores that I was shopping for viruses, but I couldn't bear the idea that people thought my heap of farm salmon looked appetizing. One woman cracked, after checking out my load, "Honey, you ought to learn to fish."

When I started to buy farm salmon for testing, I rooted around to locate and include the skinniest fish and the ones with open sores and deformities. After *Salmon Confidential* came out, such fish disappeared from the markets. Also, shoppers in the stores began to recognize me. I received a lot of smiles and thumbs-up. A few people even paid the cashier for me, saying it was the least they could do. Somehow they all knew not to mention the testing inside the stores.

I also went to sushi restaurants, hoping to find the freshest samples there. I'd take a seat, order farm salmon sashimi, and then with tweezers and a scalpel take slivers of the flesh and plop them into vials. Then I'd check out the Styrofoam coolers stacked in the alleys behind the restaurants, noting the names of the companies printed on them so that I had some idea of the source of my samples. The coolers from Cermaq had *Cook before eating* printed on them. Really? No one was cooking farm salmon in sushi restaurants. But perhaps this kind of warning protected Cermaq in some way.

Health Canada actually exempts farm salmon from regulations that apply to other fish served raw, which has to be frozen to very low temperatures to kill parasites. Their rationale is that farm fish eat pellets that are heat-treated to kill parasites. However, farm salmon are exposed to all the wild species living in and around their farms. There is a free exchange of parasites and bacteria between them, and farm salmon eat some of those wild fish too, ingesting their parasite load. A large percentage of BC farm salmon are infected with a bacteria, *Tenacibaculum*, which causes them to get a condition called mouthrot. People who eat farm fish sushi in British Columbia are eating that fresh from the pens.

One of my best Atlantic salmon samples came from an eagle that grabbed a dead farm salmon out of a mort tote on a farm off Port Hardy. The fish was heavy for the bird, which caused it to fly low over the water as I followed in a friend's boat. As soon as the eagle got to shore, it got into a fight with another bird over the fish. They slashed and tore at the dead fish, screaming at each other, and then the fish slipped out of their talons, hit the beach rocks and slid into the ocean, where it sank. Anissa leapt off the boat onto the rock where the fish hit and collected the heart, a gill arch and part of its liver. Thanks, eagle! This sample was PRV-positive, as was nearly every Atlantic salmon we tested.

In December 2013, my research group published the first paper reporting on the presence of PRV in British Columbia, based on evidence from samples we'd gathered, in *Virology Journal*: "Whole-genome analysis of piscine reovirus (PRV) shows PRV represents a new genus in family *Reoviridae* and its genome segment S1 sequences group it into two separate sub-genotypes."

While we'd only sequenced fragments of the ISA virus, our team was able to sequence the entire genetics of PRV. Unlike ISAV, PRV is a very durable virus and doesn't break up into pieces in fish that have been dead for several days, such as those I purchased in the markets. PRV is also quite resistant to temperature change; we found the intact virus in farm fish dead in a tote sitting on a dock in the heat of summer. Having its whole sequence allowed us to not only confirm that this was PRV, but also trace where it came from. When the lab entered the genetic sequence we found in BC fish into the international virus registry, GenBank, it matched a PRV sample taken from a farm salmon suffering from the HSMI disease in Lofoten, Norway. It was like running a fingerprint match.

Interestingly, when a virus travels beyond its home community—in this case from Norway to British Columbia—its genetic sequence changes slightly over time through gradual mutation. Virologists describe this record of mutation as a genetic clock; comparing the BC and Norwegian sequences of PRV in GenBank allowed virologists to roughly estimate how long the virus we found had been outside Norway. While the Norwegian virus had gone on to mutate in the more than 900 salmon farms in Norway, the strain in BC appeared to be the PRV strain that occurred in Norway at the beginning of that country's outbreak.

In 2013 when we published this result, few people in the province had heard of PRV. In preparation for the publication of our results, I raised money on GoFundMe to send Twyla, who was heavily pregnant, to Norway to film experts there describing the impact of the virus. The Norwegian researchers were very open about their findings in the interviews they gave her, including Dr. Nylund, who said, "It is always a cause for concern when you move a virus from one ocean to another." Others described how, as the viral load increased in fish, so did the damage to the fish's organs. I posted Twyla's short video, *Asking Norway*, on social media and included it in the press release we put out when the paper appeared.

While there was almost no response from people concerned with the state of wild salmon stocks about this spreading epidemic from Norway—the information was too new to them—a group of government and Marine Harvest scientists collaborated on a paper in the journal *PLOS ONE* that disputed our findings, saying they had "ruled out" a recent introduction of PRV to British Columbia. We contacted the journal and presented the evidence that neither government nor the industry had actually ruled out the possibility that PRV had been introduced recently to the province, and eleven months later they had to publish a correction: "After careful reconsideration, the authors feel this conclusion is overstated." And we were also able to publish a formal comment presenting further evidence that PRV is exotic to British Columbia.

In the ongoing war over the impact of salmon farming, no one who disputes my science ever brings up this correction. Government and industry instead refer to the finding in a paper Dr. Marty published in 2014 in the *Journal of Fish Diseases*, reporting PRV in a steelhead captured in 1977 that had been preserved in paraffin by DFO. Dr. Marty argued that the presence of the virus in the steelhead demonstrated that PRV was in the province before the salmon farming industry began. He did not provide a genetic sequence to corroborate his claim, and that sample tested negative in future retesting ordered by the court during one of my lawsuits.

Despite the growing evidence to the contrary, government and industry scientists and their PR teams kept repeating that there is a local, endemic strain of PRV in British Columbia and that it is harmless. At the time of this writing, they still have no proof of such a strain and they do not address the finding of a Norwegian strain. But by claiming that the PRV in the province is a local, harmless virus, they are able to carry on legally transferring Atlantic salmon infected with PRV to the farms. Section 56 (b) of Canada's Fishery (General) Regulations prohibits DFO from issuing a transfer permit for any fish infected with a "disease agent" into the marine waters of Canada; if PRV is harmless, it is not a "disease agent."

When science runs counter to government policy, there seems to be nothing you can do to have it acknowledged. But when science supports such policy, there is nothing you can do to stop it from being misused. When I am accused in the media of irrational bias against the salmon farming industry—or fearmongering, as it is sometimes called—all I can say is that I don't wake up every morning with a blank slate. My views are the sum of my experience. I have nothing against aquaculture, but it is clear from decades of research that wild salmon are not surviving exposure to the unnatural levels of pathogens that pour out of marine salmon feedlots. Nothing in wild salmon's evolution has prepared the fish for immersion in the effluent stream from salmon farms. The federal government's consistent failure to legislate a sealed pathogen barrier between wild and farm salmon has made this situation much worse. The 2016 paper that Dr. Marty published in collaboration with Marine Harvest and DFO with the subtitle "Western North American PRV fails to cause HSMI" provided government with the science it needed to allow the heavily infected salmon farming industry to continue. If there was no disease, no one was breaking a law and no one had to enforce that law; it didn't matter that other DFO and international scientists were saying the opposite.

I knew there would be a lot of emails going back and forth between government and industry on this subject, so I began filing more access to information requests. It was easy. I simply went to the government website, identified the department, topic, dates and people involved, paid five dollars, clicked send and waited. Thousands of pages of emails arrived on disks in the mail. Each page had been scrutinized, and thick lines blacked out any material deemed sensitive or a privacy concern. But it was not hard to piece together that much of what was being said inside government was profoundly disturbing. The bureaucracy in DFO and the CFIA seem heavily invested in hiding things they know the public is not going to like about salmon farming.

In early January 2017, I was reading through another package of DFO communications about PRV when I came across a series of emails Dr. Marty had written the year before, in which he pulled the rug out from under himself. Despite having published a paper with Marine Harvest reporting that PRV failed to cause HSMI in British Columbia, he'd written emails a few months later that appeared to say the opposite. I'm going to quote directly from one dated May 21, 2016, sent by Dr. Marty to Pacific Salmon Foundation veterinarian Dr. Emiliano Di Cicco: "In February 2008, [redacted] provided BC vets a continuing education session . . . . When she showed images of HSMI, I immediately recognized the lesions as similar to what I had been seeing microscopically in some BC fish. However, the aquaculture veterinarians said that they were not seeing a clinical pattern that was consistent with Norwegian HSMI (all the Atlantic salmon companies have Norwegian connections, so I assume that they are well aware of the clinical signs of HSMI). Therefore we decided that what I was seeing was probably not the same as Norwegian HSMI."

I stared at this a long time. "I immediately recognized the lesions as similar to what I had been seeing microscopically in some BC fish." It appeared to me that four months after Dr. Marty published a paper stating HSMI had never been found in North America, he was now saying that it does occur, that he had found it himself eight years earlier but had decided at the time that it wasn't HSMI because the fish farm industry's veterinarians told him it wasn't.

Dr. Marty didn't stop there. On May 23, 2016, he wrote an email to Dr. Kristi Miller: "I do not want the SSHI [Dr. Miller's research team] to be seen as a project that takes credit for discoveries that were previously reported by other scientists . . . . Microscopic features of the 2013 outbreak reported by DFO last Friday [in a paper by Miller] were first reported publicly by another researcher (me) in 2013." Was this the reason for his stunning reversal of opinion on the existence of HSMI in BC farm salmon—he didn't want anyone taking his credit?

Two pieces of information clicked together like the halves of the stone tool Billy Proctor had found. When Dr. Gary Marty had reported the HSMI lesions to the fish farm company Mainstream in 2008, the company told him it was not HSMI, and that was the last time he reported any signs of the virus. Yet now, internally, at least, he was suggesting it had indeed been HSMI and that he continued to observe these lesions in farm salmon.

In December 2017, eleven months after I found these emails, I wrote to Dr. Marty asking if he had seen HSMI in BC salmon. He answered that he'd seen heart lesions that were "HSMI-like." I wrote again to ask him what the difference was between "HSMI" and "HSMI-like." Dr. Marty said I would have to pay his lab $150 an hour to receive his answer, and he sent me a link that allowed me to make a formal request. I made the request. On January 26, 2018, I received Dr. Marty's response: "There is no difference." He said he sent the samples for a second opinion to Norwegian scientists and they said the lesions in the BC salmon were within the range of what they would diagnose as HSMI. He billed me $275.63.

If my name was on a scientific paper stating that HSMI had never been found in British Columbia and one of my co-authors started saying that actually he *had* found it and now wanted credit for that discovery, I would take this up with all my co-authors, contact the journal, tell them we had made a serious error and ask that the paper be retracted, or at the very least amended. Instead, none of the co-authors blinked. This paper remains a pillar in DFO's legal defence that PRV is not a disease agent, meaning that salmon infected with it can, legally, be transferred into marine pens. I also contacted the journal, *PLOS ONE*. A year later, I was told the journal was still investigating.

Meanwhile, Dr. Kristi Miller was learning about how PRV interacts with Pacific salmon. In 2011, Creative Salmon, which operates in Tla-o-qui-aht territory off Tofino on the southwest coast of Vancouver Island, called her. They are a small company owned by Japanese interests and the only one to continue farming chinook on the BC coast. Many of the chinook salmon in their farms were turning yellow and dying, and they wanted to know why.

Miller's tests quickly homed in on PRV as a potential cause. Then, in collaboration with Dr. Emiliano Di Cicco, she and her team learned that when the virus enters the red blood cells in chinook, the virus uses the cell to make so many copies of itself that the cells rupture en masse.

The hemoglobin explosion from the ruptured blood cells overwhelms the fish's liver, causing jaundice, which turns the fish yellow, then causes organ failure and death.

Among the internal documents I was reading, I found a comment by Miller that a pathologist with the Province of British Columbia had advised Creative Salmon not to allow her to publish this work. (She wrote, "the histopathologist from the province convinced the industry not to sign off on the report . . . if PRV was to be included in the analyses.") Ah yes, I thought, if Dr. Miller published that PRV was causing chinook salmon cells to explode, PRV would be designated as a "disease agent." Dr. Marty was a "histopathologist from the province." It took Miller and Di Cicco seven years to finally get this work published, but they did it. In response, Dr. Hugh Mitchell, an aquaculture veterinarian from eastern Canada told media that Miller and Di Cicco's work was not science, but "activism" and "fearmongering." The BC Salmon Farmers Association said Miller's data did not support her conclusions. None of the critics provided any detail to back up their comments.

In 2013, the same year my research team published our first paper on PRV in British Columbia, I got a tip from an anonymous source saying that Marine Harvest's Dalrymple Hatchery, just north of Campbell River on Vancouver Island, was infected with PRV and young fish from there were going into a farm off Port Hardy. Farm salmon eggs are incubated in hatcheries on land and the young salmon are reared in freshwater in tanks for up to a year before they are old enough to transition to saltwater.

I wrote to Marine Harvest asking them please not to put fish infected with PRV into their farms. I went to the hatchery, stood in front of its gate and made a short iPhone video that I posted to let people know what was going on. Where were all the fishing organizations, including the union, who had started the fight fifteen years earlier to stop Atlantic salmon from introducing a dangerous virus to our coast? When I contacted these former allies, I got no response.

So I went to Ecojustice, a law firm run as a charitable society that pays lawyers minimal salaries to defend cases important to our environment. They can't take every case, and I felt very lucky they took mine, which would test the law that prohibits transfer of fish carrying a "disease agent" into the marine waters of Canada, including net pen salmon farms. We soon learned that there were two conflicting regulations in play here. One, section 56 of the Fisheries (General) Regulations, straightforwardly prohibited fish infected with a disease agent from being transferred into the ocean. The other, written into the salmon farm licences, said it was okay to put infected fish into the ocean if the company veterinarian thought the risk of spreading disease was low. Which rule should take precedence in a case like this?

To find out, we sued the minister of fisheries and oceans and Marine Harvest.

It took two years, but in 2015 we won. Federal Court Justice Donald Rennie delivered a blistering decision in which he struck down the part of the licence giving the company the power to make such a decision and he ordered DFO to initiate PRV screening of farm salmon before transfer into the farms. DFO, Cermaq and Marine Harvest appealed this decision, but when Dr. Miller reported that PRV *was* causing disease, the Department of Justice warned that all parties might want to reconsider their position. They dropped the appeal and took a different path.

Four successive federal ministers of fisheries—Gail Shea (the only Conservative on this list), Hunter Tootoo, Dominic LeBlanc and Jonathan Wilkinson—have so far been convinced that they do not have to implement Justice Rennie's decision. DFO said that as a result of the ruling it had reconsidered its policy not to screen farm salmon for PRV. But after reconsideration, it reached the same conclusion—that there was not enough scientific evidence to treat PRV as a disease agent—and so it allowed the companies to continue as before. It ignored Miller's findings.

In response, Ecojustice and I sued the minister of fisheries for a second time. Millions of farm salmon infected with a virus that appeared to be from Norway were still pouring into the waters of the BC coast, and yet the Canadian government allowed the practice to continue. How many wild chinook salmon had experienced massive cell rupture after swimming past salmon farms, and how many Fraser sockeye were getting heart lesions from this virus as other DFO research suggested?

A scientific paper published in 2017 reported that the southern resident orca, already a small population of less than a hundred individuals due to the heavy toll from decades-earlier captures for marine parks, was declining at an alarming rate. In recent years, 69 percent of pregnancies failed to produce live babies as a result of starvation. In 2018, Tahlequah, a young mother whale, carried her stillborn daughter for seventeen days over two thousand kilometres in what was called a "tour of grief." She was followed by millions of people on social media. Why were these whales too starved to procreate? Researchers identified the steep decline in chinook salmon in the Fraser and nearby Columbia Rivers as the cause of the whales' decline. Dr. Miller's work linked PRV with disease and death in chinook salmon; my research found that more salmon were infected with the virus in the lower reaches of the Fraser River than farther upriver, which suggested that PRV-infected wild salmon are having difficulty getting up the river.

Was viral infection why the Indigenous fishermen told me "the fish aren't moving up the river like they should"? Standing over pools with long-handled nets, they stared into the rushing water for hours waiting for the right moment to scoop up a fish. They grew to recognize individual fish by the scars on their backs and other signs, and they noticed that many fish never left the pool to continue their migration. This is exactly what the Norwegian scientists suggested: PRV-infected wild salmon could be too weak to swim up rivers.

Six years after the Cohen Commission was convened, the 2016 run of Fraser River sockeye was the lowest on record since counting began in 1893. In 2019, the run dropped again, and in 2020 it dropped still further. I was racing a virus our government had given a head start.

Part IV

The Uprising

17.

A Ship

IN THE SPRING of 2016, Captain Paul Watson, founder of the activist/ conservation group Sea Shepherd Conservation Society, posted on Facebook: "We are sending a ship to help Dr. Alexandra Morton protect whales from fish farms."

Paul Watson saves whales. Whales were starving to death due to lack of wild salmon, and since salmon farms appeared to be killing large numbers of wild salmon, I had written to Paul about salmon farms. But we had never talked about him sending *me* a boat. I messaged him to please remove this post. While I admired Sea Shepherd's bravery and activism, it was hard enough to get people to believe my science without being associated with a group that had a reputation for ramming ships in the Antarctic to protect whales. I worried that the post alone would eliminate any chance of a helpful conversation with government.

Paul didn't answer me and he did not remove his post. His silence gave me time to get over the shock, to think and to ask the people I trusted most—my children, Twyla, and some of the researchers I worked with— what they thought. I realized that the doors to government were already firmly shut and had been for twenty-seven years. In the documents I'd received through my access requests, I had seen a few briefings about me written for politicians. They presented me as obstinate, perhaps pig-headed, when in reality I simply have a lot of experience with the subject of salmon farms, they put wild salmon at grave risk; to change my mind they would need to tell me something true that I didn't know. Instead of seeing me as a resource, the bureaucrats (and as a result their ministers) regarded me as somewhere between a waste of time and too dangerous to associate with. For a politician trying to walk both sides of the line—the safest path for them, they seem to feel, but the most dangerous path for the survival of the natural world—paying attention to what I had to say was too risky. When Vaughn Palmer, a columnist with the *Vancouver Sun*, suggested that I was telling the provincial minister of agriculture, Lana Popham, what to do, she never acknowledged another letter from me. The industry knows I am very persuasive, because I speak the truth based on my enormous depth of experience on the subject of salmon farms. I assume they get nervous when I am in the company of government and they try to make sure that rarely happens by branding me as a radical.

Maybe it was time to do something different.

I got in touch with the nations of the Broughton to let them know that I had been given access to a large boat, and I asked if they were interested in using it to amplify their voices on salmon farming in their territory. Having been to many meetings with local Indigenous leaders, I knew they felt deep frustration and pain at having their territories misused to raise farm salmon when they had been saying no to the industry for thirty years. I knew many were without food fish now. Fish had not only been a staple of their diet for the past ten thousand years, but it is a critical part of their identity. They messaged back. They were interested in using the boat.

I reached out to Paul, this time asking, "When can the boat get here?" He said it was in Mexico, working to save a tiny porpoise called the vaquita, but could be in British Columbia by early summer.

Now I was nervous, and there was a lot to be nervous about. My biggest concern was that I wouldn't be able to fully utilize this eighty-foot sailboat and crew for a whole summer. I did not want to waste this opportunity or the generosity offered. Since my children had left home, I had also been living a very solitary life, so I worried that I would not do well in close quarters with a group of strangers.

I decided to use the vessel to audit every salmon farm en route from Vancouver to the Broughton. That meant doing a visual inspection: How many farms were stocked, how old were the fish in their pens, how did the fish look? What could divers see from outside the nets? What could we see with a drone? With that audit completed, I would take the ship to the First Nations and await their instructions.

The sailing vessel *Martin Sheen* arrived in Vancouver on July 15, 2016. Sea Shepherd names its boats after the big supporters of its fleet; the actor Martin Sheen is one of them. The ship was beautiful, with her tall mast, dark ocean-blue hull, wooden decks, sleek design and carved figurehead of a woman leaning out from her bow.

Sea Shepherd planned a press conference with actor Pamela Anderson for the launch of the expedition, which we were calling Virus Hunter, to be held in False Creek. *Oh dear*, I thought, *what have I gotten myself into?* Pamela asked to meet with me so she could hear directly about the impact of salmon farms before the cameras were turned on her. I liked her immediately and I was disappointed with myself for having prejudged her. Like me, she was doing everything she could to protect parts of this planet. David Suzuki, a giant in the fight against climate damage, also joined the press conference. Cameras crowded the deck of the *Martin Sheen* to hear David's powerful comments on the urgency of taking action. Then Pamela said a few words before she stepped aside and gave the spotlight to the Dzawada'enuxw Hereditary Chief Willie Moon, from Kingcome Inlet deep in the Broughton.

Chief Moon was both the elected chief and a hereditary leader. In his remarks, he made it clear that the Canadian and provincial governments had ignored the Dzawada'enuxw for thirty years when they repeatedly insisted the salmon farms get out of their territory. Now, he said, wild salmon were so scarce that after ten thousand years of feeding his ancestors and the animals, everything was suffering. He thanked

Sea Shepherd and said he looked forward to working with them when they arrived in his territory.

Another nation felt differently. John Smith, chief of the Tlowitsis, whose territory is along the southern border of the Broughton, was quoted in the international aquaculture news service *IntraFish* forbidding the *Martin Sheen* from entering Clio Channel, where Grieg Seafood was operating two salmon farms. While other nations in the Broughton, the Dzawada'enuxw, Mamalilikulla and Kwikwasut'inuxw Haxwa'mis, had refused to sign contracts with the salmon farmers, the Tlowitsis had reached an agreement with the industry.

The next day we cast off and headed north. I asked the skipper, a Frenchman from Madagascar named Francois "Fanch" Martin, "Where are we going first?" He looked at me as only a Frenchman can and said, "That is what you are going to tell me." After staring back at him for a moment, I pointed on a map to the first salmon farm, near Earl's Cove. That is where we would head. Five farms and a week later, we were cruising by the micro-community of Surge Narrows in the Discovery Islands, halfway up Vancouver Island, surrounded by a fleet of tiny boats like a pod of dolphins. The people around here mostly lived off-grid, like we did in Echo Bay. They were highly self-sufficient, independent thinkers and as comfortable on the water as otters. There were no roads connecting them, so they all moved by boat. Many of their boats were homebuilt from interesting and innovative designs. I loved the way they surrounded us, cheering and waving flags and signs reading *No More Fish Farms*, *Put the Farms on Land*, *Trudeau Do the Right Thing*, *Okisollo Community Supports ALEX!*

Okisollo Channel, part of a network of waterways near Surge Narrows, is one of the narrowest stretches of the migration route of the Fraser River salmon; because it is so narrow, it concentrates the effluent of the farms, causing greater exposure and risk to wild salmon—in particular the Fraser River chinook and sockeye. When we arrived at the Venture Point fish farm at the west end of the channel, I told Fanch that we would be spending as much time here as possible. Cermaq, the second-largest of the three Norwegian companies in British Columbia, ran this farm. (Though Cermaq was now owned by Mitsubishi, the head office was still in Norway.)

The Venture Point farm is where the fish that produced opposite results for HSMI from Dr. Kristi Miller's team and Dr. Gary Marty came from. Miller's team found it and Marty did not. The cohort of fish they had examined had already been shipped to market. The fish now in the farm were the next generation; we could see that hundreds of them were barely moving in each of the twelve pens, their backs out of the water and exposed to the summer sun. A bank of gas-powered air pumps roared with hoses that snaked away from them and down the aluminum walkways, four running into each pen. Fish were clustered around the air bubbles rising from the hoses; others had their heads against the netting at the edge of the pens to be the first to breathe the new oxygen-rich water flowing into the pens. Many fish were lifting their heads above the surface, gasping, desperate for more oxygen. As we watched, fish were giving up, rolling over and floating to the surface belly up.

One of the crew sent up a drone. The images it was able to capture provided a clearer picture of the condition of the fish in this farm. Just under the surface of the water, thousands more were behaving similarly to the ones we could see.

I phoned DFO's Aquaculture branch and asked them to come out and assess this farm to see if I was looking at fish suffering from PRV infection. The papers out of Norway reported exactly this behaviour in PRV-infected Atlantic salmon. I said we would wait for them. The farm workers, seemingly unsure what to do with us watching the fish, stopped working for two days. The employees took pictures of us taking pictures of the fish. A couple of the farmers posted angry comments on Facebook about our monitoring, but in my view, if they need to farm salmon in privacy, they should put their farms somewhere private. They could move into tanks on land, erect tall fences around them and post *Keep Out* signs—even get some guard dogs. One of the few things all countries agree on is the right for boats to move freely over the water. This includes near salmon farms.

I called DFO again twenty-four hours later to alert them to this farm full of salmon in visible distress and dying just as the Fraser River sockeye were migrating past them to the river to spawn. DFO inspectors needed to get out here to take samples so they could assess whether a pathogen was killing these fish, and then they needed to test the wild salmon to see if it was spreading.

For the two days the workers stayed out of sight, they didn't clean up the dead fish. Then suddenly, they began running the uplifts, which suck the dead from the bottom of the net pens into large blue totes that sit on the walkways. Once the totes were full, the workers lifted each fish out of the tote and put it in a large plastic garbage can. As they did this, we took pictures. The skin was peeling off many of the fish and the flesh underneath was so opaque it looked cooked. We saw fish with open sores and deformities, emaciated fish, plump fish and very rotten fish.

The next day I called DFO again. It should have been easy for the nearby DFO Aquaculture office in Campbell River to send someone out to take some samples to evaluate the risk these fish posed to the migrating wild salmon. If I had been calling about a fisherman catching a few sockeye without a licence, I am pretty sure a DFO officer would have shown up immediately. Here were a million salmon in a farm where hundreds were dying daily. Was a pathogen flowing into the ocean currents? Where was DFO?

A diver from Sea Shepherd went into the water with a video camera and swam up to the pens to get some video of the fish through the nets. When I viewed the footage later, I realized there were hundreds of thousands of herring outside the nets feeding—I could see their gills flash silver as they opened their mouths. The herring would wander off a few metres and then come rushing back to the nets when the feeders were turned on, which was audible underwater. What were they feeding on? Only a few days into the trip, I was already learning a lot.

When I later did an access request for the DFO conversations about the voyage of the *Martin Sheen*, I received 1,524 pages of inter-department emails, wondering where we were going next, discussing everything we posted, guessing what we were up to. But no one from DFO could send a boat out to check the dying fish in this farm.

After about a week, we had to leave to sail north to the communities up the coast who were preparing to welcome us. The captain and crew ran a tight ship. Maintenance was ongoing. I felt completely safe with them, but also something else. The crew members were all so different; they came from France, Argentina, Vancouver Island and the United States. But they had each decided to donate part of their lives to doing something to make a difference. I had grown accustomed to facing a chronic level of low-grade hostility, to always being the outlier. I did too much activism for the scientists' comfort; I was too focused on the fish to fit into political environmentalism. I guess I am too intense for people in general. But on board the *Martin Sheen*, I was among people who were a lot like me. While they weren't scientists, they also lived outside the box and were ready to go the extra mile. The sensation of fitting in was unfamiliar and unexpected. I liked it.

As promised, we stopped at First Nation villages where we met with many friends to see what they wanted to accomplish with the boat. We received an emotional greeting from 'Namgis in Alert Bay, and a warm welcome from Gwayasdums, on Gilford Island.

One chief stood in front of everyone in a gymnasium and said to me, "If you had come here earlier, none of this would have happened to us." His words burned. I'd never thought of myself as significant to these communities. I was deeply regretful that there had been something I could have done, but hadn't. I could see that I'd been too focused on counting the lice, on finding labs to test for viruses; maybe the solution to this mess could be found in connecting to the people. In fact, that's why I'm writing this book: so that others can avoid the mistakes I've made. So much of our world is already so damaged, there isn't any more time to waste.

At the head of Kingcome Inlet we tied the ship to a small wood float, mooring near the base of a sheer rock wall. On the rock were faded paintings of coppers—a cultural symbol of truth, justice, wealth and balance. Seeing those coppers took me back to February 2013, when I'd agreed to walk with Hereditary Chief Beau Dick and his family the three hundred kilometres down Vancouver Island, in order to break a copper on the steps of the BC legislature. It was an ancient and powerful shaming rite, directed at the provincial government for betraying its promises to the nations.

A little further up the inlet there was a huge, freshly painted copper by Dzawada'enuxw artist Marianne Nicolson, high on a sheer rock bluff. She'd perched on a small platform to paint it. This nation is remote, ancient and alive. Its culture, present and past, exists uninterrupted at the head of the inlet, where there are totem poles so old that they are gradually decomposing alongside large modern buildings.

A small skiff appeared between the waves of golden grasses of the estuary carrying hereditary leader Joe Willie towards us. Joe was completely at ease in the dangerous waters of the Gwa'yi (Kingcome River), which was chocolate brown, swirling and opaque. The tips of a huge root mass bobbed in the current, long skinny fingers warning that a massive tree lay just below. Hitting one of those could spin the boat broadside and tumble you into the swift current. On one end of the root was deep water, on the other the log and an accident; Joe knew which was which.

The valley is a narrow floodplain squeezed by steep mountains. The houses in Ukwanalis are built on stilts because the river claims the valley for brief periods every few years. A totem pole in black, red and white with wings outstretched at the top stands beside the stark Anglican Church, which was built in 1934. Since the government had outlawed Indigenous ceremony, the villagers of the day told the church they wanted to erect a totem pole to celebrate the King of England. That is how they got approval to raise the pole, which was designed to become a beacon to the people that their culture was still alive, not to celebrate the king of their oppressors. This community had endured the theft of their children, who were incarcerated in church-run residential schools and abused to the point that many died; most survivors dealt with consequences that reached into the next several generations. An earlier smallpox epidemic had killed more than half of the Indigenous community here. Still they kept the ember of their culture burning. Today it is blazing back to life.

No strangers ever just wander by this Dzawada'enuxw village, because it is so remote and guarded by often violent inlet waters and a dangerous river. The people here are among the most fiercely independent of the First Nations of British Columbia; they go it alone. It is a highly democratic society, where issues of concern are brought to the entire community to decide on. The members instruct their leaders, and these leaders go to extraordinary lengths to follow those instructions. Although I had lived in the archipelago for three decades, here I was acutely aware of being an outsider.

Forty of the seventy people living in the village at that time attended the meeting with us. They were unanimous. They wanted their leadership to get salmon farms out of their territory; the hard part was how to go about it. The Kingcome River delivered much of their food supply, but the eulachon and salmon were declining to the point that this nation did not have the food they depended on from the river. It was like all the markets in a town closing and boarding up their windows. But the diminishment went deeper than the loss of food. The failure of the river to provide was a loss of culture, identity and sovereignty too. I don't think there is anything I can compare this to for non-indigenous people. The members wanted the wild salmon back. And so they hammered out a plan. Step one was to serve each farm with an eviction notice and so they sent their council member, Melissa Willie, back to the *Martin Sheen* with us to begin the process.

I gave Millie (as Melissa was called) my cabin in the bow of the boat and moved onto one of the narrow couches in the wheelhouse. I came to love sleeping there—I could see the stars, and the snoring of the crew was much less audible. When we stopped at each farm, Millie climbed into a small inflatable and the crew ferried her to the aluminum walkways. She was fearless, stepping onto the no man's land of the floating pens to hand the employees an eviction notice, saying the company did not have the permission of her nation to operate in their territory and requesting them to leave. It is not an easy thing for a woman to step into the environment of male workers who were not at all pleased to see her. At one farm, she encountered a nephew. She made it clear the farm had to go, but to show she held no grudge against him, she hugged him.

Tamo Campos, who was on the *Martin Sheen* to create short videos for us to share, recorded Millie as she went farm to farm. "We have to stand up before we have no salmon left," Millie told his camera. "I took my son to a fish farm protest twenty-five years ago, when he was just a baby. Nothing has changed. It's only gotten worse. I think it is time that we forced them to leave our territory." As she spoke I remembered what a ray of sunshine my baby daughter had been in the fish farm meetings Billy and I attended; my daughter was now in her early twenties.

Millie also went to the mort floats, the small rafts anchored away from the farms where the dead fish are stored until the barge comes to collect them, braving the putrid odour that enveloped us whenever she lifted the lid. This was where the record of damage was stored. I had always wanted to look in these totes, an enthusiasm not shared by the others.

I noted the range in size of the fish that had died in the farms. There were a lot of undersized ones: many fish simply were not growing. Norwegian scientists blamed these "non-performers," as the industry called them, for the bulk of the sea louse problem; since they didn't eat the food pellets soaked in delousing drugs. I also saw many wild fish mixed in with the dead farm salmon, including sculpins. That surprised me, because sculpins are bottom-dwelling fish; they must have come up through the bottom of the net pens following the scent of food when they were still small enough to slip through the mesh. There also appeared to be young wild salmon, though they were too decomposed for me to identify the species; everything was rotting and generally coated in wriggling maggots. The dead farm salmon showed large open sores and pimply rashes. Nothing like this scale of ongoing death had ever happened in these once-pristine little bays before. I really wanted to take samples to identify what pathogens existed in this stew of misery and death. But I knew if I did, the farm operators would charge me with theft.

The water was a strange turquoise blue that summer. Though it looked beautiful to the crew, who felt at home in tropical seas, it was all wrong for this archipelago. My plankton net caught *coccolithophore*, an algae bloom triggered by an imbalance of nitrogen and phosphorous. It consumes surface nutrients, leaving less food to fall to the sea floor to feed the benthic ecosystem. *Coccolithophore* blooms are stimulated by nutrient pollution, usually associated with agriculture and city sewage. There are no cities in the Broughton—the human population is in steep decline—and there is no land-based agriculture. However, the million or more salmon in each farm excrete waste by the ton every day, rich with nitrogen and phosphorus. The tropical blue was a warning that these waters were saturated with fecal waste.

At anchor near the Glacier Falls farm, I had a vivid dream in which Indigenous women lined the shore near the farm, their backs turned and their arms upraised. While most were in the traditional black and red ceremonial blankets, one wore a dark blue blanket with silver disks sewed onto it. In my dream, I reached for my camera, but it was broken; I couldn't find any of the other photographers on board. I couldn't shake the dream—images of the women as they mourned the damage, showing only their backs to communicate that unseen powers were at work.

On August 16, three hereditary leaders—Willie Moon, Farron Soukochoff and Joe Willie—joined Millie as she boarded the Cermaq farm in the Burdwood Islands. They were in their regalia. The clouds hung low, and the day was dark grey. The image on Farron's back, a wolf with gleaming abalone eyes, shone as he strode down the walkway along the outside of the pens. I felt a shock of hope jolt through me. The people of this land were drawing a hard line. The Dzawada'enuxw were done with the Viking invaders.

These leaders told the workers that they had no quarrel with them, but that this farm was going to have to leave. I wanted to step onto the aluminum walkways with them too, so I could finally look directly at the penned fish, but this was between the chiefs and Cermaq. I was aware of how historic this moment was; these farms had become a battleground to save the life of the archipelago. Joe Willie's face showed pure disgust and anger as he leaned over the pen, staring at the weaker fish that congregate in the corners. He was a fisherman with a lifetime of knowledge of the fish of his territory; the corners of his mouth were pulled down and his eyes narrowed at what he was witnessing. Tens of thousands of people viewed Tamo's video of this moment on Facebook. First Nations family ties link many villages, and excitement rippled among the nations as they shared the video. The Dzawada'enuxw were on the move. And that was no small thing.

The next step in the plan developed by the community was to use the *Martin Sheen* and local boats to conduct a series of cleansing ceremonies on the farms. As an example of the level of thought and integrity at work among the Dzawada'enuxw, they decided they would not release feathers, which play a part in many of their ceremonies, because they did not want to be viewed as "polluting" the farms.

Sixty or so people boarded the first farm at Sir Edmund Bay (owned by Cermaq) near Kingcome Inlet. Then on another day they boarded the Burdwood farm (also Cermaq) in the heart of the archipelago, and on a third day, Midsummer (Marine Harvest), at the western edge of the Broughton. They circled the walkways counter-clockwise, some participants symbolically sweeping the air with freshly cut cedar boughs while others drummed. Babies peeked out from under button blankets. These were ceremonies, but they were also a warning. The people were not going to tolerate the misuse of their waters any longer.

This was a message that the industry should not have ignored. The archipelago was unceded land, which means that Canada had not bought it from the nations; there was no treaty that signed these lands over to non-indigenous hands. According to Canada's own laws, these salmon farms were illegal occupants, since they were here without consent from the First Nations whose territory they were in. Even the original architect of this disaster, the Science Council of Canada, when it launched the aquaculture industry in a ballroom in Vancouver in 1984, had specifically warned government to engage in "consultation with Indian people to avoid claims that 'future settlements may be jeopardized.'" In addition, government's arrangements with this industry were in jeopardy because there was an underlying constitutional flaw in the permits that it had granted to the farms. It was the non-indigenous governments that had gone rogue, free-wheeling off the tracks laid down in Canada's constitution and laws.

The First Nations were neither vandalizing the farms nor engaging in violent protest. They were only insisting that the laws of Canada be upheld. They were behaving lawfully. The government agencies that allowed the farms to locate in the Broughton were the ones that were breaking the law. Here in Dzawada'enuxw territory, and in much of the Broughton, the divide between industry and the nations was as sharp as a blade of steel; there were no documents binding them.

At the third farm, Midsummer, I asked if I could board during the ceremony and lower an underwater camera on a pole inside the nets and was told I could. After decades of circling the farms in my speedboat, trying to understand what was going on inside, I found it shocking to look straight down into the water of the pen. As a farmer stood right beside me, I parted the bird net slightly and slipped the camera on the pole into the water among the fish drifting near the surface. The fish were barely alive, emaciated and sculling in random directions; many of their eyeballs were white, which indicated that the fish were blind. I turned the camera towards their tumours and open sores. Salmon were stacked like firewood right up against the nets, accessing the clean oxygen-rich water. The water was laced with stringy, mustard-coloured strands, fish diarrhea, I realized when one fish let loose a stream of it in front of the camera. A school of transparent young wild fish were pinned into a corner as Atlantic salmon darted at them with their mouths open. The young fish were in the smelt family, maybe eulachon. I wanted to scoop them out, identify and release them, but I couldn't touch them.

The young fish farmer beside me could see that I was capturing the evidence that would bust a long-standing myth that Atlantic salmon don't know how to feed on wild fish. I felt sorry for him and said, "Just tell your boss there was nothing you could do about this. You were surrounded by 'Indians'." A glimmer of relief crossed his face as he turned and walked away. Twyla turned my footage into a short video that almost a hundred thousand people viewed. It was a horror film.

Next the Dzawada'enuxw asked that the *Martin Sheen* carry a contingent of chiefs and councillors southward, making stops in communities along eastern Vancouver Island. In each place, they were received by local nations; together with hundreds of other residents, including politicians, they walked through the streets, then gathered to describe the work they were doing to clear their territories and restore their fish.

This leg of the journey was a rare opportunity to live side-by-side with many strong hereditary leaders. They wanted to make sure that the other nations knew why they were taking these actions on the farms. For me these weeks were like a boot camp in the nationwide move towards reconciliation with the Indigenous Peoples of these lands. Misunderstandings hit me like a bad fall; I did not see them coming and they hurt. I thought I had been listening to these leaders, but in fact I was filling in too many details from my own head. This was a tense situation. The boat was full to capacity, with people sleeping on most flat spaces; we were well off the beaten track and there were land mines between us. If you step onto the front lines with people who have been brutalized for generations, you are going to feel pain. But that pain taught me things I would never have figured out otherwise.

I offered to get off the boat, because they didn't need me for this stage of the fight. They told me to stay. Gradually I realized we were not friends, we were allies. Every time I stepped on the rake of our relationship and got smacked in the face, I picked up the rake and waited until I was told how to use it and where to put it. The hardest lesson I learned was understanding that when I looked into the eyes of a First Nation person, I saw someone I wanted as a friend; they saw a member of the race they hated for trying to exterminate them. Starting from that realization we began to work better together.

At every gathering I melted away, kneeling on the ground out of sight to let the power swell and sweep on without me. I had been the face of the opposition to fish farming for a long time, but it was essential that no one mistake who was leading this fight now. This was the Musgamagw Dzawada'enuxw, determined to restore wild salmon by enforcing their long-standing rejection of this industry.

The Sea Shepherd crew provided remarkable stability. During this storm of humans trying to figure out how to work together to save a part of their world from other humans, the boat ran smoothly and the meals appeared on schedule, but it was more than that. Because they were veterans of many battles across the world, they knew what it takes to step onto the front lines to protect this planet, and they embraced us. The power of kindness cannot be overstated, and this crew was kind. Where kindness is constant, new thoughts and ways of being can emerge. We all wanted the same thing, but we needed to learn how to dance together. Living aboard the *Martin Sheen* eventually worked its magic.

My knowledge kept growing. When the chiefs talked about going back to their own form of governance pre-contact, it sounded like a terrible idea to me, given that it looked to be inherited and all male. I got up the courage to ask William Wasden Jr., whom everyone called Wah, "Why do you want to go back to a time of kings?" He laughed hard, but then he explained. "*Chief* is not our word and neither is *king*," he said. He told me that a chief is just the head of his family. The role is inherited, yes, but it is also earned, and it can be lost through recklessness. The head of each family has the responsibility to come to agreement with the other leaders, before anything is decided for the nation. As for the women, I realized a lot of the power was held by them; they were making many, if not most, of the decisions. One of the standard jokes on board, drawing smiles and nods, was the warning, for example, that no man dared cross Musgamagw Matriarch Pauline Alfred. I don't know exactly how female power worked among the nations, but it was real.

As I lay at night in the wheelhouse, restful snoring chorusing softly around me, I thought about what I was witnessing. Through this turmoil, far outside their comfort zone, on a ship run by an environmental group, walking through the streets of town after town, these leaders were carrying out the orders given to them by their people, who lived in a remote valley at the head of an inlet. I had never seen a government like this.

After this first season on the *Martin Sheen*, I cut off the two feet of hair I had worn for my entire life. I no longer want to stand out. When Margaret Wente had called me a "folk hero" in 2010, I think she was being sarcastic, but I realized that was what I was becoming in this fight. People increasingly stopped me on the street to tell me I gave them hope. People often said, *I can't believe it is you, don't give up* and *Keep up the good work*. Online and in the media, I was called "warrior," "queen" and "saint." With this uncomfortable acknowledgement, I realized that when people assign superpowers to you, they not only expect you to use them, but they think *they* don't have the same power. People felt I had this issue handled, when clearly I did not. Working with the Dzawada'enuxw made me understand it was time to step back from the public eye as much as I could and, instead, make sure my more powerful allies had everything I could offer.

18.

Sparks and Dry Tinder

IN 2017, THE *Martin Sheen* made a second voyage into the fish farm fight. My dear dog Ahta, partner in all my sea lice research and the long walk down the island, had died at the age of thirteen, and a little husky cross with sweet brown eyes became my new sidekick. I named her Arrow, after the Harry Nilsson song. So now it was me hugging my Arrow goodbye, leaving her with Sabra Woodworth, a friend who opened her home to me whenever I was in Vancouver. I stepped on board with my microscope and cameras on July 28.

Before we set off, I had received letters from three elected council members from nations with signed agreements with the salmon farmers warning us not to enter their territories. I sought advice from the hereditary leaders I knew and they all told me that the elected councillors only rule the reserves. To be in the territory as a whole, we needed permission from the hereditary leaders.

One of the letters had come from a band in the Discovery Islands, so I reached out to Tsahaukuse—George Quocksister Jr.—hereditary chief of the Laichwiltach, who had been one of the most successful seine boat skippers in the area before the collapse of the salmon run. He said he would come aboard and escort us for a couple of days through his territory. He then contacted his cousin, Hereditary Chief Arnold Chickite of the We Wai Kai Nation, and got permission for us from him as well.

On August 2, with George on board, we approached Marine Harvest's Sonora farm, at the east end of Nodales Channel. As the *Martin Sheen* glided up to the farm, it was clear that the workers had harvested the salmon; they had shortened-up some of the nets so that the floor of the pen was only a couple metres below the surface. The day was still, sunny and hot, and yet it looked like rain was falling in these pens. I knew we were probably looking at trapped herring, dimpling the surface as they tried to feed on zooplankton, and George, with his keen fisherman's eyes, saw them too.

"Hey," he yelled to the worker closest us, "what kind of fish you got in there?"

Without hesitation, the worker replied: "There are no fish in this pen."

None of us standing on the deck of the *Martin Sheen* at that moment knew it at the time, but that thoughtless denial was a spark dropped onto dry tinder. Significant change would come from this moment. George, who had heard many stories from fish farm workers over the years about all the baby fish that were trapped and killed in the farms, headed for the wheelhouse, muttering, "Lying bastard."

He called DFO, his member of the legislative assembly, his member of Parliament, the police and the band fisheries. Only his MP, Rachel Blaney, called him back; she said there was nothing she could do. He turned to Carolina Castro, the Sea Shepherd's campaign leader for this season, and said, "I'm going to go on the farm and take a look."

"Take a camera with you," she replied. George got in the inflatable and motored to the farm. The worker hurried to where he was about to dock and stood over him, arms crossed. He told George that he was not going to let him step onto this farm. George came back to us. He paced, fumed and stared at the little dimples on the water for about half an hour, then said, "I am going to put on my regalia and then I am going on that farm."

Minutes later, wearing his cedar headband, intricate button blanket and ceremonial apron that jingled with every step, with a GoPro body cam attached to his chest so that he could record everything that happened and another GoPro on a pole to dip into the pen, George headed back to the farm. Once again, the farmer towered over the inflatable as George tied it to the farm, but this time George just ignored him. He stepped around the farmer up onto the aluminum walkway, lifted the bird net slightly and lowered the pole camera into the water. From where we stood, we could hear the farmer telling George he had to leave, but George calmly kept filming. The man walked away, probably to get instruction from head office, and George kept filming.

When George came back to us, he was choking on tears he didn't want us to see. We cheered him as he climbed back on board. Then we viewed the footage. We saw thousands of herring dashing back and forth in a great school, panicked to be trapped at the surface in the hot summer sun. Sea Shepherd's videographer quickly edited a three-minute video and posted it on social media.

George decided that he would stay with us and board the next farm we visited. So two days later, after donning his regalia and cameras, he walked throughout the Marine Harvest's farm at Hardwicke Island, near Johnstone Strait. He held the pole camera in the water for about five minutes in each pen. He did the same thing at the next farm too, which was Althorp. While the farmers shadowed him, filming George with an iPad while he filmed what was going on in the pens, they remained pleasant. George was pleasant back.

It was Canada's 150th anniversary year and federal and provincial governments had been loudly affirming their commitment to reconciliation with the Indigenous Peoples across the country. Only months earlier, close to ten thousand people had marched in the streets of Vancouver with First Nations; the new NDP premier of British Columbia, John Horgan, had walked among them with Robert Chamberlin at his side. If the fish farm companies had harassed George, they would have caused a public relations nightmare. Alba Treadwell, a Sea Shepherd crew member, who kept her eye and camera on George the whole time he was on a farm, had outfitted him with a microphone that fed sound into her camera so she could monitor his interactions with farm staff as she filmed. Most of the farms had surveillance cameras too, so any incident would have been well-documented, if either side decided to go to court.

I thought I'd been able to see a lot of what was going on in the farms from my boat for all these years, but the footage George brought back revealed a situation that was so much worse than I expected. Every minute I watched educated me further. The stringy fish diarrhea drifting throughout the pens entered the mouths of other fish as they breathed water over their gills. This was an open door for disease transmission, as fecal matter was coming into direct contact with the bloodstreams of fish. The fish were aggressive with each other. In the crowded pens, big fish opened their jaws and engulfed the midsections of smaller fish, tossing them aside in a violent headshake. I could see the nervous darting of these smaller fish, which tried but never succeeded to get away from the bullies. I understood the research papers describing the elevated stress levels in these pens.

I noticed many of the salmon had misty grey patches in the centre of their eyes, a symptom that had not been present in the young wild salmon outside the farms in 2001, when I began my sea lice research, but was becoming more common. In the farm salmon streaming past George's camera, the patches ranged from cloudy to completely opaque; when they were white, the fish were blind. Whatever was causing this discoloration was affecting wild salmon too.

While I saw many fish with grotesque deformities, such as twisted or missing lower jaws and misshapen spines, I was most drawn by the disease symptoms: the blisters, open sores and raw wounds where tails had fallen off. Since the impact of each pathogen is connected to financial risk, the fish farmers had to know about these signs of disease in their pens. The companies would have to communicate the risk of losses to their shareholders. However, until I published my 2017 paper on the higher rates of PRV in wild salmon that were exposed to salmon farms, almost no one had looked at the losses these farm diseases might be causing in wild salmon populations, and the ecosystems and livelihoods that depend on them. Now that I'd seen into the pens, I realized that sea lice and PRV were only the tip of the iceberg.

An extraordinarily high number of wild fish was also apparent in the pens. In January 2012, I had won a lawsuit against Marine Harvest for their illegal bycatch of herring and salmon. The company was fined five thousand dollars and told not to do it again. But in every pen that George lowered the camera into, there were large schools of herring. Legally these fish were still in the ocean, but the looming question was what happened to them when the farm salmon were sucked out of the pens. We had already seen herring being held after the harvest of the salmon in the Marine Harvest Sonora farm. Why hadn't they been released? How many wild fish were getting vacuumed into the packers as they were harvesting the salmon?

Simon Ager, who was doing the diving for Sea Shepherd that summer, filmed even larger schools outside the nets, attracted to the farms. What happened to these fish? When the farms were emptied, did they know how to swim off and be wild herring again, and if they did swim safely away, did they carry farm diseases with them? What was the fate of the wild fish in the pens? Were they killed or released at harvest? Were they being turned into farm fish feed pellets?

I knew from the international salmon farming media I followed that the industry was voicing strong concern about the decline of the wild fish stocks they said they depend on to make farm fish feed. Would these farmers really throw away tons of free, oil-rich herring already caught in their net pens? In Simon's footage, I could see the herring outside the pens turn in unison and swim right up to the nets at the sound of the pellets rattling down the long plastic hoses into the pens. The pellets are too big for a herring to eat, but in the process of tumbling through the hoses, tiny pieces break off into a dust that is the perfect size for herring to swallow. I could see that dust floating out of the rotating feeder spigots. Were the wild herring addicted to that pellet dust?

When we sailed north, George stayed on board. At the next town we bought him a few new items of clothes, as he only had the one pair of sweatpants he had arrived in. With the permission of hereditary leaders Rick Johnson and Willie Moon, the *Martin Sheen* entered the Broughton Archipelago. At every farm—Port Elizabeth, Doctor Island, Sargeaunt Pass, Humphrey Rock, Glacier Falls, Burdwood, Midsummer Island, Swanson Island, Sir Edmund, Wicklow and Maude Island—we saw thousands of herring in the footage that George continued to shoot. The more footage of farm salmon I viewed, the more disease symptoms I noted. There were also differences between the farms. In some farms many salmon had gills so swollen they were flared like a ruffled collar; in others the fish showed open sores, ranging from the size of a quarter to a fifth the size of the fish's body. On August 10, I wrote: "There was an entire pen of fish with their noses towards the net, emaciated, open sores, blisters, sea lice, bulged eyes, missing parts of their faces. Oil droplets and flesh bits were pouring out of the pens."

Herring glittered in and around every farm. The herring fishery had closed for good in the archipelago just before I had moved there, thirty-four years earlier, yet the number of herring had continued to decline. Clearly, fishing was no longer the factor driving these stocks down.

I remembered my neighbour, Glen Neidrauer, who worked as a DFO fisheries officer, out front of my floathouse in his boat, *Port Lincoln*, yelling at his boss, who had arrived in another boat and ordered Glen not to measure the herring spawn on the Burdwood salmon farm. Glen was furious: it was his job, he shouted, to measure *all* the herring spawn in the Broughton, and that included spawn on the damn farms. For instance, when herring spawned on log booms, Glen reported it to DFO and the logging companies were not allowed to tow those logs out of the area until the herring had hatched. But when herring eggs were laid on fish farm anchor chains or nets, DFO officers were not even allowed to look at them.

On August 11, the hereditary and elected chief Don Svanvik, of 'Namgis in Alert Bay, requested that we show the footage from inside the salmon pens at their council hall. I had edited the hours of images into a sample of what was in each farm. I showed it first at a gathering in Kingcome Village and the people asked me to turn it off partway through. Seeing the condition of the farm fish left them in tears. They connected the way the salmon were suffering to the way they had suffered during their incarceration in the residential schools.

We headed into Clio Channel where Grieg Seafood had signed a deal with Chief John Smith, one of the leaders who had written to warn us away. However, we had the young, outspoken Tlowitsis Hereditary Chief Ernest Alfred aboard; he wanted to film the fish in the farms in his territory. Along with the blind, blister-encrusted and emaciated fish, the camera revealed many others with disturbing, poached-egg-like tumours protruding from the corners of their mouths. Many of these fish were missing their lower jaws; I wondered how they were managing to eat. They really did not look like salmon. Ernest was horrified, his handsome face blotched with rage and sadness as he viewed the footage he had shot.

Part of the damage done to BC Indigenous nations after the devastation of the smallpox epidemics included moving them from their traditional villages into larger towns like Alert Bay. There, many more had died of diseases such as tuberculosis, and the white authorities could better monitor their banning of First Nations cultural practices. Potlatches, held over several days around a roaring cedar fire in the Big Houses of each First Nation, were where the business of passing leadership roles down to the next generation was done, along with naming children, conducting coming-of-age ceremonies and marriages and other essential customs. Potlatches were outlawed for nearly seventy years, from 1884 to 1951 (though some were held in secret, usually during stormy weather so that government agents couldn't get to them). The first arrests for the crime of holding a potlatch were in 1921 on Village Island in the Broughton Archipelago, where forty people were charged with speech making, dancing and handing out gifts, a form of payment to the people who attended to remember the cultural transactions that had taken place.

Many Indigenous people point out that while Canada now says it recognizes the rights and title of the nations, companies take advantage of the gaping holes left in their social fabric by this colonization. For example, they make contracts with people who may not have the right to grant access to their lands, since the signature of one man cannot convey permission from a nation. I am just the biologist here. But knowing some of the history and a little of the culture helped me ride the wave that was building. As we shared the footage with the communities, the impact was like an explosion in a mineshaft. It moved fast and with force, but it was not yet visible. I could feel that inexorable pressure to act was rising. But how? Plans formed and crumbled.

On August 21, a total solar eclipse occurred. Many First Nations viewed this as a powerful omen of change. On that day a fish farm in Puget Sound in Washington State crumpled in a catastrophic structural failure, releasing 250,000 Atlantic salmon into the ocean. This triggered the end of salmon farming in Washington. The Lummi Nation fishermen caught an estimate twenty thousand of these Atlantic salmon. Timothy Ballew II, chairman of the Lummi business council, said this escape put the native species at risk. His tribe was furious and they did not let go of this. Seven months later, the state legislated that its salmon farms would have to close by 2025. They closed much sooner.

We screened our footage at the community meeting in the bingo hall in Alert Bay the next day—August 22. Residents had pushed folding tables together and set up chairs all around in the hall. People filled the room, with many standing in the back, interested but not fully committed.

As the images from inside the farms played, the room filled with fear that whatever was wrong with the farm fish had spread to their fish, and with anger at having been trampled again and again by government and industry, which had forced this sickness into their waters. Everyone realized that the wild salmon that had always been there were truly almost gone; it wasn't just a matter of a bad year for fishing, the decline was ongoing year after year.

After we screened our footage, Carolina Castro, from the *Martin Sheen*, stood up and in her Brazilian accent said gently to the community, "I just want you to know we will stand by you and offer support in whatever you decide."

The energy and calming presence of the *Martin Sheen* crew, who sensed what was happening in this room, eased the heavy, looming sense of the enormity of what had to be done. Like having a big brother there to walk beside you past the bullies, they took the pressure off just enough that one person was able to speak. It was Ernest Alfred.

Ernest stood and, in his quick, emphatic cadence, said, "I don't know what the rest of you are going to do, but I am going to occupy the Swanson fish farm the day after tomorrow, so I better go pack." He nodded, as if startled that he had actually said that, and then strode out of the room. Everyone watched him go. The mood changed, enlivened by Ernest's pledge of forward motion.

A schoolteacher and a hereditary chief, Ernest was stepping onto a well-worn battlefield. The lines were drawn, the science was in. The Broughton nations and the public at large wanted the farms out. Government and industry defended the status quo. George had struck the spark. Now Ernest became the blaze. I hoped this was it—that finally we would make the difference that would save the salmon. I followed Ernest out of the room.

On August 24, 2017, Ernest Alfred, a young woman named Karissa Glendale, the filmmaker, snowboarder and activist Tamo Campos and I piled cameras, sleeping bags and other camping supplies aboard Hereditary Chief John Macko's fishboat, *Pacific Endeavour*. Blackfish Sound lay still in shades of pastel blue as we crossed over her; humpback whales were at work feeding. When we got near the Marine Harvest farm, Ernest, Karissa and Tamo climbed into a small skiff.

Marine Harvest had filed charges against many of us the previous year after we'd held the cleansing ceremonies. They dropped the charges against everyone but me, since I was not Indigenous and those I boarded with did not view me as their guest: this was only my home, not my territory. I learned that being on the front lines means that while you may stand as a group, you must be prepared to face the consequences alone. This is important as you can never expect others to fight your battles. The company warned that if I stepped on one of their farms again I would be arrested, and so I stayed aboard Macko's boat. Tamo's grandfather is the famous and fiery David Suzuki, and Marine Harvest seemed to have adopted the policy of ignoring Tamo for fear of the uproar charging him might cause. Ernest carried an old, hard blue suitcase. Karissa had her belongings in a garbage bag. Their outboard wouldn't start. Ernest pulled on the starter cord again and again, until it was flooded and the only thing to do was wait. As the skiff started drifting towards the farm, Ernest pulled again and the motor caught. The mission was under way.

Ernest and Karissa wore their ceremonial blankets inside out to signify grief and mourning. As they stepped onto the farm, Karissa crossed her arms and tilted her chin up, signalling she was ready for whatever they decided to do to her. It was a challenge as ancient as woman. An employee walked towards them, maybe assuming they wanted to do another cleansing ceremony.

He asked, good-naturedly, "How long are you staying?"

"Until this farm is gone," Ernest replied in an equally good-natured tone, while Tamo filmed.

As Karissa and Ernest began setting up their tents, the farm employee turned and walked away. He needed instructions. The three hauled lawn chairs out of the skiff and got comfortable in the warm afternoon. A short time later an RCMP police boat pulled up to the farm. Two officers went first to speak to the farmers and then approached Ernest, who smiled warmly and extended his hand to one of them. He had taught kindergarten to the man's children.

The officer asked, "How long are you staying?"

Ernest replied, "Until this farm is out of 'Namgis territory." He then told the officer the farms were operating in the Broughton Archipelago without First Nations permission, and had been for the past thirty years. By the law the RCMP was meant to uphold, the farms were the trespassers.

The officers told Ernest, Karissa and Tamo they had only come to check on everyone's safety. This was an issue between the nations and Marine Harvest, not a police matter, they said, and they left.

That evening, the *Martin Sheen* glided gracefully into view and dropped anchor near us and the Swanson Island salmon farm. At the top of her seventy-five-foot mast was a cellphone booster antenna. Now the world would be able to watch.

I believe that without the tens of thousands of people who were able, via social media, to keep an eye on us over the coming weeks and months, the outcome of these occupations would have been different. Marine Harvest (which had made the name change to Mowi earlier that year to leave behind some of the negative press of its past) had always gotten their way. I believe that if no one had been watching, they would have taken a heavy-handed approach and moved to end the occupation of their farms immediately.

19.

Endurance, Chaos and Resolve

IN THE EARLY morning fog, I puttered over in the ship's skiff to bring Ernest, Karissa and Tamo coffee—and my gratitude. As we talked, the feeders came on, with a roar of the generator followed by the clatter of pellets tumbling through the hoses and the *wiisshhh wiisshhh* of the mechanical arms rotating in the middle of the pens to fling pellets into the water.

The next day the Kwikwasut'inuxw Hereditary Chiefs Wesley Smith and Chaz Coon came from the nearby village of Gwayasdums, and then members of the Dzawada'enuxw Nation arrived. They all set up lawn chairs on the farm, demonstrating their approval. This was critical. The next day, Chief Willie Moon travelled the sixty kilometres from the head of Kingcome Inlet in an open skiff to stand with Ernest and Karissa. Chiefs Joe Willie and Eric Joseph also visited the farm, further affirming the widening support of families and clans.

In the fight to protect wild salmon, an ancient powerful government was re-emerging. It had been badly damaged, but it had survived and it was reforming. Indigenous governments are among the only ones with the clear mandate from their people to restore the living world. Non-indigenous governments are pulled in all directions by corporations, international trade and myriad interests. Indigenous governments are rooted to the land where they were formed over thousands of years.

Is it any wonder the aims of these two different governments are often so different?

A bureaucrat named Ken from the provincial Ministry of Agriculture called me, fishing around for how serious this occupation was. "First Nations have been put on the agenda at an upcoming meeting on salmon farms with the minister of agriculture," he said.

Probably a little too late for that, I thought to myself as I gave him Ernest's number.

My role in the fight to protect wild salmon from salmon farms had changed dramatically. I was no longer out in front, but was part of the support team for this simple, powerful act of resistance on one of the farms that was killing wild fish. I was there to witness, communicate, support the bravery of others and do what I could to serve this moment of truth standing up to power—the transformation of these nations from victims back to their role as keepers of this place, sweeping the fate of wild salmon into their embrace. Because of this occupation, the wild salmon of the Broughton would be given a fighting chance to survive. It was a turning of the tide, from ebb to flood.

By day three, there had been no response by government or industry, and so I launched an online crowdfunding campaign to support the occupation. It was clear this action was going to take a while; the fall rains were coming and the people on the farm needed shelter. I have built several houses with friends in Echo Bay, and so I knew how to draw up a plan for a tiny house that would fit snuggly on the aluminum walkway between the pens. I placed the lumber order in Port McNeill, and others arranged for the boat and crew to pick it up. The building supplies were delivered to the farm along with a carpenter, Antonio, from Alert Bay in a fisherman's herring punt. Foreseeing how difficult it would be to build a structure on the narrow walkways, Antonio had pre-cut the lumber.

He arrived in the early evening and got busy with Karissa's help. By dark, a small building spanned the walkway between two pens with a door on either end. The next day they sheathed it in plastic and they were ready for the rains, which hit hard that night.

Ken, the bureaucrat, called Ernest again to ask whether this occupation was about moving the one farm he was standing on or all twenty-two farms in the Broughton? (The industry had gambled when it had placed almost a quarter of the entire BC salmon farming industry in Musgamagw Dzawada'enuxw territory.) Ernest told him that moving one farm was not going to stop the death of wild salmon by sea lice and disease—the occupation was aimed at removing all the farms.

The next day the Dzawada'enuxw boarded Mowi's Wicklow farm twenty-two kilometres north of the Swanson farm. At Wicklow, Macko brazenly tied *Pacific Endeavour* right to the farm. I left the *Martin Sheen* and hitched a ride with Chief Moon on a bear-watching tourism vessel that was heading up there. When we arrived, I jumped aboard *Pacific Endeavour* and started to make coffee and sandwiches for the ten or so people from Kingcome Village who were setting up tents.

For decades, I'd approached these farms alone in my speedboat to record sea louse outbreaks, do plankton tows and film fish dying, watching helplessly as more and more Atlantic salmon were poured into these waters. Now several cellphones live-streamed the setting up of the new camp and it felt like the cycle of death was going to end. A reporter from Canadian Press called Chief Willie Moon the moment he stepped onto the farm. Moon, whose true name is Okwilagame, told the reporter, "We were asleep, now we are awake; salmon farms are going to get out of our territory."

That night I slept on the deck of Macko's boat, on a flattened piece of cardboard wedged between the fish hold hatch cover and the gillnet drum. There was nowhere I would have rather been. I could hear the caged fish plopping all night long a few metres away, and the snoring of chiefs from the cabin. Laughter drifted out of the tents of the young women on the farm. My heart was singing.

Ernest began posting short cellphone videos of his days on the aluminum walkways of the Swanson farm, amassing a following of thousands of people. He was a natural. "Marine Harvest, you have a problem," he stated in his Big House voice. Molina Dawson from Kingcome Village, who had walked down Vancouver Island in the Get Out Migration, appeared with her gear in a bag and bravely moved onto Swanson with Karissa, and Ernest pitched a tent. The little plastic house was the kitchen, office and a place to keep the growing amount of donated supplies.

As a non-indigenous person in this uprising, there are parts of this story that are not mine to tell. I am not exactly sure how some things happened. While I have had the honour of being culturally adopted, dressed (meaning, given regalia) and named Gwayum'dzi by families of Dzawada'enuxw and Kwikwasut'inuxw, Indigenous societies remain mysterious to me. When I walked with Beau Dick and his family on his mission to break the life-holding copper on the steps of the pro-vincial government, I realized there were times when my companions felt things I simply couldn't. The biologist in me tried to figure this out. I asked them to explain it to me. They looked at me in disbelief that I couldn't feel *it*. In this uprising, I experienced the same sense of mys-tery many times; these humans were connected to each other and the place in ways beyond my comprehension.

The Broughton Archipelago once supported ten thousand people with her generous production of nutrient-rich seafood. There was an Indigenous saying that when the tide went out the table was set. In order for so many people to live here peacefully, each community established the camps they needed to thrive. Summer camps; winter villages; places to dry different species of fish, to dig clams and to collect cedar bark. The boundaries between territories were living lines that responded to seasons and resources. When non-indigenous governments began sell-ing access to resources in these territories, they conjured hard boundar-ies, making mistakes and imposing a false reality. They didn't care what the history was or what was best for the people whom they were tres-passing against. They wanted to stake a claim, find an "Indian" to sign off on it and collect the proceeds from the resource.

The Mamalilikulla, originally of nearby Village Island, where fallen totems were slowly rotting back into the earth, came to the Swanson farm and drummed. To an outsider, it looked like a simple show of solidarity, but this was much more. The Swanson farm sat in territory disputed by the Mamalilikulla and the 'Namgis Nations. This visit by Hereditary Chief Art Dick signalled that he was putting aside that dispute for now, uniting with the uprising to get the fish farms out. Art had been a First Nations fishery guardian. His first-hand knowledge of the fish and the protocol of his culture was a powerful blend. Setting aside the territory dispute was a very big deal. If a First Nation did not have access to the resources it needed to survive the people would perish, so maintaining such territorial borders was born out of ten thousand years of life-or-death importance to the people. Now, in 2017, it was a different kind of life or death, so they set aside a dispute that was hundreds of years old. In doing so, Art worked to remove the tactic called divide and conquer from hostile hands that might have wanted to disrupt and extinguish this uprising.

I got a call from the *Seattle Times* for comment on a press release issued by the Fraser River Shuswap Nation in support of the occupations, signed by Chief Wayne Christianson. We had not heard about his support. The news that the nations of the mighty Fraser River, the biggest salmon river in the world, were backing this stand brought a surge of energy to everyone.

A few weeks into the occupation, Mowi called a meeting with the 'Namgis elected council to put four options on the table. The people occupying the farm at Swanson Island in 'Namgis territory included members of that nation, but they could not speak for the nation. The elected First Nation governments were invented and imposed by the Government of Canada, and these band councils have to interact closely with the federal and provincial governments on matters like education and health on the reserves. While the hereditary leaders have the true say over the territory, they had been sidelined and ignored. The elected band councils are increasingly in a very difficult position as the intermediary between traditional and non-indigenous governments, particularly at moments like this. Everyone out at the occupations wondered what would happen at this meeting. Would the council cave? And then we heard. As the entire council sat there with their arms crossed, the elected chief councillor, Don Svanvik, who is also a hereditary chief, leaned towards the company reps and calmly said, "You don't understand: We want you to take your fish and get out of our territory." They didn't want to hear any other options.

First Nations from Campbell River happened to be in Port McNeill when the lumber headed to Swanson Island to build the cabin was loaded onto the herring punt, and they began talking about occupying the farms in their territory. The Kwagiulth to the north held a meeting about getting the farms out, too. The difficulty for nearly all other nations on the coast is that they had accepted industry money. When the industry arrived, no one on this coast knew the impact it was going to have on wild fish. They had signed the contracts. Members within these nations were angry about these deals, describing the money as "trade beads"—the cheap glass beads white traders had used to buy valuable furs and other resources from First Nations. Tamo, who had been on the front lines in the Sacred Headwaters of the Klappan Valley in northern British Columbia with the Tahltan Nation as they stood between their lands and the oil and gas industry, was struck by the extraordinary unity in the Broughton. The community members, their elected and their hereditary leaders all agreed the farms must go.

I brought the people occupying the farms freshly charged GoPro cameras daily, and they continued documenting the fish in the pens. They decorated the dull grey aluminum farm structures with painted fish sent to them by supporters from Vancouver as a show of solidarity. They hosted visitors from their nations who came aboard for a few hours and posted images of their presence on social media, demonstrating support. The occupiers served them coffee and food from their makeshift kitchens. They explained what they were doing to the pods of curious kayakers who paddled by. People who couldn't be there followed the occupations closely on Facebook. Every time Ernest posted a short talk, thousands more people viewed his videos, and conversations moved across his posts between supporters and those opposed to the occupations.

The power of the short video cannot be underestimated. Mainstream media largely ignored the occupation, despite the fascinating images of the people on the farms; the contingents arriving in regalia, faces streaked with paint, standing in the bows of old beat-up speedboats; the images of the fish themselves; and the stunning beauty of the place. I had been fascinated by the social phenomena of the Occupy movement and vividly recall an interview at ground zero on Wall Street in which a reporter asked a young woman, "Are you disappointed in the lack of mainstream media covering your event?"

She shook her head. "We have our own media. We really don't need you."

It was the same here. While mainstream media coverage would have been good, the message only needed to reach the other nations and the provincial government, which acted as the landlord of this industry.

Early into the occupation I checked on the tenure status of all the farms. While the tenures for most sites outside the archipelago were good for another few years, the Broughton tenures were all expiring on the same day, June 20, 2018—less than a year from now. I informed the nations, and they decided that the province was not going to renew these salmon farm tenures in their territory ever again. First Nations people and allies in the cities of Victoria and Vancouver began occupying the offices of politicians in solidarity. Pictures of people holding up statements of support all over British Columbia, and in Washington State too, appeared on Facebook. I know that the companies and government pay attention to Facebook, because every time I am in court with the salmon farming industry, the contents of my Facebook page appear as exhibits in their court documents.

I don't know why all the Broughton tenures were all set to expire years earlier than the other tenures in the province. But whoever renewed them had put the industry in the Broughton on a short leash; the timeline was so perfect it felt like a gift.

On September 4, I hitched a ride with Hereditary Chief Mike Willie—he was a wilderness tourism operator and ran a big Zodiac—and

Macko. Headed from the Swanson occupation to the Wicklow occupation, we stopped by the nearby Mowi farm at Midsummer Island. We'd heard that this farm was preparing to restock despite the very clear demand from the Musgamagw that the industry leave their territory.

Mike called out to a worker on the farm, "When are you getting the fish?"

The worker, from Alert Bay, yelled back, "Very soon."

With that confirmed, we set off for Wicklow. As we arrived, the enormous 150-metre-long smolt-transport vessel, *Viktoria Viking*, passed us. It was low in the water, heavy with farm salmon. I pulled up the Norwegian-registered vessel on MarineTraffic.com, where, sure enough, its destination was reported as Midsummer Island. *Very soon* was right.

Mike and Macko made a few calls to other hereditary leaders, and with their approval, we hastily took down the tents on Wicklow and packed them aboard *Pacific Endeavour*. Mike's Zodiac had to leave as it had a charter the next day, so I hopped on to Macko's boat with Tamo and Jasper Snow Rosen, as he set a course for Midsummer with the gear. When we arrived, Tamo filmed the *Viktoria Viking* leaving the farm to fetch another load. Given the mood of the nation whose territory they were exploiting, this was a stunningly stupid move by the company.

At ten o'clock on the night of September 6, Macko and I were at the Midsummer farm aboard his boat, along with Tamo and Jasper, when the *Viktoria Viking* reappeared. Macko's foot drummed on the deck, releasing just enough of his anger to keep it under control. Tamo, Jasper and I filmed the Norwegian ship disgorging 100,000 Atlantic salmon into one of the twelve pens on this farm, and we posted the images. When the boat returned the next day, Hereditary Chiefs Willie Moon, Wesley Smith, Macko and Chaz Coon, as well as Chief Moon's daughter, Sherry, and Karissa, were waiting for it. They were all in regalia.

The crew of the Norwegian ship wore deep frowns as they stared down from the wheelhouse. Perhaps distracted by the contingent of warriors facing them, they lost control of the huge vessel and ran over one of the farm's large steel anchor buoys. Seconds later the buoy shot out from under the ship into the air towards the farm. Fortunately no one standing on the flimsy aluminum walkways was hurt. The boat backed away to reposition and came in again, as the fish farm crew tried to block the warriors from getting too close. The walkway was so narrow the chiefs and the women were forced to walk single file. Sherry Moon, in the lead, didn't hesitate. She looked right through the man blocking her way as if he wasn't there and gracefully sidestepped him. The chiefs and Karissa followed.

Ignoring the First Nations warriors standing below them, the crew of the *Viktoria Viking* swung the huge transfer pipe over the heads of the people whose territory they were violating. The fish that poured down the pipe had already spent several months in another farm in the archipelago, Glacier Falls; illegal bycatch—thousands of herring—also spilled out of the pipe with the salmon. Like all fish farm packers, the *Viking* had no fishing licence displayed on its wheelhouse, even though every other vessel on the BC coast carrying herring would have to display one. Macko, realizing that emotions and actions were escalating dangerously, turned to the Mowi farm manager, and said, "We are done for today." The group returned to the *Pacific Endeavour*, their anger at everything scraped raw again. We silently realized that the heady early days of the occupation meant nothing to Mowi. For them, it was business as usual.

The company was invested heavily in courting public opinion. They sponsored youth sport teams, emblazoning their logo across the chests of children. When one girl, Freyja Reed, refused to wear the Marine Harvest logo on her elite soccer uniform in 2015, she was kicked off the team by other kids' parents who didn't want to lose the industry's funding. The company donated equipment to local hatcheries, set up farm salmon barbecues for many community events and donated to museums and churches. It was a tactic that worked. Many local people actually saw me, one lone woman with extremely limited resources, as the aggressor and Mowi as the kindly company lending a hand to impoverished communities. Nasty words people use when they are angry at women filled the online comment sections under news stories about me. However, when the images of Sherry, Karissa and the chiefs under the transfer pipe of the *Viktoria Viking* spread through social networks, the professionally crafted corporate image shifted. Mowi now looked more aggressive than smart.

On September 8, the *Viktoria Viking* returned with its fourth load of young salmon. Each load filled a single pen. Since the farm had twelve pens, that meant seven more loads to go. We were ready. Sherry used her cellphone as a mirror as she painted two dark red warrior streaks down her face. As the *Viktoria Viking* loomed over him, Chaz Coon, a hereditary chief in his eighties, yelled, "Sacrifice me! Tie me to the bow of the boat!"

The skipper and his crew peered down, looking angry and incredulous. How was this *still* going on?

As Chief Willie Moon stood defiantly where the pipe needed to go, they lowered it towards him anyway. A unit from CTV's investigative program, *W5*, had come on board the *Martin Sheen* for a previously scheduled interview with me and they were filming everything. Soon the police arrived to assess the situation. Since no one was out of control, they made no arrests.

That was the last smolt delivery to the Midsummer farm for three months. Someone in the corporate hierarchy at last realized the disastrous optics of showing such disregard for human life and such disrespect for the Indigenous owners of the lands. In the following days, Molina Dawson fearlessly moved onto the Midsummer farm and brought stability to this occupation. Other young women tag-teamed, making sure that she was generally not left on her own. We built another plastic house, and Nabidu Willie, Cassandra Alexis, Sii-am Hamilton, Lindsey Mae Willie, Shawna Green and Julia Smith spent weeks rotating in to keep this farm occupied. There was no plan, and no one knew how long people would have to live in these uncomfortable conditions. Under the glare of the workers and the surveillance camera high on a pole above the farm, there was no privacy. The constant dust from the pellets caused your lips to crack and your eyes to redden. Soon the stress of being away from children, jobs and home also showed. Everyone was hoping the province would announce that the Broughton tenures would not be renewed when they expired. But government remained silent.

As the weeks passed, Nimmo Bay Resort and the Buffer Zone, two local lodges, donated warm clothing, food and transportation. When the winter storms began, Ocean Outfitters in Tofino donated the use of a high-speed boat and a captain, an expense of thousands of dollars that made all the difference in keeping the occupation going through the winter months.

The Tiny House Warriors, who erect houses for people occupying pipeline routes, built a second house on the Midsummer farm. Supporters arrived with solar panels they hooked up to keep the occupiers' radios and cellphones charged, and a wood stove was installed. An inflatable unicorn, brought to the farm by the young women to lighten the heaviness of the work they were doing, joined the occupation. The Anglican bishop of Vancouver Island, Logan McMenamie, stepped on the farm in solidarity, as did David Suzuki. George Quocksister Jr. lent us his old prawn boat, *Sea Pride*, and she became the winter base of operations for the Midsummer occupation. I rafted my speedboat to the *Sea Pride* and lived there.

Before winter had set in—and only four days after the third load of smolts was delivered—my friend Jeff Jones called me. Jeff was a neighbour as well as a lawyer, and he'd worked with me pro bono to lay charges against the industry for the release of sea lice and illegal bycatch. When you are up against several governments and a whole industry, it's an invaluable gift to have a lawyer as an ally and a friend. Jeff had originally been the one to approach me, saying, "Alex, I need a client to fight the fish farms." Usually it's the other way around. But Jeff went to work every day in his speedboat; he and his wife, Marianne Mikkelsen, loved this coast fiercely and this was how they chose to help protect it. Jeff, who had helped me avoid the legal traps that dotted my path for years, was calling now to tell me he was dying. He was gone three days later.

That same week, Twyla Roscovich drowned, leaving behind her four-year-old daughter, who was the same age my son had been when my husband drowned. I mourned for what her daughter would face and for my own profound loss. Twyla was not only a brilliant filmmaker who brought the fish farm fight to millions, she was someone I had come to depend on emotionally. Most people are too burdened with their own lives to offer others emotional help. Twyla was a gifted healer who noticed when the steady losses, year after year, eroded whatever it is that keeps me going. People call me a warrior, but inside is a woman who sometimes needs help. She noticed this and, sifting through my experiences by making me talk about them, found the ones that had caused damage and helped me heal.

In the middle of this fight, I sealed up my grief at the loss of these two close friends and stored it away carefully, like an unexploded bomb. I could not mourn now. I did not have the resilience to both mourn and fight. I knew Twyla and Jeff would have wanted me to concentrate on the uprising. With each new pitch of the wave I was riding, I consulted with them internally. I pretty well knew what they would have said, and that helped a little.

I threw myself into my work. I picked up Karissa from whichever farm she was staying at, and together we tracked the progression of disease in the farms, in particular the open sores that exposed growing areas of pink flesh. Karissa, only twenty-three, was solid and calm each time she stepped onto a farm with the GoPro and filmed. She was good at noticing the range of symptoms the fish showed and being sure to get clear shots of them all. I nosed my boat into the farms and without my boat touching the farm, Karissa jumped off with the pole camera and filmed.

When the farm at Sir Edmund Bay, owned by Cermaq, was harvested, the workers left the nets in the water. George was the first to notice that, while empty of salmon, they still held herring captive. It was de facto a herring farm. Karissa and I kept track of those herring. Every time we visited, I asked the farmers that came out to monitor us, "What are you going to do with these fish?" The workers, of course, did not answer. Karissa climbed back into my boat after one visit to document that the herring were still being held captive and quietly said, "That's one of my best friends working on that farm."

"You okay?" I asked, and she nodded. It was complicated.

One day we returned and the herring had vanished. Until I learn otherwise, I believe the herring trapped in salmon farms are being rendered into feed for the farms, which is not allowed in Canada. Whatever their fate, the salmon farms were essentially fishing for herring in regions where the herring are in collapse and other herring fisheries are prohibited.

20.

The Boulder Starts to Slide

OVER THE YEARS, I'd often said that dealing with fish farms was like trying to catch a greased pig. Terrible analogy, really, but that's what it felt like. No matter where I published my science, how many lawsuits I won, whether I was on *60 Minutes* or the front page of the *New York Times* science section, or how many people marched or paddled with me, there had been no getting hold of this industry in order to stop the harm. They successfully slipped away from every measure that could have made the industry acceptable to First Nations and Canadians in general.

Imagine my surprise when after fifty days of occupation, British Columbia's premier, John Horgan, agreed to meet with the nations of the Broughton Archipelago in the Big House in Alert Bay, 'Namgis territory, at 10 a.m. on October 10, 2017.

Hope ran high as representative chiefs of eight nations in and surrounding the Broughton gathered together in their most sacred regalia. Present were four tribes of the Musgamagw Dzawada'enuxw, along with the Mamalilikulla, Ma'amtagila, 'Namgis and Tlowitsis. A cedar fire roared on the earthen floor in the middle of the Big House. Its smoke defined shafts of sunlight streaking down from the opening in the roof where the smoke escaped, igniting the colours of the regalia. The Big House was full. Packed rows of benches rose in tiers around the walls. Volunteers had gone out to the farms to hold down the occupations so that Molina, Ernest, Karissa and others from the front lines could attend. The heads of these families gathered here to impress upon the provincial government that it must not renew the salmon farm tenures.

Elected Chief Robert Chamberlin, who had been battling this industry for the longest of all the chiefs, stood wearing an ermine headpiece. Elsewhere, conflict was escalating between elected and hereditary leaders over fish farming. Rumours circled about huge signing bonuses coming annually to councillors who had aided in the signing of contracts with the industry, some of whom might not even still be on band councils. The Broughton was lucky in that her people, elected or hereditary, spoke with one voice against the farms.

Premier Horgan arrived with four cabinet members in tow, including his minister of agriculture, Lana Popham, and the local MLA, Claire Trevena. I wondered who had advised Horgan to dress in casual clothes. When he and the others took their seats in the only chairs in the house, they faced a line of twenty chiefs in full regalia. Then Horgan announced that he was here to hear their "stories."

Stories! This felt condescending. From the stern expressions of the men standing in front of the premier, it didn't look to me like they had gathered to tell him stories. They were there to meet government-to-government in order to find a path forward on how salmon farms were going to be removed.

They handed the premier a stack of my published scientific papers, saying the province didn't need any more science to prove that salmon farms were destroying wild salmon. (I still savour that moment; it meant that I had not wasted the past thirty years.)

Just before this meeting, Lana Popham had sent a firm letter to Mowi—the first and only letter I had seen from a non-indigenous government that stood up to the industry. Popham put the company on notice about the upcoming deadline to renew the Broughton tenures, pointing out that the government was "entering into sensitive discussions with some of the First Nations in the Broughton Archipelago" and that the company's tenure renewals were not guaranteed. She warned

Mowi that if the company chose to restock farms on expiring tenures, they needed to be aware they might have to "return possession of ten-ured sites." Did the company's shareholders even know that a significant number of its tenures in western Canada were not "guaranteed"? After decades of dedicated bootlicking from previous provincial parties, I don't think Mowi was used to being talked to that way. Popham was a brave and straightforward woman.

After delivering my papers to Horgan, the leaders of each nation voiced their concerns one after the other. Chief Moon demanded that Horgan prohibit any restocking of farms whose tenures were about to expire, given that farm fish require two years to grow before harvest and all the tenures were due to expire in eight months. Since the occupa-tion began, the companies had been leaving farms empty to the south of the archipelago, but they were restocking the farms in Broughton. This made it seem that the industry was doing everything it could to make it hard for the government not to renew the tenures. The industry certainly did nothing to defuse the situation.

After hearing out the chiefs, Horgan stood among them to deliver his response. What we all heard from him was that nothing was going to change at the provincial level. As the knot of chiefs around Horgan tightened, the diminutive Lana Popham rose to stand beside him. Chief Bill Wilson, Hemis Kla-Lee-Lee-Kla, a lawyer influential in amending the Constitution of Canada to enshrine Aboriginal Rights (and former federal minister Jody Wilson-Raybould's father), took the microphone and advanced on Horgan. He posed a simple question: Was the premier going to allow Mowi and Cermaq to restock farms on tenures that would expire in a few months?

Hundreds of people on the surrounding benches fell silent, listening hard for the answer. Dzawada'enuxw filmmaker Lindsey Mae Willie had her camera focused on the premier. Horgan could not walk away from Wilson and the chiefs who now ringed him and so, in that moment, he took the side of the Indigenous leaders and said, "If those leases are up in less than two years, they should not be able to restock them."

There was a collective sigh. Everyone knew there was a good chance Horgan would retreat from those words—politicians break promises all the time. But what is said in the Big House becomes law. The nations' leaders had represented them properly and had achieved what they could that day.

Claire Trevena had become skilled at ducking all things fish farm over the years she'd been the local MLA. While the uprising was in her riding, so were the head offices of the three Norwegian-run companies that dominated the BC industry. She'd faced crowds eleven years earlier who carried signs with her name and a skull and crossbones on them threatening her for trying to get salmon farms out of the ocean and into land-based facilities. When she'd awarded me the Queen's Diamond Jubilee medal in 2002, she hadn't mentioned the words *fish farm* when describing why I was receiving the honour. She could not be seen rewarding me for fighting this industry. Here in the Big House, after Horgan had made his promise, she moved through the crowd telling people that if the government did not renew the tenures, the companies could sue them. This made me wonder how, exactly, this industry was threatening government.

I went home after the meeting to provision my boat. That night I heard an unfamiliar noise. I looked out the back door and saw a plane flying very low and slow right up the road to my house, then over me and on, over the Swanson camp. Then it banked and flew over Midsummer Island, before it continued up Knight Inlet. It had a triangular pattern of lights on its belly and a big orange light in front of that.

When I arrived at Swanson the next day, I heard that RCMP officers were amassing in Port McNeill, where two large black Zodiacs were sitting at the dock. The parking lot of one of the town's hotels was full of police vehicles. I also heard that the *Viktoria Viking* had gone north to get another load of farm salmon. Everyone was on edge. What farm was the *Viking* preparing to stock? And what would we do about it?

21.

Keeping Up the Pressure

THROUGHOUT THIS UPRISING, the occupiers and allies were under the guidance and the watchful eye of some of the hereditary leaders. Chief Arthur Dick told us, "Don't bring shame on the nation." What he meant was no violence, graffiti or vandalism. And Chief Don Svanvik said something that took me a while to understand. He said, "At the very worst, I want people to feel indifference about what we are doing."

That did not sound right to me. I hoped people *would* care, and that they'd step up to the plate and lend a hand in all the ways people can. But eventually I realized he meant for us to be careful not to cultivate hate or anger. He knew wide support was essential, but not hatred; he wanted the worst response to the occupation to be indifference. Still, the hereditary chiefs asked us to keep up the pressure, a vague instruction.

I split my time between living in my speedboat at the farms, travelling to related events and some time at home, now and then, to rest, edit footage and get warm. It's energizing to be on the front lines, but I was sixty years old and knew that at some point my body would crash if I wasn't careful.

For Molina and the others on the Midsummer farm, it was bone-deep uncomfortable to live on the aluminum walkways. At Swanson, there was a cabin on the land behind the farm that Mowi had built and abandoned. In early October, Ernest, with other hereditary leaders, entered the cabin and took it over. The cabin had no running water or electricity, but it was on solid ground and had a wood stove and a roof that didn't leak. A group, including Ernest's mother, Tidi Nelson, arrived and cleaned it out, including the mouse droppings. Ernest's call sign on the VHF radio became *Staycation*.

The folks who showed up at the Swanson camp to help were extraordinary. There were family members and members of local First Nations, but there were also people who had been to the front-line occupation camps throughout the province that were trying to prevent construction of pipelines that would contribute to the growing climate crisis: Lelu Island on the north coast, the Unist'ot'en camp in the interior, and Camp Cloud in Burnaby. Activism tourists from Germany, who used vacation time to assist global efforts such as these, also showed up. They believed that the simple act of sitting in a small cabin on a remote island was important to the future of all life on Earth. Every day that someone was able to remain in place was another day of the occupation. I was amazed when day seventy dawned cold and frosty. It was winter, and this action had started in the heat of summer.

These volunteers and friends cooked, cut firewood, cleaned, built drying racks for clothes and kept a watchful eye on the farm. Mowi had harvested their fish at the Swanson farm during the occupation, as per their production schedule, and it now stood empty. No one wanted Swanson to be restocked.

The stress began to wear on Ernest. When I returned after a few days away in October, I realized that he looked hunted, with dark circles under his eyes. At every noise he jumped to his feet to check the farm, camera in hand. His phone rang constantly, with calls from politicians, reporters, Indians in Washington State, his leaders and his wife, Nic Dedeluk. The farm kept surveillance cameras pointed at him and the others. No one knew when the heavily armed RCMP officers who were staying in Port McNeill would appear, maybe from the woods behind the cabin at night.

It was also very hard on Ernest that other chiefs, who were not taking the risks he was, had entered into talks with the provincial government about the farm tenures with no communication back to him. The occupation provided the pressure that had brought government to the table with the chiefs, but no one doing the occupying was kept informed about what was unfolding behind closed doors. We all feared the talks might fail; the leaders might give in too soon. Ernest had not returned to his job as a schoolteacher and did not know if he would still have a job when this was over. He was taking this action for everyone, but felt shut out, which significantly compounded his stress.

Ernest was lucky to have the support of his wife, Nic, the fisheries manager for the 'Namgis, who ran supplies out to the camp in various boats, often in very foul weather. His mother, Tidi, housed and organized the flow of supporters who needed a place to stay in Alert Bay while they awaited transport out to the farm. She met with a group (mostly women, including Ernest's aunts) every week in Alert Bay about managing the logistics of the occupation. Nic left her dog, Lucy, with Ernest. Lucy was the unflagging keeper of happiness at the occupation; she also kept an eye on the local bear, which foraged daily on the beach at low tide, and became Arrow's best friend.

When winter storms started hitting the farms, I thought constantly about the young women holding down the Midsummer occupation. The ocean current roared through that farm like a wild river and the place was open to the wind. The aluminum walkways bucked and heaved in that wind like a rug being shaken out.

As the weeks wore on, tribal divisions emerged between the two occupations. What had seemed like one action to me was clearly two: the Musgamagw camped on Midsummer and the 'Namgis camped at Swanson. The women on the Midsummer farm, many hardly more than teenagers, were invited to rotate through Ernest's cabin at Swanson, but they wouldn't, staying put in the storms, snow and pelting rain. There was a frightening incident in which a group of men who worked for Mowi strode down the walkway towards the northern edge of the farm and one of the occupiers' little houses, each of them carrying a knife. The women had no warning, no idea what they had planned and nowhere to run. They texted and called for help. I was nearby and raced towards them.

The farm staff pushed past the women and slashed the ropes that tied a twenty-five-foot banner that asked in two-foot-high letters *GOT PISCINE REOVIRUS?* to the farm's railings. The sign had been visible to everyone passing the farm, and I would discover that, yes, this farm did have PRV. Without a word to the women, the farm staff carried the banner away.

The occupiers had called the RCMP. When the police arrived, I watched their vessel go to the farm's crew quarters first, remain there for about thirty minutes and then leave without ever speaking to the women.

This broke my heart. The RCMP had declared many times that they were there to make sure *everyone* was safe. This looked like racism and sexism to me. I loved these women for their remarkable bravery and smiles, for the sacrifice they were making and for who they are. Molina, Nabidu, Cassandra, Sii-am, Julia, Shawna and Lindsey—*respect*.

When David Suzuki had visited these young women, he'd asked them, "Where are the men?" They smiled in quiet pride and told him they didn't know. Men did spend time on the farms, but most paced like caged animals. They wanted to be doing more than just sitting there, and yet just sitting there was the powerful act that was forcing change where nothing else had worked.

The women settled into a rhythm of enduring grace. I used the crowdfunding to make sure they each had cellphones to keep them a little safer and also to buy them winter boots. I brought them firewood from my house. They told me that they could feel their ancestors as they occupied the farm. If their ancestors could have spoken to me, I hoped they would have told me to try to keep them safe.

While I still couldn't set foot on the farm, I rafted my own boat to the old *Sea Pride* as often as I could. One night, several of the farm workers crashed their work skiff into my speedboat hard and threw an application for an injunction against me into my boat. And so I was served . . . again. I am not convinced that they actually meant to hit me, but I didn't see them coming till the last minute and the encounter left me shaking as I thoroughly checked my twenty-five-year-old fibreglass boat for cracks.

An hour later my boat tipped slightly under the weight of someone coming aboard. Instantly I was ready to protect myself. It turned out to be Martin, an occupier from *Sea Pride*, carrying two cast iron frying pans pancaked together. He lifted the top one to reveal a single freshly baked, still-warm chocolate chip cookie. Martin, who rarely spoke, said, "I figured out how to bake without an oven." *Kindness.*

By the middle of October, the crew of the *Martin Sheen* were gone. I was consumed with worry. Worry someone would get hurt, worry that we would give up and all of this would have been for nothing, worry that the wild salmon would go extinct. We didn't know what was being said in the government-to-government talks, now being called the *G2G*. I knew the outcome of all the talks that had gone on before these. How long before we could abandon the occupation and be certain there was no chance of failure? How long before someone got hurt? How much longer could we sustain this?

On October 13, 2017, *Viktoria Viking* passed the Swanson camp, headed up Knight Inlet in the pre-dawn light. Ernest and I went after it in my boat. Two black inflatables came streaking out along the far side of the bay as we turned towards the farm in Port Elizabeth following the ship. As we approached the farm, we saw an RCMP officer watching us from an upstairs window of the floating crew quarters that were tied to the farm, the RCMP logo emblazoned across his cap. When we drew close, Ernest asked the farm workers on the walkways if he could speak with the officer. They laughed and the officer refused to come out.

Ernest posted updates as I collected hundreds of scales that were twinkling out of the nets, knocked off the young farm salmon as they tumbled down the pipe from the boat into the pen. These scales would later test positive for PRV, the Norwegian salmon virus I had been tracking, meaning that these fish had become infected while still in the hatchery, and not from wild fish.

Two reporters who were monitoring Ernest's feed online called to interview him. We were just barely in cell-range and I had installed a booster on my boat. He pointed out that the BC minister of agriculture and eight First Nations had asked Mowi not to restock the farms on soon-to-expire tenures, such as this one. Just three days earlier, the premier had said in the Big House that farms with expiring tenures should not restock. Mowi cared nothing for any of this. I uploaded pictures of Ernest and the *Viking* to the reporters.

When the boat had disgorged its load of a hundred thousand Atlantic salmon, it backed away and two black Zodiacs zoomed into the bay again and up to the crew house. More than one RCMP officer had been on the farm that day, it turned out, as we learned when they came out of the staff quarters, got into the boats and took off. My camera caught the face of one officer who was lying down in the boat with just his forehead and eyes visible. Why was he hiding? Was he someone we knew?

The Zodiacs came at us and then split, passing close on either side of my boat. I wondered whether the manoeuvre was meant to be aggressive.

The next day, forty people came to the Swanson camp in a winter gale, including Grand Chief Stewart Phillip, David Suzuki, Chief Bill Wilson and Chief Robert Chamberlin, all ferried there by my dear friends, Bill and Donna Mackay, in their storm-worthy forty-eight-passenger vessel, *Naiad Explorer*. The gathering was uplifting for everyone.

I lay awake that night, October 14, in my boat at the Swanson camp under a mountain of blankets, my dog curled up beside me. Everyone here was stretched taut. The RCMP were clearly expecting us to react to Mowi's disrespectful restocking of the Port Elizabeth farm. What did they expect us to do? I could see on the vessel traffic website that *Viktoria Viking* was heading north from its hatchery in Sayward again, loaded with more smolts, probably destined for Port Elizabeth. What was my role? I had to make up my own mind, listen to my instincts. All I could hear in my head was, *It's your turn.*

John Geraghty, from Sointula, had arrived that day in his aluminum crew boat, *Strider*. The dorsal fin of the large male orca, Strider, from Corky's A5 pod, was painted on the cabin. Bonny Glambeck and Dan Lewis from Clayoquot Action in Tofino were at Swanson as well, seasoned allies who were also trying to protect wild salmon from salmon farms. Nabidu Willie, Ernest, and many others were gathered around the wood stove on their sleeping bags.

By dawn, the wind had come up, making Knight Inlet too choppy for my boat. The next morning, Ernest and I asked John if he would take us up the inlet to witness another load of Atlantic salmon being poured into the Mowi farm in Port Elizabeth, Musgamagw territory, like a lethal injection into the archipelago. John agreed. Bonny, Dan and Nabidu came with us.

When we got to the farm, I asked John to drop me off. He looked at me to make sure he had heard right and then, with zero commentary about how this was not safe, took the boat close enough for me to step off. The instant I stood on the farm, I knew I was doing the right thing. Thirty years of trying to prevent fish farms from killing the wild fish outside the pens had made no difference. There were so few wild salmon left even the sports fishermen didn't waste the gas to come to the Broughton. I was haunted by the stories bear tour operators told of bears facing starvation during hibernation. It was time to get past my fear of the injunction and raise the ante.

The RCMP were already in place. A police negotiator approached me as soon as I stepped foot on the farm. He said I would be arrested if I moved past him and the line of heavily dressed officers. I slipped between them and walked up to the pipe; together we watched the juvenile Atlantic salmon pouring into the pen.

"How do you see this going?" he asked.

"Arrest me, put me in one of your black Zodiacs and take me to Port McNeill," I said.

The officer retreated, huddled with the farm crew and came back to me. "There will be no arrests today," he said.

"Okay, then I am here to observe." I advised him and the other police present, with their bulletproof vests and firearms, that they were over-dressed. I had no plans or capacity for violence. Then Ernest jumped onto the farm as well, and we stood there together watching the unload-ing process.

After several hours, the *Viking* was empty. As soon as it backed away from the farm, the police piled into their black Zodiacs and sped off without a word. The wind was continuing to rise, a typical October day in Knight Inlet. John came by to ask what we wanted to do. Ernest needed to get back to Swanson, but I was going to stay. I asked Nabidu if she would look after Arrow for a few days. As Ernest boarded the boat, John threw me a garbage bag full of supplies to get me through the night. Then he left too.

I walked the farm and noted where I could find a weak cell signal. The newly arrived salmon were floundering. Some were swollen like balloons, others listing to one side. The majority were circling the pen. In the next pen over, fish that had been in the ocean pens for several days were leaping and seemed to be feeding. They had spent over a year in a hatchery and would spend two more years here, the slowest-growing farm animal in production. After looking into each pen, I climbed into a sleeping bag, pulled the garbage bag over it up to my armpits to keep dry, then hunkered down behind a large plastic box labelled *Spill response kit* in the lee of the wind. I was warm and dry enough.

I gazed at the little salmon in the pen beside me. As eggs they were released from their mothers with a knife. Hatched in trays, reared in steel tanks in the town of Sayward on the east coast of Vancouver Island, they migrated to sea in the belly of a Norwegian registered ship. Now they were going in circles in a pen seven thousand kilometres from the ocean they belonged to. The shock of being hurled into saltwater at the end of a pressurized tube had been too much for many of them. Gulls, standing ready to do the job of removing the sick and damaged, cried out in hungry frustration. They could see the fish, easy pickings, lying on the surface, just the right size for them to swallow. But they could not reach them through the bird nets stretched taut over each pen. There is nothing right about salmon farms.

After a while, Craig, the farm's security guard, came walking towards me carrying a small wooden chair. It took him several minutes to carefully position the legs so that each rested on an intersection of the aluminum grid-work and wouldn't fall through, tipping the chair. "Please leave," he said to me once he'd settled. "It's cold out here and I don't want to have to sit here watching you."

"My ride is gone," I said. We both looked up the inlet at the endless rows of grey waves in the failing light.

Eventually I asked him how he ended up here. Craig said he used to work in a mall near Vancouver, but took a job with Mowi for a change of pace. He repeated that he was cold and told me to leave again. I explained why I was here. Again he told me to leave. Finally I suggested that he go and sit in the office and watch me on the security camera, pointing to the dome-shaped camera high above us on a pole. Off he went, but he left the chair.

I looked around and noticed a small float with a three-sided generator shed on it. It would be oily, but it was dry and out of the wind. I decided that was where I would sleep. I was looking forward to it getting dark. I had never had a chance to look into a farm at night to see how the fish respond to the massive underwater lights that many farms use to fool the fish's internal growth regulators so they keep growing through an eternal, industrially produced summer. Fishermen, who knew how lights attract wild fish because they used to use lights at night themselves, worried that the lights were also being used to draw fish into the pens to feed the Atlantic salmon.

I wasn't worried about anything happening to me. I was sure Mowi wouldn't want that kind of publicity. But I remembered to call Greg McDade, who was handling Mowi's still-active trespass charges against me. I didn't want him to hear about what I had done before he heard it from me, especially since I'd told him at the beginning of the occupation that I would not put a foot on the farms, a promise he had communicated to Mowi.

Greg sounded irritated; he had every right to be. I had broken my word and his too. But, I told him, this was the last chance we would get to protect this place. I was concerned that Mowi would just let the occupation roll on until people got hurt, fell ill from stress or had to resume their lives to pay their bills; my presence was a way to increase the pressure without risking anyone else. Hereditary leaders had told me to keep up the pressure, I said, and . . . the phone cut off. I sat there in silence for a moment or two, then took a selfie and just barely managed to upload a low-res version of it onto Facebook, giving my location. *Protection*, I thought.

Just after dark, I was heading for the little generator shed when I heard a high-speed boat approaching. The shot of adrenaline that jolted me was quickly replaced by disbelief as I heard voices and laughter carried on the wind. It was Ernest, Sherry Moon, Julia Smith and Karissa. I couldn't believe it.

As they pulled up, I called, "What are you doing here?"

"We are not going to let you do this alone."

They tied up and unloaded a tent, blankets and my winter boots, which I had left in my boat at Swanson. Then they proceeded to string lines between the pens to put up the tent. They were pros at this by now.

My loner heart was grateful. That night I felt something rare. Solid allies, people who really have your back, are one of life's greatest gifts. We five lined up like sardines in the tent, shared stories and laughed into the wee hours.

Just before dark the next day, the farmers and Craig, the security guard whom Ernest soon nicknamed Mall Cop (my First Nation friends gave everyone a nickname), came down the long walkway from their quarters in the pouring rain. They served us each with a soggy pile of papers—an application for an injunction to the Supreme Court of British Columbia that accused us of trespass, nuisance, intimidation, conspiracy and having caused Mowi loss and damage. The copies of the application were missing every other page, and they got most of our names wrong. But not mine.

That night I took my camera and went to observe the effect of the high-powered underwater lights on the fish, both farm and wild. Using bright lights to commercially fish for herring was prohibited in the early 1980s, because the lights worked too well. Massive schools of herring were drawn to them, along with octopus, young salmon, halibut, cod—everything in the sea. The fish farmers claimed the Atlantic salmon were so domesticated they wouldn't eat herring, but the Atlantic farm salmon I've autopsied have dozens of needle-sharp, inward-curving teeth, the perfect equipment for catching herring. If such well-developed teeth were not benefiting farm salmon, the intensive industry breeding programs should have stunted these teeth, as the fish also used them to attack and cause damage to each other. Not good for business.

Each pen was lit by four submerged lights. During the day the Atlantic salmon swam in one big circle, but at night they moved in four circles, one around each light. The salmon formed the deepest layer of fish. Above them were herring. The herring didn't circle, but they couldn't stay away from the lights and streaked over them. They flowed like a river, passing over the lights, then turned and swam back through the trailing edge of their school, tying knots that unravelled, unwound, coiled and straightened as the fish sought to stay in the light and avoid the salmon. Above the herring, only a few centimetres below the surface, swam tiny stickleback. They move like hummingbirds, darting forward fluttering their pectoral fins and then suddenly coming to a complete stop and hovering. Each about the size of a triple-A battery, they swam in schools of a few dozen.

Ernest had caught a ride back to the Swanson camp with some RCMP officers who had dropped in to check on us, so that night, as the storm worsened, it was Sherry, Julia, Karissa and me. With each gust the tent flattened on our faces only to pop up as the poles snapped back into place. I couldn't sleep and so I read the rain-soaked injunction application with my headlamp, one hand holding up the tent. I learned more about the stock transfer that was under way. Mowi explained in the document that once the hatchery staff in Sayward triggered "smoltification"—the process by which all salmon switch from the freshwater where they are born to saltwater—the fish had to go into saltwater in about a week. If they missed that window, the document said, the fish would never be able to enter saltwater. (Mother Nature is all about timing, and apparently the industry had not yet bred this internal clock out of farm salmon.) The *Viktoria Viking* could carry approximately 180,000 fish per trip. The injunction application said that over the course of the journey from the hatchery to the farm, saltwater was gradually introduced into the tanks in the boat "until all of the fresh water is replaced with saltwater." This meant that water from the hatchery, along with whatever pathogens were in it, was being released into the ocean as the vessel travelled along the coast.

I lay back and thought for a moment. This had to be why Norwegian scientists had reported that smolt transport vessels were one of the most efficient disease vectors in the Norwegian salmon farming industry. When I sued the minister of fisheries, Mowi had provided the Federal Court with documents reporting that all but one of their hatcheries was infected with piscine orthoreovirus. This meant that, as it travelled through Johnstone Strait and Blackfish Sound, the *Viktoria Viking* was leaving a trail of highly contagious virus particles behind it.

I cannot fathom the reckless self-interest at work here. How did Mowi justify its release of an infectious foreign virus into some of the most productive ocean waters left on our planet? As a society, we casually toss around the term *going viral* while passively allowing dangerous viruses to do just that. Is it worse if the companies were doing this intentionally or if they just didn't care? The company's intentions don't matter when it comes to the fate of the wild fish, but they would matter in a court of law, where intention is everything. I hope that one day this industry will have to face a reckoning with the First Nations and all Canadians for the damage they have done.

The injunction application stated that young farm salmon could safely spend five to seven days in the boat, and that Mowi was chartering the *Viktoria Viking* for $25,000 per day. The company also said that if the fish were not pumped out of the boat after a week, they would be turned into the gardening soil product called Sea Soil.

We four women lay in the tent with the aluminum grating imprinting into our backs. "What should we do now?" I asked.

Julia replied over the shriek of the wind: "Tomorrow we should shoot our exercise video. Aerobics while occupying a salmon farm." I had to smile. These women had no bandwidth for showing fear. They may have felt it, but they were not going to voice it. And if they weren't, I wasn't going to either.

Three hours later a bright light filled the tent, waking us instantly. We could hear the industrial racket of a smolt packer approaching the farm. Since we were all sleeping fully dressed against the cold, we piled out of the tent like zombies and walked to where the boat had docked. Craig was there, as well as the farm workers. Julia went first down the narrow outer walkway, followed by Karissa, Sherry and me. Julia stopped beside where they were lowering the pipe, prepping for an injection of PRV-infected farm salmon into the waters of Knight Inlet. An angry First Nation man who was crew on the packer started yelling at us and was hustled below decks by other crew. The RCMP appeared out of the dark in their Zodiacs, from wherever they had spent the night. Had our national police force become an armed escort service for Mowi?

As RCMP officers moved in to crowd Julia away from the pipe, one of them leaned close to her and said, "Sometimes the older people get the younger ones to do their dirty work." Her jaw set in pure stubbornness. As if anyone could tell this woman what to do. I had a moment where I wondered how many times her parents had faced this look. Julia and Karissa are both the same age as my equally fierce daughter; I knew the look. I was struck to the core by their grace under fire. Karissa would later say she wanted to throat-punch the guy who was muscling Julia, but in the moment she honoured her ancestors and did not bring shame to the nations with any type of violence. She and Julia stood their ground, remaining silent while I filmed the scene with my phone. As the fish fell into the pen, tears slipped down Sherry's beautiful face.

Later, in the media, we would be accused of risking Mowi's investment in the farm smolts by delaying the transfer out of the boat that
night, but that is not what happened. If we delayed the unloading process at all, it was only because the boat crew waited to start unloading
until the RCMP had surrounded the pipe. We had no means to delay
them. We were there as witnesses, and we only watched as hundreds of
dead Atlantic salmon shot out of the pipe, their sides and bellies flashing
in the floodlights mounted on the ship's mast. Everyone saw them: the
crew, the farmers, the police. I caught the eye of one of the officers and
thought at him, *Now you see what this is about.*

No one moved to stop me as I lowered the underwater camera on a
pole and pointed it towards the dying fish that were spewing out of the
pipe and spiralling downwards. The camera recorded thousands of scales
being knocked off them as they tumbled.

Later that morning, Ian Roberts of Mowi put out a press release,
which he forwarded to Chief Willie Moon in an email that read,
"As there were protestors on site at the time, likely with their own version of events, I thought it best to provide you with the facts directly."

Here are excerpts of that press release:

> Marine Harvest Canada is reporting elevated mortality during
> its salmon smolt delivery this morning at its Port Elizabeth farm.
> Delayed delivery and possible mechanical problems with the
> delivery vessel are thought to be likely the cause . . . .

> The company has had to adjust its delivery schedule to daylight
> hours to address safety issues concerning activists protesting at
> the delivery site, which has resulted in fish being held for up to
> 10 additional hours within the delivery vessel. Another hour was
> delayed this morning within the delivery vessel. Another hour
> was delayed this morning when protesters attempted to block
> the delivery.

"These delays have caused additional stress to the fish, which may have added to the mortality this morning," says [Production Director Dougie] Hunter. "We will now return back to our normal delivery routine which is best for the fish." Estimates by site staff indicate less than 5000 fish (weighing 150 grams) died from the 180,000 fish delivered.

"We are aware that some protesters witnessed the delivery this morning and may suggest the fish died from disease, but we know this isn't the case," Hunter says. "The fish delivered were in good shape leaving the hatchery, but unfortunately some looked in poor condition when unloaded this morning. Our staff are very upset that this has occurred."

They were blaming us for the dead fish. I don't know why they said they were delivering in daylight hours. It was pitch-black and pouring rain when they had started.

When the vessel left, we decided to leave as well. We faced arrest if Mowi's injunction application was successful. As we were gathering our things, the RCMP officers came to talk to us. They told us that they knew we posed no threat of violence, that they knew we were trying to save the life of this coast and that they did not need to be here. They said they were not coming back. They were telling the truth: we never saw anyone else from the RCMP over the next two hundred or more days of the occupation. Though Mowi went on to hire a private security firm, at least the taxpayers were not footing that bill. I went back to the Swanson camp to pick up my dog, who had spent the time frolicking with her new best friend, Lucy. I got in my boat and headed home to deal with washing and drying a mountain of soaked clothes and blankets.

Two days later, on October 19, I took the first ferry to Vancouver Island, then drove the hour and a half from Port McNeill to the dock in Sayward. There, Mowi was loading more smolts destined for the Port Elizabeth farm into a packer called the *Orca Chief*. A long translucent orange hose ran from the boat, across the wharf, to the road. A truck with two large tanks came down the road and backed up to where the hose end lay. Staff waiting on the dock buckled the large hose to an outlet on one of the tanks, and water and fish started to pour from the truck into the ship. I went to the edge of the wharf to watch the fish pour into the boat. As I stood there, Carla Voyager, my sister from one of the Musgamagw families that had adopted me, and Chief George Quocksister Jr. arrived from the south. They witnessed it all with me, as I filmed. Many of the young Atlantic salmon were dead, floating upside down in the vessel's open holding tank; they were dying before they reached the farm. Filmmaker April Bencze, who was volunteering all her time to the occupation, later helped me put together a short video on how farm salmon migrate from the hatchery via trucks, hoses and ships, with many dead on arrival. After we released the video, Mowi stopped making a fuss about protesters being the cause of death of the fish being transferred into the Port Elizabeth farm.

As I watched Mowi continue with business as usual, I clung to the knowledge that leadership of three Broughton nations were at the table with the province. All we had to do was *keep the pressure up*.

I went back to photograph the smolt loading for four consecutive days. In the transfers that occurred at low tide, the young fish were dropped a distance of fifteen feet as the pipe hung straight down from the dock to the deck of the ship. The pipe then bent ninety degrees and ran towards the hold, where the fish were flushed into a tank of water. The salmon tried to avoid that fall by swimming back up the pipe.

On December 6, Tavish Campbell set up a camera underwater in front of the effluent pipe from the farm salmon processing plant in Tofino and live-streamed the images of farm fish blood water pouring directly into the waters of Clayoquot Sound. The environmental group Pacific Wild hosted the live feed and patched me in to speak about the test results from the blood samples that Tavish had collected, along with a few of the young rockfish feeding on effluent. All the samples, both the blood and the wild fish feeding on the effluent, were PRV-positive.

Tavish also filmed the blood water from the Brown's Bay Packing plant north of Campbell River and sent me samples. It was also heavily infected with the infective "live" PRV.

Over a million people viewed a short video Tavish made from this footage, sparking a wave of outrage and disgust at the news that farm fish viruses were pouring into British Columbia's largest wild salmon migration route. Tavish's work added significant pressure to the already besieged BC government. The Brown's Bay plant eventually admitted that while it could add chlorine to kill pathogens, it only used chlorine when the companies told the plant that they are sending diseased fish for processing; it's illegal to release chlorine into the ocean. (The province has not yet ordered the Brown's Bay Packing plant to cease pouring Atlantic farm salmon blood into the Fraser River sockeye migration route.)

On November 24, the Heiltsuk Nation in Bella Bella on the central coast of British Columbia, north of the Broughton, issued a press release announcing that they were on their way to Alert Bay to support the occupation. "The days of industry running amok in First Nations homelands are over," said Chief Councillor Marilyn Slett. "Our nations have both a right—and a responsibility—to exert control when atrocities like fish farms are decimating the wild salmon." In the release they also announced termination of a stewardship protocol agreement with Mowi over the company's Ocean Falls hatchery, saying, "Marine Harvest's business can no longer be condoned by Heiltsuk."

Representatives of four northern nations—Haida, Gitxsan, Wet'suwet'en, Heiltsuk—soon arrived from the north, no small journey in winter. All of us were buoyed by their presence. As they stepped onto the farms, these greatly admired leaders, including the Haida political activist and carver Guujaaw and Chief Namoks of the Wet'suwet'en, raised their fists and the image streaked across Facebook, Instagram and Twitter. They said that the farms felt as dead as the tar sands. Members of other nations, still locked into contracts with the salmon farming industry, saw these images and "liked" them. Arguments erupted in the comments below, but the support outweighed the hostility. Government and industry observed silently.

One of the northerners provided us with timely food for thought. "Yes, we won at Lelu Island," she said. That was where they had stopped the development of a port to ship LNG (liquefied natural gas) abroad that would have killed the large salmon runs of the Skeena River. "But relationships were destroyed that could take a decade to heal."

I knew what she was talking about. An ill wind had infiltrated the camps, accusations seeping among us like noxious gas as the community of people involved grew, ebbed and changed. Money started it. Donations were flowing into the GoFundMe campaign. I provided a full accounting of how it was spent, but that did not clear the air. Anger, heated by exhaustion and stress, threatened to slice us apart.

The directive not to bring shame to the nation was not heard by everyone. A contingent of people moved in a different direction. They jumped into the pens and provided us with stunning footage of what looked like the advanced stages of mouthrot in farm fish. But doing this between court hearings on one of the injunction applications played into the hand of the companies. Cermaq won the right to exclude people from the ocean around their farms, an alarming precedent in Canada.

I was asked to attend a meeting where I was told that I was the problem because I was too independent—a familiar theme. But I hadn't been expecting such a charge here, where we were all the David against several Goliaths. If we didn't stick together, there was no hope of protecting the wild salmon we were fighting for.

I write about this to warn others. Front lines are highly unstable. Maybe it's just the stress that causes the divisions. As we humans strive to change things, sometimes we forget whom we're fighting. Leaderless uprisings are powerfully resilient, but perhaps humans are not built to exist without hierarchy for long and seek to dominate each other and restore a pecking order. Or was something else at work?

Three years earlier, on September 9, 2015, I had been asked to join a fish farm occupation in Ahousaht territory, Clayoquot Sound, on the southwestern coast of Vancouver Island. A group of warriors led by the soft-spoken Lennie John sent home the fish farm workers who were anchoring a new salmon farm in a bay called Yaakswiis. He and the warriors took over the site, set up tents on the partially anchored farm and tied a small cabin cruiser to the structure so there was a place to cook. When I arrived, ready to cook, clean and learn, I found an extremely volatile situation. Then it turned out that the most vocal member of our group—the angriest, the most verbally abusive towards the RCMP who visited—was working for Cermaq. After this came out, the man left. But the occupiers, most of them Ahousaht, still had to deal with the fact that their leadership had a signed contract that bound them to Cermaq, stating that the leadership had to side with the company in the event of conflict.

I was there with Joe James Crow and his partner, Sacheen Seitcham, and two others, Anushka Azadi and Wyman Stanlick; their bravery under Lennie's calm leadership made a deep impression on me. Harsh words were spoken between community members who gathered in the village. Ahousaht is much bigger than the villages in the Broughton, with a thousand members moved by strong undercurrents I could feel but did not understand. In the end the occupation was handled in a remarkable way. In a ceremony, a chief took control of the farm and asked the occupiers to leave. Obeying their chief, they did. The chief then negotiated with Cermaq, which agreed to remove the farm from the bay. We piled into Lennie's boat before dawn and watched as the tugboat came and took the farm away. Joe James's deeply stern face changed as I witnessed the first and only smile I ever saw him give, and Sacheen, never without her red lipstick, cried into the wind and rain. As Lennie watched, he said in his deep, calm voice, "Look what a handful of warriors did. Imagine what a nation could do." Unfortunately the company only moved the farm to another site nearby. Still, a victory is a victory.

As a result of that experience, I knew there was a very real possibility that people working for the industry had infiltrated our much bigger occupation in the Broughton. I suspected the companies were concerned that the occupation could turn violent and wanted a heads-up on what was being planned. But I began to wonder what might be spurring some members of the group to repeatedly suggest radical actions that fell well outside our instructions from the hereditary leaders.

Thankfully those ideas never took root. But discontent flared, maybe as a natural by-product of sustained anxiety or perhaps manufactured to destroy the uprising. Either way it hurt people. Key people left and never came back. I was accused of stealing and lying. I couldn't sleep. I felt detached from my life, with no support to be found. Some whispered that witchcraft was involved, after a symbol was found on the building at the Swanson camp. This was frightening in the dark days of the winter storms.

In my experience, when non-indigenous people form front-line coalitions with First Nations, two things happen. One, the Indigenous people have deep bonds going back thousands of years; the heady action on the front lines releases a tightly coiled spring of hurt and hate caused by racism, and gives rise to a Red Power stance that swells into rejection of all that is not Indigenous. And two, the non-indigenous people striving to enter into a strong relationship with their Indigenous partners during such an explosive moment enter into a contest of sorts. To be accepted, others must be rejected. I don't fully understand this dynamic, but I have seen it several times. This contest plays out entirely among the non-indigenous, and it was this dynamic that threw me to the side. I was not to be trusted, I was told. Now there were two battle lines—one between us, and one between us and the companies. It broke *us* into two. This was catastrophic. The clarity of the mission, the love and co-operation, the energy—all shattered.

I don't like contests. I generally step aside and try to let them go on without me, for better or worse. But I felt I had to try to stop this devolution before the emotions undid all our progress. I put together a slide show of the powerful images captured by the Sea Shepherd's photographer, Simon Ager, and by Tamo Campos, along with some of my own. I added music and posted it on Facebook. I wanted to hold up a mirror to all of us on the front lines, showing us that we were brave, beautiful, powerful and relentless, and winning a future for our children, the fish and the whales.

If only one farm site had been occupied, this phase of discord would have been the end of the salmon farm occupation in the Broughton. It would have stranded the chiefs at the table with government by removing the source of the urgency for the province to act. Tabatha Milian, who'd arrived with the Tiny House Warriors in the summer and stayed at the Swanson camp, helped keep the effort alive. She kept the Swanson camp clean and functional and demanded a certain standard among those who passed through. She embodied the female capacity to be immovable, yet to hold that ground quietly. She re-established stability. And so we managed to regroup and the movement survived; the pressure on government was maintained. But as the northerners had warned, the wounds remained and I lost people I loved.

I share this part of the story, with many names and specifics removed so I don't cause more hurt, in order to pass on what we learned. It can feel like everything is falling apart, but if the thread, no matter how thin, is unbroken, it doesn't matter in the end that you came close to collapse, only that you kept going. Humbled and sad, I went home for a few days in December and once again dried out the collection of soggy blankets and clothing that had accumulated in my boat. I had a hot shower in town (I lived without running water) and wrote in my journal, "I'm okay." Then I went back to the fight.

On December 13, 2017, I published the paper with my colleagues on the spread of piscine orthoreovirus along the coast of British Columbia. It reported that 95 percent of farm salmon sold in markets are infected and 45 percent of wild salmon heavily exposed to salmon farms in Broughton and the Discovery Islands are infected. But in the northernmost reaches of the province, as far away as a salmon in BC can get from the farms, only 5 percent are infected. We also found that the rate of PRV infection was 50 percent higher in salmon in the lower Fraser River than in the river's upper reaches, which raised the concern that infected fish might not make it upriver through the strong rapids at Hell's Gate. We framed these findings as a warning that the salmon farming industry appeared to be spreading the virus and that more research was urgently needed to measure this threat to wild salmon. Even finding PRV in just 5 percent of salmon in the northern reaches of the province was concerning, as the virus appears to be from Norway.

One of the most worrisome things about this ongoing research effort was the data we were gathering on the ISA virus. Although we were unable to confirm that ISAV was present in British Columbia—as per the government's definition of "confirmation," which would have required access to the fish in the farms—the ongoing detection of ISA virus fragments by world-standard test methods revealed the same pattern of infection as PRV: it was significantly more common in wild salmon that were near salmon farms. When we had published the ISA virus technical data on exactly what the tests were detecting in *Virology Journal* in 2016, Dr. Marty and Nelle Gagne of Canada's reference lab for fish had failed to convince the journal to retract it. The science was solid.

Despite this, no scientific journal would allow us to build on that paper to report on where we detected these virus fragments. This ran counter to scientific discovery. Published scientific papers are like bricks. You build with them, slowly adding pieces. ISAV is much more fragile than PRV and so we only found segments of it, but the tests were consistent; whatever it was, it kept appearing and there was a relationship between where we found fish that tested positive and the salmon farms. However, journal after journal refused to review the paper as long as we included the ISAV results, because we had only detected the virus, not "confirmed" it. To have our new paper accepted for publication, we'd had to remove the ISAV results, leaving only the PRV results.

This is one of the dangers in a world so heavily under the influence of international trade. ISAV is a reportable virus; countries in which it appears have to report it, and countries that don't want it can, without fearing trade repercussions, reject product from contaminated regions. This in turn means companies can be financially impacted by detection of this virus. So, to protect them, rules were put into place as to exactly what constitutes a "positive" result confirming presence of such a virus. In the case of ISAV, these rules have not kept pace with the development of powerful new scientific tools that detect minute levels of virus fragments at the molecular level, which is what we need to do to prevent outbreaks. We have to believe the science.

PCR virus tests use a precise clip of genetic code and look for just that sequence, like the child's toy where a star, square, circle or triangle shapes are matched to precisely cut holes. The lab I was using went a step further and sequenced the fragments they detected so we could see that the pieces we had found matched ISA virus sequences identified in Norway (HPR5) and Chile (HPR7b). The test required to confirm a reportable virus was a clumsy, old technology that required massive amounts of live virus to produce a positive. The only place to find that level of virus is in farm pens where there are no predators, but we were not allowed to go there. So the repeated molecular test results were simply ignored.

The fish farmers had reacted badly to the first paper; clearly, they were sensitive to the dangerous optics of being seen as spreading a Norwegian virus. The BC Salmon Farmers Association said our data did not support our conclusions, ignoring the fact that the paper had passed scientific peer review for a journal that specialized in viruses.

The day after publishing the PRV paper, on December 14, I was in court in Vancouver facing new Mowi trespass charges that I had picked up when I occupied the Port Elizabeth salmon farm. Molina and Ernest were present to see what would happen; they faced similar charges. Greg McDade raised the point that since the federal government only has jurisdiction over the water, and the provincial government over the seafloor, no one had the power to enforce an injunction against the people on the farms. We did not win, but it was a moot point, because I was no longer on the farm.

Then Mowi also won their injunction against the Midsummer Island occupation. The cabins on the farm were slid onto skiffs and moved to a nearby beach, and Mowi finished restocking the farm. The biggest fish farming corporation in the world, publicly traded on the Oslo exchange, was unable to adapt to a future that was glaringly obvious. Being bullies had always worked for them. They did not or could not accurately assess what it meant when Ernest kept repeating in his video posts, *Marine Harvest, you have a problem.*

In an extraordinary gesture, a group of remarkable people came up from Salt Spring Island to run the Swanson camp so the regulars could go home for Christmas. I went to see my children and my two-year-old grandson. I felt my tension ease a little every day as I baked cookies, helped decorate the tree and built a snowman. But my mind couldn't let go and it kept processing away in the background. When Mowi sought an injunction against the last camp, the one at Swanson, would they actually restock that farm? And would the internal talks between the province and the chiefs be far enough along at that point that the occupation would no longer be needed?

My New Year's resolution was to remember, *I am a person.* I was changing. Year after year of believing I was just about to crest this mountain of opposition had kept me giving 110 percent for far too long. Exhaustion was creeping up through the floorboards of my soul. I'd kept thinking that I could take care of me later, figure out how to make some money so I could build some savings, even go back to studying communication in whales and be that grandmother who is greeted with small, messy hugs.

I recall Jane Goodall thanking her parents for giving her a body that was full of energy. I had my parents to thank for that same gift. When the young and brilliant activists I had the pleasure of getting to know came to visit, I mostly learned from them, but I also counselled them to take care of themselves or they would be useless to the fight for our planet. Clearly I was not taking my own advice. I needed to stop every now and then to play my guitar and savour the pleasure of the music. I needed to tend my garden, which had become a neighbourhood U-pick because I was so rarely home at harvest time. I needed to get into my speedboat now and again to go out to simply watch the animals—whales, eagles, bears.

I see that the term *forest bathing* is now used to encourage people to walk in the woods and let the breath of the trees permeate you. This is important. At every opportunity humans need to feel the power, order, beauty and greater life force of the natural world, to remember that our survival depends on us fitting into it, to remember that when we fight for nature, we are on the big team. It was essential that I get out again into the wild so that I could keep my compass true, to avoid becoming used up, bitter, hardened and weak. My first commitment to myself was to get running water in the place that I had built with friends overlooking the archipelago. Four years of carrying buckets needed to end with a hot bath.

On January 21, 2018, members of the Kwagiulth First Nation asked me to come with them to serve eviction notices to two Mowi farms just north of the Broughton off Port Hardy. This was a significant development because, like the Ahousaht with Cermaq, this nation was bound to Mowi by contract. Donna and Bill Mackay, ever generous with the *Naiad Explorer*, offered to transport us, given that you rarely knew what sea state you might face up off Port Hardy, an area much more exposed to the wind than the Broughton is. As we were pulling into the dock at Port Hardy to pick people up, a white van parked at the top of the boat ramp rolled down its window and a long lens appeared. This was surveillance, by whom I didn't know, but I waved and smiled.

The chiefs who had travelled here on the *Naiad*—Ernest Alfred, Arthur Dick and others—were met by Kelly Robertson; his father Billy Bird (Wit'satle'su); Tony Roberts Jr., the councillor in charge of fisheries from the Wei Wai Kum in Campbell River; David Knox, hereditary chief of the Kwagiulth; and James Wadhams, known as Digity. The leaders from the Mamalilikulla, Dzawada'enuxw, We Wai Kai, Tlowitsis and Kwagiulth Nations formed a knot and began a heated exchange. I stepped back. This was not my business. The regalia on the men glowed against the shades of grey rain as the fine drizzle fell over them. Then suddenly they were done discussing. They had made the decision to head out and serve the eviction notices.

As the *Naiad* approached the first farm, just outside Port Hardy, a small, battered speedboat came alongside us. David Knox, Ernest and Digity climbed into it, along with filmmaker Alex Harris, whom I had invited to come along in order to capture this historic moment for these men. Ernest and David sat on the bow of the boat, tension etched in their faces, as it idled towards the farm. Then Ernest began to sing, his clear voice drowning out the sound of the outboard engine. Digity held the paper eviction notice and David held the carved wooden talking stick with an orca on it. When they got to the farm, a worker accepted the eviction notice, which read in part, "We the traditional chiefs and respected elders of the Kwakiutl have written this letter to inform you that all agreements with Marine Harvest have been cancelled due to the great concern of our traditional territorial lands and waters and the impact that your industry has had."

As the men came back to the *Naiad*, Digity was smiling broadly. Back on board he said, "I'm as happy as a sockeye leaping out of the water."

On our way back to Port Hardy, an A-clan resident orca pod appeared alongside us. Resident orca in January are not a common sight on this coast. Bill Mackay cut his engines and the chiefs began singing to the whales, their deep voices calling out in a simple rhythm. As we floated on the grey sea, ruffled with small whitecapping waves, an adult female and a young whale swam under the boat and surfaced right beside us, salting us humans with their explosive blows. The biologist in me has given up trying to account for the way whales show up at significant moments, but I recognized that these whales and these people have known each other for ten thousand years.

In the end the Kwagiulth Nation as a whole was not ready to remove the salmon farms from their territory, and so this mission was merely symbolic. But there were witnesses: the Mowi workers, these leaders and these whales.

On January 30, 2018, Premier Horgan and his cabinet met with the Broughton nations' leadership in more formal, still private but highly publicized government-to-government talks in Vancouver. The salmon farm tenures were due to expire in five months; I held my breath to hear what they would announce.

Stories trickled out. We heard that the province had arrived with an offer that the First Nations flatly rejected. The politicians asked for a moment to meet on their own, a request the leaders granted. When they returned to the table, the governments released a joint communiqué with the participating nations stating that "all Parties confirming a willingness to engage in a consent-based process consistent with the United Nations of Declaration on the Rights of Indigenous Peoples with respect to wild salmon and existing open-pen aquaculture operations in the Broughton Area."

For those of us who had been keeping the pressure up, this was a huge disappointment. It had been three months since Horgan had come to the Big House in Alert Bay. Closed-door meetings between the Broughton nations and the province had been under way since then. I am sure that everyone thought the occupation would not last through the winter months, and perhaps the province hoped that when the occupation ended, it could quietly renew all the tenures. Both Chief Robert Chamberlin and 'Namgis Councillor Kelly Speck were involved in the talks, and they were a force to be reckoned with. Robert had years under his belt working with government to literally rebuild his village, Gwayasdums, including new houses, a water system and a Big House; Kelly had worked in the provincial government as a senior bureaucrat. Nothing got past those two. There had to be some sign of hope in this, but it was not the end point we, on the outside, longed for.

In the end the Dzawada'enuxw abandoned the talks because they were asked to keep the discussions confidential, which went against the grain of their community tradition of making decisions together in open dialogue. Instead, they sued the federal and provincial governments for granting permission for the salmon farms to be in their territories in the first place. This meant three very different processes were now in play, aligned in the attempt to save wild salmon in the Broughton: occupation, government-to-government talks and two lawsuits.

Prime Minister Justin Trudeau held a town hall meeting in Nanaimo in early February, which I live-streamed at home. I spotted Ernest and Karissa sitting in the front row in their regalia; it made me smile to see these two warriors sharing the screen with the prime minister of Canada. Ernest had a question about the salmon farms ready, but I suspect Trudeau had been briefed about who was who. As this spectacular young chief sat a couple of metres away from him with his hand up, Trudeau never so much as looked at him. Instead, the prime minister pointed over Ernest's head to call on another man. I couldn't believe my ears, when this man asked, "Prime Minister, are you going to stop allowing farm salmon infected with piscine reovirus in fish farms on this coast?" I didn't even know this person. I was so pleased that it was a stranger asking the question.

When Trudeau promised to do a review of whether PRV was a threat to wild salmon, I slumped in my chair. This would be, by my count, the seventh government review of the impact of salmon farms. All the previous reviews called for innovative change, such as moving the farms off wild salmon migration routes, reducing sea lice in the farms and moving the industry into closed tanks on land. But every one of these reports had been shelved. I didn't expect any better outcome from the review Trudeau promised, and I would learn later that I was right.

On February 12, the occupiers at Swanson reported increased activity at the farm that made it clear that Mowi was planning to restock even this site. China hats, as the blue plastic objects placed in the bottom of the pens to suck up dead fish from the bottom are called, had been dropped off on the empty site and the number of staff increased. At the same time, 'Namgis leadership were working to file an injunction against restocking this farm. It was a race.

At this moment the first sperm whale to visit 'Namgis territory in thirty years appeared. As someone who intended to spend her life working to understand non-human intelligence, I had always wanted to meet a sperm whale. A human's brain weighs about 1,350 grams; a sperm whale's brain is 9,000 grams. What are they thinking? What are they *capable* of thinking?

OrcaLab, run by Paul Spong and Helena Symonds, maintains a network of hydrophones that broadcast underwater sounds on orca-live. net, but also over VHF radio. They picked up Yukusam, as the 'Namgis named this exalted visitor to their territory, on their Johnstone Strait hydrophone. I never saw him, but I listened to his phenomenally loud clicks day and night. Yukusam stayed in the area from February 11 until March 18, when he was spotted a few times south of here and then vanished out to sea.

Perhaps our biggest ally in the supreme effort to pull salmon farms out of wild salmon habitat came from Washington State. Following the massive escape of 250,000 farm salmon in August 2017, the US Indigenous fishermen had been outraged to catch thousands of Atlantic salmon in their rivers. They and many Americans in the region demanded an end to Atlantic salmon farming. I teamed up with the US-based Wild Fish Conservancy, which was collecting many of the escaped Atlantics, to collaborate on testing them. All the fish turned out to be infected with a variation of PRV that I had only seen once before, in a salmon fillet labelled "Icelandic" sold by Whole Foods Market in West Vancouver. When Wild Fish Conservancy raised this with the Washington Department of Fish and Wildlife, the agency reported that Cooke

Aquaculture was indeed importing its eggs from Iceland. The agency followed up and confirmed the Atlantic salmon in the Cooke farms were infected with the same virus as the hatchery in Iceland.

On March 2, 2018, a Washington State vote on whether or not to phase out Atlantic salmon farming altogether was scheduled to be live-streamed from the state legislature. It had been slated for early in the day, but the bill disappeared from the roster. When it reappeared hours later, it had twenty-five amendments attached to it like sea lice. Every one of them would have to be voted on individually and defeated before the final vote on the bill. As the five o'clock end of session loomed, the sponsors of the bill got permission for the sitting to run long.

These amendments were meaningless items, such as one calling for a study of how to make fish farming less of a threat to orca. That was a nice sentiment, but what the orca needed was more wild salmon, and what the wild salmon needed was less farm disease. Then a dishevelled state senator came running in, papers gripped in his fist, insisting that the whole bill was in violation of something called "Rule 25."

The audio feed went off. I watched people wander the floor while the possible rule violation was considered. Suddenly everyone was back in their seats: there was no violation.

The voting on each amendment droned on. Every one was defeated, so the bill did not have to be delayed in order to be rewritten. Then the bill passed, with sixteen out of thirty votes in favour and one abstention. Farming Atlantic salmon would be prohibited in Washington State when the last licence expired in 2025. My phone started to ring, beep and ding as people got in touch to share the news. I hadn't been sure if salmon farming could ever be legislated into retreat. Now, thanks to the people of Washington State, we knew it was possible.

On March 7, Mowi sent its security guard, Craig, and another employee to serve Ernest Alfred with legal papers at the cabin on Swanson Island. Karissa went down the ramp to the dock to tell them that Ernest had left the day before to drive his mother down-island to an eye surgeon, but the two men seemed convinced that Ernest was hiding in the camp. Ignoring the fact that another occupier was filming them with a phone, they put their shoulders against Karissa and tried to force their way past her. An athlete, she braced herself and resisted.

"I am a licensed security guard and you need to move," said Craig, inches from her face.

"You are not a security guard of this place," she replied calmly.

"We don't need your permission to go up."

"Yeah you do. This is my territory."

When he saw the footage, uploaded within minutes to Facebook, Ernest was furious. He called Mowi and told them to stop assaulting young women. With an unparalleled flair for the dramatic, he said he would meet them at high noon in the town square in Alert Bay in two days.

At the appointed time, nine nations from territories from Campbell River to Bella Bella stood drumming in the square. The influential young Chief Wah was present as well as a contingent of Matriarchs, as the company served Ernest yet another injunction notice.

On that same day, representatives of the federal minister of fisheries contacted my lawyers at Ecojustice to reaffirm that the ministry would not screen farm salmon for PRV, despite the Federal Court case we'd already won against him, and the second lawsuit I'd filed on October 12, 2016, which was working its way through the courts. Cermaq and Mowi had once again been granted status as co-defendants with the minister of fisheries, because, as they argued, the industry would be "severely impacted" if they were prohibited from transferring PRV-infected fish into their pens. Now, Cermaq contacted Ecojustice to demand my personal financial records for the past three years as part of the discovery process.

The promise of progress kept eroding. On a call with the provincial Ministry of Environment about my test results that showed high levels of PRV in the blood water shooting out of the pipe from the Brown's Bay farm salmon processing plant, the ministry confirmed it was not going to do anything about the pathogens being released, not even the human gastrointestinal bacteria, *Enterococcus*. Tests done by the province had found levels of this bacteria so high that they were off the charts. My brief review of the scientific literature revealed that the salmon farming industry was experimenting with feeding *Enterococcus* to farm salmon to produce a probiotic effect that apparently increases growth and resistance to sea lice. Was that why the levels of the bacteria in the blood water were so high? Apparently no one in the BC government cared that this pipe released its bacterial load into a bay that featured a recreational beach. Three decades of investigating salmon farming and there was still something new and appalling to be uncovered.

I asked the Ministry of Environment what strain of *Enterococcus* they'd found and whether it was antibiotic resistant. Were the farmers actually feeding it to farm fish in BC? What about all the people eating raw farm salmon sushi? The ministry responded that, because it was a human health concern, the bacteria was the responsibility of the Vancouver Island Health Authority. When I inquired with that body, they in turn said they didn't know if anyone was testing the waters in Brown's Bay for the bacteria. If they were the health authority, shouldn't *they* be doing the testing?

On March 9, the 'Namgis filed their injunction to stop Mowi from restocking the Swanson farm, based on the threat represented by the company's introduction of fish into their traditional waters without screening for piscine orthoreovirus. On March 23, the injunction was denied by Justice Michael Manson of the Federal Court of Appeal. Curiously, Justice Manson ruled against the injunction because he said that Mowi had not been given enough time to find an alternative site, but he stated in his decision that infected farm salmon posed a threat of irreparable harm to wild salmon. The fact that Mowi couldn't have helped but be aware for the *past seven months* that the 'Namgis did not want this farm restocked was outside the scope of the court. This was a blow, but the 'Namgis had also filed a suit parallel to mine to stop the minister of fisheries from issuing permits for farm salmon transfers into their territory without screening for PRV. When the court decided to hear the cases together, our lawyers joined forces.

The eagles were just starting to show up around Blackfish Sound to fish for the herring that move onto the coast to spawn every spring. I was interested in studying whether herring caught by eagles were more frequently infected with PRV than the herring that did not get caught. Does PRV slow the herring down, making them more susceptible to predation? To do this I needed to take samples at the same time from both the herring in the sea and the herring caught by the eagles.

Catching herring in the ocean was easy. I just had to wait for the diving birds—auklets, loons and murres—to chase the herring until the fish rushed together and formed a tight ball, every fish in the ball writhing to hide deep inside the mass of fish where the birds couldn't reach them. It was easy to drift up to the school in my boat and dip a few out with a small hand net.

The ones caught by eagles were another matter. Eagles work hard for their catch, swooping out of the air, stretching their short legs to snatch the slippery fish out of the water with their talons, but they frequently drop them as they land in trees. Once a herring was dropped, it was gone, because the eagles couldn't manoeuvre their two-metre wingspan between the trees to retrieve it. As I kept an eye on the eagles, I felt tremendous sadness for them. There were not enough fish to go around. In my first years in the area, I saw clouds of gulls and eagles pulling herring out of the water for hours. Now there were brief moments when thirty or so gulls clustered on the water trying to reach the herring as the eagles swooped overhead, rarely making contact with the water to grab a fish. The birds were going hungry. I thought about the tons of herring in and around the salmon farms. Cermaq could have lowered its nets and let the herring out of the Sir Edmund farm, but they didn't.

Recent research suggested that elder herring may lead the way to the spawning and feeding grounds, and that the presence of such elders may be critical to herring populations, because they hold the memory of when and where to migrate. Scientists think that a lack of old fish who know the way may be one reason that the North Atlantic cod have not recolonized their traditional spawning grounds, even as their numbers are slowly rebounding from the overfishing that DFO carelessly permitted in the early 1990s. Killing off the elders—the biggest of the fish—interrupts the transmission of essential information between generations. What happened to the herring clustered outside salmon farms when the farms stood empty between harvest and restocking and pellets of food were no longer being sprayed into the water? Did they know where to go to feed?

There were ten of us present on March 26, 2018, when Mowi began restocking the farm at Swanson Island. Tsatsaqualis, a Matriarch and Elder, along with Karissa Glendale and Sii-am Hamilton, a young Indigenous activist who'd been part of the Midsummer occupation, set out in a small inflatable boat towards the approaching smolt packer, *Orca Chief*. Maia Beauvais, a kayak guide from Salt Spring who had spent quite a lot of time at the camp that winter, was at the helm. I followed in my boat. The three Indigenous women stood in regalia and raised their hands gesturing for the boat to stop, but soon Atlantic salmon poured once again into 'Namgis territory. True to the hereditary chiefs' instructions, the women took only symbolic action. I filmed their plea against the industrialization of their home waters, and then I collected hundreds of the minute scales that were pouring out of the restocked farm to test for PRV. The images of the women were shared hundreds of times, spreading through Indigenous, fishing, environmentalist and local communities. *The world was watching.*

When the boat returned two days later to stock another pen, Ernest was there. Transmitting on the company VHF channel, he ordered the vessel to halt so that a ceremony could be performed. The crew complied. Ernest stood in the inflatable, singing as he released down feathers into the breeze. Then, having communicated his objection to what was happening here, he let the ship continue. Fifteen farm staff stood protectively around the transfer pipe behind a newly erected nine-foot electrified fence designed to keep people off the farms. Later Mowi would complain about how much money they had spent protecting themselves from us, but the 'Namgis were losing far more than money.

In April, Mowi also restocked the Wicklow farm. After everything we had done and risked, the young salmon migrating out of Musgamagw and 'Namgis rivers would face a full house of stocked salmon farms, even as farms stood empty to the south of the archipelago. The sense of failure was crushing. I called Hereditary Chief Art Dick to make sure that he knew this was happening. Though he was inside the government-to-government talks over the farm tenures, at that point he couldn't even tell me whether there was any hope that the tenures would be cancelled. I wanted to know what I should do now. What more could we do to stop the extinction of the wild salmon runs?

Men acting for Mowi found Sherry Moon in a coffee shop in Port McNeill and served her legal papers; Mowi had applied to BC's Supreme Court for an injunction to restrain her from stepping onto another farm. They were picking us off one by one. We began fundraising to hire more lawyers.

On April 14, I headed out in my boat towards Echo Bay to check on the young wild salmon migration. Steaming black coffee in hand, I savoured the sheer beauty of speeding across Blackfish Sound, which was wearing the colour of pearls on her smooth surface that day.

The salmon were almost invisible. Seventeen years earlier the entire shoreline of Tribune Channel had been alive with young salmon from the Ahta, Kakweiken and Glendale Rivers—millions, far too many to count. Their little green sparkly backs, smooth for the pinks and dotted with black for the chum, looked like the water itself as they all swam in one direction. Somehow they knew to cross the large open expanses at the mouths of Thompson Sound and Bond Sound, staying true to their course to the sea. In the spring of 2018 I could barely spot them. With a growing sense of dread, the question *Am I looking at extinction?* repeated in my mind.

Gone were the schools of thousands I used to float among and observe. One day I had been lucky enough to witness a school of salmon make the decision to continue their migration and all suddenly pour out of the bay, rounding the corner out of sight. Moments later, the bay started to refill with tiny newcomers from the east. Everywhere the tiny pink and chum salmon went, their entourage of predators went with them—kingfishers, mergansers, and the plump and voracious chinook and coho smolts. This year the migration was so small even the king-fishers did not attend. People who have not seen all this and who don't know the fish often tell me, *Don't worry, the salmon always come back, they'll be fine.* Really?

Some scientists believe that because we never counted how many there were before, we can't be sure they are gone. They accuse me of always seeing the worst, but by now I am an expert at seeing the missing. It feels like that dread that grows inside when you wait for a loved one whose arrival is overdue. I knew that the pink salmon return to the gen-erous little Ahta River in the summer of 2019 would be *very* low, because I saw those young salmon off when they headed to sea. I have seen too much to believe the opinions of people who are not actually looking at the fish.

Five days later I was in the Ecojustice law offices being interrogated by lawyers from Mowi and Cermaq as part of the examination for dis-covery in my second lawsuit against the minister of fisheries over PRV screening.

The DFO's lawyers were there too, but they sat completely mute as I was grilled, hoping that I would give a response that the defendants could use against me at trial. I tried to talk about the issue at hand,

PRV and its risk to wild salmon. Instead the lawyers were attempting to show that, by suing government, I was after money. Such a line of questioning revealed more about their intentions than mine. Dedicated to the independence necessary to be able to speak freely, I'd always lived on minimal income. I had no savings. I lived from 2014 to 2019 without running water, because I couldn't afford to drill a well at my home on a bluff overlooking the archipelago. Months after this interrogation by Cermaq and Mowi lawyers, my bank account was hacked. I don't know who did it, but I smile when I imagine the hacker's reaction to how little was in it.

On April 28, I got a message from Mack Bartlett and Julia Simmerling, who used to do research at Salmon Coast Field Station, my place in the Broughton. They were now managing Cedar Coast Field Station in Clayoquot Sound, a brand-new facility owned by Simon Nessman, a male supermodel who built it because he wanted to do something to help protect this coast. The appearance of these small non-government field stations is a godsend to this coast. In general, they demonstrate a great spirit of sharing data, co-operation in field studies, and integration with First Nations and the local communities. The science is high-calibre and high-intensity. Mack and Julia sent me the numbers of lice they counted on a few chum salmon fry they had taken a brief look at. They'd found up to fifteen lice on a four-centimetre fish, enough to kill the fish several times over. I packed my camera and gear in the car and took off with my little Arrow hanging her head out the window to sample the breeze.

Mack picked me up the next day at the wharf in Tofino, and we headed out on a calm sea that was all shades of light blue. While Broughton smells mostly of damp, earthy forest, these waters carried the scent of open-ocean saltiness. I spent the day photographing tiny salmon dying of sea lice using a narrow, clear plastic box that allowed me to really see the fish without harming them. These fish did not have a chance. The lice were crawling all over them—on their eyeballs, attached to their sensitive gills, the female lice puncturing holes in them. I watched the little fish panic whenever they listed over to one side and shake themselves to regain their balance. Most of the saltwater fishing lures I have seen are made to mimic the movements of a crippled fish; the big fish are programmed to target any fish that moves differently from the others. These little fish were hard-wired to move in unity with their schoolmates, to keep up, to not be the last fish or even the outside fish in the school. They knew it was dangerous to list over to one side, sinking slowly.

That night I stayed at the field station on Vargas Island. The setting was idyllic, an old homestead surrounded by tall grass, with brilliant yellow daffodils sprinkled under the twisted fruit trees. I didn't want to be the angry biologist; she makes wearisome company, I know. So I sat on the beach where I had photographed the dying fish and cried to release the anger, the sorrow and the pity before I joined the others in the house that evening.

On the way home, I met with a man who had contacted me to say he had some information I might find useful. I made arrangements to meet him at a restaurant, where I had a friend join me. After he arrived, he said he wanted to go somewhere more private and we three ended up in the woods. My dog, generally eager to go off exploring, sat on me the whole time. The man told me he wanted money for images of things that went on in the farms, but he didn't have the images and I didn't have the money. I never heard from him again and had to wonder if it was some kind of set-up. Another time a man phoned to say he had something that would shut the salmon farming industry down tomorrow, but he wanted a million dollars for it. I asked him to give me some idea what kind of revelation he was talking about, but he wouldn't. He told me that with the kind of money I was making, a million should be no problem for me. I hear this a lot.

I told him I had no money. "Think about it," I said to him. "Who is going to pay me big money to fail for thirty years?" He said I had a point and hung up.

Over the years I have received angry messages from fish farmers who have been told I am making several hundred thousand a year to put them out of a job. I always reach out to each one to explain that the industry they work for came into the village I was living in and destroyed our way of life. My neighbours were completely displaced from their fishing grounds, with no compensation; when the province started granting fish farm tenures, we got chased out because government would not grant tenures to the people already living in the area. It was an aggressive and nasty invasion. Many of them admitted, "Well, I agree with you on that. They are bastards."

When Mowi won their injunction against the Swanson camp occupation, everyone was supposed to be gone by May 6, 2018. Typical of Ernest, he intended to comply, but he wanted to make sure that Mowi knew they were no longer in charge here. The backbone of the occupation, Ernest's mother, Tidi, and his wife, Nic, made arrangements for the seventy-five people who answered Ernest's call to show up at Swanson in a fleet of boats of all sizes and shapes—local tourism operators, pleasure boats, crew boats, fish boats. Forming a procession, we slowly circled the farm. As everyone watched, a group of hereditary leaders, including Ernest's brother, K'odi, a thoughtful man who was very involved in the background of the occupation, knocked on the front door of the floating crew quarters tied to the farm to deliver the nations' final eviction notice. But the Mowi employees had locked themselves in and pulled the curtain across the sliding glass doors.

I can understand how our large gathering might have appeared frightening, but after 280 days of occupation of this and other sites, there had been no violence on any side of the dispute. Did they really think that violence was going to happen in front of so many witnesses? Mowi, though they knew about this event, made no effort to end this standoff on an honourable note—to show respect for the people whom they had defeated in court. The chiefs were dressed in regalia and children were present, along with residents of all the surrounding towns and villages. Everyone watched as no one from the company would answer the door. The chiefs ended up taping the eviction notice to the door.

Then the flotilla headed to the cabin where people from many parts of the world had sheltered while occupying the farm. We collected around a fire to hear from Indigenous leaders from all over British Columbia, including Grand Chief Stewart Phillip. He had told me years before that the hardest part of activism is when the people have to go home. He was right. By now the fish farm had become a home. The people who had stood ground here had dug and planted extensive gardens, which were ready to produce food as the weather warmed. The roof of the cabin was layered in solar panels donated by Bearfoot Renewables from Salt Spring Island. We had a satellite dish donated by Ocean Outfitters in Tofino to improve communications beyond the marginal cellphone service. This event was a message to Mowi. The people would abide by the court ruling, but the fight for the life of these waters was not over. Not at all.

The government's mishandling has caused the salmon farming issue to morph from an ecological issue to a social issue. After decades of doing the science, participating in government reviews and meeting with politicians, the only thing that brought the province to the table with the nations was 280 days of occupation. We had done what we could, and now we had to pass the baton to the ones who were at the table negotiating. I knew Chiefs Robert Chamberlin, Arthur Dick, Richard Sumner, Don Svanvik and Rick Johnson, Councillor Kelly Speck and their lawyer, Sean Jones, were in for one hell of a fight. The solution seemed obvious to those of us on the outside—the province just had to let the tenures expire—but of course, it was not that simple.

In late 2018, the city of Tromsø in Norway began trying to do the same thing—to let the tenures of the fish farms in the district expire without renewal. Two fish farm industry lawyers popped up in the Norwegian media warning the city that allowing the tenures to expire might be illegal due to the industry's "political expectations." These words leapt off the screen at me. Such expectations are both unwritten and outside the law, but clearly industry lawyers viewed them as more powerful than the tenures.

On May 7, the day after Mowi removed the last people occupying their farms in the Broughton, Dr. Kristi Miller and her colleagues succeeded in publishing their paper on the impact of PRV on chinook salmon in the journal *FACETS*. The title of the paper stated what many of us feared: "The same strain of *Piscine orthoreovirus* (PRV-1) is involved with the development of different, but related, diseases in Atlantic and Pacific salmon in British Columbia." The virus strain was the one from Norway that we'd reported in 2013. In the internal documents I was obtaining, I saw that this research had been suppressed by DFO and the province since the Cohen Commission aquaculture hearings wrapped up seven years earlier. This was evidence that PRV is a "disease agent" and that it was killing chinook salmon. That meant it was illegal to transfer fish infected with PRV into marine farms in Canada.

I was disgusted and angry that I had fought four federal ministers on this virus for five years, and sued them twice, and all while people in DFO and the provincial Ministry of Agriculture had known PRV was killing chinook salmon. Our federal government refused to uphold the law and refused to honour the demands of First Nations. They just left this Norwegian virus to "go viral" and explode the blood cells of the magnificent chinook salmon.

Miller and Di Cicco's paper was attacked and ignored by all the usual suspects. The salmon farmers said their data did not support their conclusions—the same line used to discredit my work. I felt the hope drain out of me. I picked up my chainsaw and bucked and split firewood until I was exhausted, day after day. I didn't want to think about this anymore. Someone I don't know sent me a T-shirt in the mail, with the words *WILD SALMON MOTHER FUCKER* emblazoned across it. It became my favourite at-home shirt. At least I could see progress as my woodshed was filled. I needed that.

22.

Political Expectations

ON JUNE 20, 2018, the day the salmon farm tenures in the Broughton expired, the provincial minister of agriculture, Lana Popham, announced that in 2022 all salmon farms in British Columbia would require consent from First Nations to operate in their territories. Of course, the NDP government would have to be re-elected for her to deliver on this promise. Glaringly absent from Popham's announcement was a decision about what would be done with the Broughton tenures.

Buried in the online version was a line to the effect that talks were ongoing with the Broughton nations still at the table. This meant two things to me. One, the First Nations were holding strong and had not caved to the pressure of the June deadline, and, two, the tenures were just paperwork. The industry's "political expectations" were the dominant contract in play.

This was the moment when the emotional toll of the last nine months finally knocked me over. I did not want to be awake. I only wanted to sleep. I went to see my beloved grandson and my tiny new granddaughter and they buoyed me. But if someone called about salmon farms, I was instantly submerged in overwhelming exhaustion. I wanted to drop to the floor on the spot and go to sleep.

It was frightening. I thought I was sick, but when I googled my symptoms, up came the terms *burnout* and *depression*. Until this moment,

I did not know what depression was. I thought myself immune to it by a stroke of lucky internal chemistry. I saw myself as being as sturdy as a Chincoteague pony from the books I'd read as a child—head to the wind, tough, unbreakable. I had seen depression and burnout take other activists down, who then vanished from the front lines forever. I always thought they would come back, but they never did. I googled "how to cure depression" and got the answers: rest, change, self-care. On the self-care front, I promised myself again that I would get running water at home this year, but that didn't help me in the short term.

The *Martin Sheen* was scheduled to return to British Columbia in a few weeks for a third summer. When I told Eva Hidalgo, the new campaign leader, that I did not have the energy to get on board, that they could do just as well without me, she expressed such heartfelt disappointment, I felt I couldn't let her down. I said, "Okay, I'll give it a try." But I was sure I wouldn't last more than a couple of weeks.

This year when the boat entered Canada from the US, Canadian border officials confiscated the passports of the crew and interrogated each of them separately. This was alarming in itself, but then they were asked if Alexandra Morton would be on board this summer. Was I now on the radar of Canada's border security? Eventually the vessel and her crew were allowed into Canadian waters under an exceptional restriction. The Canadian border authority ordered that *Martin Sheen* had to be outfitted with a device that would report its position at all times. This is common for commercial vessels but not private boats. Since Sea Shepherd wasn't interested in hiding, they accepted the restrictions. My access request for DFO's communications around our travels the previous year had produced two thousand pages of email to and from people trying to guess where we were going and what we were doing. It would be less time-consuming for the government if there was a vessel-tracking device on board.

It was with mixed feelings that I hugged Arrow goodbye and left her with my friend Sabra in Vancouver for a summer of long walks and trips to the dog park, loaded my gear onto the *Martin Sheen* and claimed my bunk in the wheelhouse. The crew loyally said otherwise, but I know I was grumpy for the first month. Exhaustion still dogged me. But eventually I fell into the peaceful pattern of life aboard, and soon I was exploring a new research method.

At every farm we visited, a member of the crew deployed the vessel's tiny inflatable so we could circle the farm very slowly, staring down into the water. At some point along the perimeter of the farm, we would spot scales, bits of flesh and salmon feces drifting out of the farm. With a fine-mesh aquarium net on a long pole, I scooped up these bits and transferred them with tweezers into vials filled with a virus fixative. Since all the farms now had nine-foot-high electric fences, the farm workers appeared to be in a cage, just like the fish they tended.

When we entered the Broughton Archipelago in July, aluminum boats whose cabins had blacked-out windows started to follow us everywhere we went. There were generally two boats behind us at all times; the one called the *Coastal Logger* was the one we most often saw. The first day we encountered the boats, they swarmed us, pointing cameras at us with lenses so long they had to be getting very detailed shots of our faces and research equipment. We did the same back to them. Although I did not recognize any of the crew, some of them were clearly local. One seemed much more European in dress and style; we saw his suitcase, which had tiny wheels, sitting on the back deck when he arrived—definitely not a local style of luggage. We were friendly in our banter back and forth with the men on these boats, but there was nothing friend-like in their approach.

I called out to the man with the wheelie suitcase, "Are you with Black Cube?"

He called back, "No, I am in a boat."

A non-response.

Why was I asking that? A month earlier I'd received a phone call from a fisherman who told me that his kid had answered an ad and got asked in for an interview. Afterwards, he told his dad that the company doing the hiring was called Black Cube. They were looking for divers, paramedics, drone operators, filmmakers and young women to act as what they called "diffusers."

"Google them," the fisherman said to me. "I don't know if this has anything to do with you or fish farms, but I thought you should have a heads-up. Check out their website. Whatever they're up to, I can't believe this is happening in Campbell River."

The website BlackCube.com struck me as so sinister I thought it was a hoax. Then I came across the MSNBC exposé on the company that had aired in May 2018. The victims of this company's surveillance said Black Cube operatives aggressively tried to uncover details of their lives, looking for points of leverage for their client. I went back to the website, where the descriptive phrases sounded like something out of a thriller: *A select group of veterans from the Israeli elite intelligence units . . . tailored solutions . . . litigation challenges . . .*

The company listed "Cyber Intelligence" as one of their services. My email had been hacked two weeks prior to receiving the call from the fisherman. I noticed because emails stopped coming in. Through the recovery process, I learned that my password had been changed and that someone in Toronto had logged in to my account. Whoever hacked my account would have had the opportunity to download every email and attachment I'd sent and received for years. Since I don't believe there is such a thing as online "security," and I wasn't planning anything illegal, I hadn't been too concerned about the breach. Now I started to wonder whether Black Cube was behind the hack.

The salmon farming industry was in the fight of their lives. The future of one-quarter of their BC tenures was the subject of ongoing talks between the provincial and Indigenous governments and they did not have a seat at that table, a position they were not used to. They had just learned that, as far as the NDP government was concerned, in the near future they would need First Nations consent to renew any of their BC tenures. An increasing number of hereditary chiefs in full regalia had boarded their farms and filmed the shocking condition of many of the fish in their pens. Who knew how much longer the minister of fisheries would keep ignoring the federal law that would prevent restocking fish infected with PRV? I was suing them, the 'Namgis were suing them and Mowi was suing me and a growing list of others for trespass. Mowi definitely had a public relations and litigation problem.

I posted pictures of the people who were following us on Facebook. That created quite a stir. Boats with blacked-out windows are not common on this coast. The day after I posted, our tails were a little more shy; they still followed us but at a distance that stretched to just over 1.2 kilometres, according to the radar sweeps. They also delivered a security crew to each farm outfitted with the same uniform pants, hi-vis vests and radios. It made sense that Mowi would put more security on the farms, but following us was a lot like stalking. It was definitely a show of force.

I started to dig a little deeper into who these people were. I found out that on June 5, 2018, Peter Thomas Corrado of Campbell River had incorporated Black Cube Strategies and Consulting Ltd. On June 18, a Peter Corrado had also applied for two business licences for Black Cube Strategies and Consulting Ltd. On July 3, Campbell River granted these licences. And on July 9, Black Cube Strategies and Consulting posted want ads for "Risk Management Personnel" in five local towns. On July 11, the boats with the blacked-out cabin windows began to follow us, each with a crew of approximately eight people. The boats had been hired from Progressive Diesel in Port McNeill.

When we came close to some Mowi farms, open Wi-Fi network icons appeared on our laptops; in one case the network was identified as "Martin Sheen." What was that about? Apple laptops can be overly friendly. When I left mine on while collecting samples at one farm, it connected to the farm's server and I lost the summer's external hard drive of photos, which was plugged into the computer at the time. Members of the *Martin Sheen*'s crew also began having serious computer issues.

The boats with blacked-out windows watched us when we were tied to the dock in different towns. They watched us at anchor, floating at the edge of the bays. They followed me one day when I was out in my own boat taking a break, even though I was far from the farms, cruising instead among the sportfishing fleet. Fed up, I turned and headed straight towards them. When I got close enough to talk to them, they slammed their windows shut.

"Stop following me," I called.

They sat there, engine idling. No one responded, though I could just make out the shadowy forms of several people inside. After a couple of minutes, I took off and again they followed me. I turned and circled around behind them. They circled behind me. We were now a merry-go-round. Finally, they took off at high speed and I followed them. My boat was much slower, but they seemed unsure where to go. They headed for the archipelago, then turned south, then north and then they just sat there, waiting for me.

I was wishing there were other boats around, but I did not want to back down now. When I caught up to them, they were floating with all the windows sealed shut.

"Hey guys, what's the plan?" I called, circling to see if I could spot an open window.

They beeped their horn, but never came out of the cabin. I told them to have a good day and safe boating, and I left. They didn't follow me. Later I posted a video I'd shot of the entire encounter.

Then a woman in a local market pulled aside the young woman who was volunteering on the *Martin Sheen* as our cook. "You should know those guys following you have a lot of surveillance gear and firearms," she told her.

A local online news service, My Campbell River Now, saw my Facebook posts and did some investigative reporting on the boats. The article stated that Jeremy Dunn, media spokesperson for Mowi, confirmed that they had hired the company running the surveillance on us, but that they wanted to be very clear that they "would not hire an international intelligence agency." So was the name Black Cube just a coincidence?

One evening some of the guys on board the *Martin Sheen* watched the nautical drama *Master and Commander* in the wheelhouse. The next day the two boats following us changed their VHF radio call signs to

"Master" and "Commander." When we heard them, we all looked at each other. *They were listening to us.*

A crew member who knew about cellphone hacking asked, "Anybody experiencing unusual data use on their phones?"

"Yes," I replied. My cellphone provider had just cut off my data, because I had inexplicably burned through several hundred gigs. I was used to managing my data while using my phone for email, and this had never happened to me before. "Why?"

"Well, then they are listening to us right now," he said.

The next time I was in town I made a report to the RCMP. I felt they needed to know what was going on in their jurisdiction. The officer seemed unsure what to do. I asked him to start a file. He told me not to go anywhere alone. That wasn't particularly helpful.

I got a call from the people who had bought my old cabin in Echo Bay, saying that crew boats with black windows were floating in front of the house taking pictures of them. They figured whoever was in the boats thought I still lived there. They filed a report with the police, as did a tourism operator who almost came to blows at the gas dock with the crew after he asked them about the blacked-out windows.

Fishermen started messaging me with pictures of the same boats cruising up to my boat where I kept it tied in the local marina. One of them chased the boats away. I was very grateful for the heads-up. At this point, some colleagues in the BC environmental movement distanced themselves from me. I wasn't sure if they didn't believe me about the surveillance or they were scared.

I wrote to the contact address on Black Cube's website saying I had some concerns about their activities. I got an email reply from a Toronto lawyer within hours, claiming I was not being targeted by them. Why would I believe that? I wrote back, "Deception is your tool." I didn't know what to think about the odd mix of surveillance and overt aggression we were facing from these people.

Despite the Black Cubers, I felt my energy begin to return. It was such a relief. On the *Martin Sheen*, I was surrounded by kindness and that healed me. Each year the volunteer crew changed, but a common thread runs through the people who do this work. I was awed by the risks they had taken to save and protect the creatures of the sea. Imagine chasing rogue fish boats literally halfway around the world! Or trying to stop Japanese whalers in Antarctica where there is no coast guard, no anyone, to help. To them, being followed by an entity like Black Cube was normal. It was a gift to be surrounded by this crew of extraordinary and generous people.

At each farm, our crew went up the mast with a camera to assess the size and condition of the fish. A research team from the University of Toronto took water samples at positions around the farm and at different depths, and then began the laborious process of gently pumping the samples through filters to catch viruses for pathogen analysis. I circled the farms in the little dinghy, dipping up scales, tissue and feces. That summer we were lucky to have Tavish Campbell as our diver. I asked him to focus on filming the waste coming out of the nets and the wild fish aggregations around the pens.

From a distance, the farm nets appeared to be covered in a miniature forest of delicate seaweed. Through Tav's lens, I saw that it was actually a massive aggregation of curious little shrimp creatures called caprellid, or ghost shrimp, which look a bit like praying mantis. They were holding on to the nets with their lower body as they pawed the water with long arm-like claws. They had rounded little pot bellies and when they caught a piece of the flesh or fat that I was also hunting for, they did a face-plant into it, while others nearby reached out and tried to steal it. They were living on the waste. Occasionally I would see thousands of them let go of the nets all at the same time and drift away. I don't know yet what they are up to when they do this: Are they dying or reproducing or just dispersing en masse? What I do know is that they were full of farm waste and ready to be snapped up by any fish big enough to get one into its mouth.

Again, we witnessed herring moving as one great living creature, all black one moment, then after a shift in direction, all silver. They turned, flashed and then darkened again and again, as they fed on the pellet dust coming out of the pens. For moments they milled around, then suddenly all at once they flowed towards the net like rain in a windstorm.

Several times, salmon smolts darted out of the shadows and grabbed and ate the piece of flesh or fat I was aiming for with my pole net. The surface of the water was greasy around the farms. I wore surgical gloves because it felt revolting on my skin.

As I focused on the waste, I became even more aware of the industrial stain seeping from these farms, spreading over the water. Gulls landed in it, then took off to land in other areas, their feathers transporting the grease. The millions of creatures at every farm eating the fish fat and other decomposing flesh became potential carriers for the born-and-bred farm pathogens.

As I worked around the farms, the Black Cubers yelled at me that I was violating my scientific licence and the injunctions, but this was not true. One evening, the owner of a local dock screamed at us to get the hell away even as his employees were guiding us in and taking our lines. Our crew did not scream back. Benoit, who was captain that summer, said, "Okay, I understand, no problem, we are leaving." And we did, as the owner kept yelling at us. People holding drinks watched the spectacle from the decks of their yachts.

This man's marina made hundreds of thousands of dollars annually from people who came to see orca, salmon, bears and eagles. While he couldn't accept the connection with the farms, he did know the wild salmon were disappearing because there were no longer line-ups of fish boats wanting to fuel up at his dock before an opening. Some people, unsettled by our collapsing ecosystems, push back with anger at the people trying to protect this world. I think what he really wanted was for things to be the way they once were. Perhaps he thought that if people would just stop talking about it, the world would revert to that more bountiful time.

In general, the response to the *Martin Sheen*'s presence was fabulously supportive: much waving, cheers, and calls of *We love you* across the water. We took Hereditary Chiefs Ernest Alfred, Arthur Dick and Robert Mountain out to witness the Black Cube Strategy boats following us and to show them what we were doing at each farm. They approved and thanked the Sea Shepherd crew for their presence in their territories. That summer we sampled farms along the five hundred kilometres from Puget Sound in Washington State through the Broughton Archipelago. No one had ever done that before. Every time we came into port, I shipped the most recent collection of samples off to the lab. The results started coming back: *positive, positive, positive*. Almost every farm was releasing PRV.

On August 2, Mowi won a partial injunction preventing me from approaching its salmon farms in any boat larger than 2.6 metres. This was odd. What did it matter what size my boat was? Even more odd was the fact the little boat I had been using, the dinghy from the *Martin Sheen*, was 2.8 metres. How did the judge come to pick the number 2.6? I made a short video about shopping for a 2.6-metre boat in Port McNeill. The only one I could find was a toy meant for children to use in a swimming pool. The clerk who was serving me sympathized with the situation and paid for my boat, warning me to be careful. Everyone knew it was not safe to be in a boat that size on these waters.

At the next farm I went to sample, I used it, rowing with the tiny plastic oars; a crew member stayed close to me in the dinghy, taking care not to enter the injunction zone. It was ridiculous. The video footage of me in the toy boat trying to continue my research was shared so widely on Facebook, Greg McDade was able to negotiate the right for me to use my own vessel, *Blackfish Sound*, instead. Mowi insisted I would have to be alone on my boat. That was fine. I usually was alone.

In the summer of 2018, fishermen contacted me because the pink salmon of British Columbia seemed to disappear. Sportfishermen don't like pinks; they are too small and usually so abundant they are viewed as a nuisance because they bite on bait rigged to catch the much larger coho or chinook salmon. After every pink salmon strike, fishermen have to bait their hooks again. But they found their disappearance unnerving.

In reality, pink salmon are a gift. They used to enter the rivers in such huge numbers that they hid the smaller populations of other species. Bears would gorge on pink salmon, leaving the chinook to spawn. In spring the newly hatched pink salmon left the river without feeding, bequeathing the sockeye, chinook and coho—species that stay a year or more upriver before heading for the ocean—all the rich nutrients from their dead parents to feed the insect life that young salmon eat.

A few years earlier, in October 2013, I had gotten a call from Sandy Bodrug and Brad Crowther, the two sportfishers I met on my first trip to the Fraser to test for the ISA virus. They said they'd found hundreds of dead pink salmon strewn on the riverbank. The fish hadn't spawned and they were the weirdest shade of yellow. I drove seven hours to meet them and they took me out to Mountain Bar, a gravel island in the river. There they were, large males with their huge humps—yellow. The smaller females, full of eggs—yellow. When I did autopsies on some of them, I saw the fish were yellow all the way through. The cartilage of their heads was yellow; their spines were yellow; their heart and liver were yellow; and their spleens were swollen and misshapen, a sign they were fighting disease.

The First Nations fishermen who were fishing with beach seines for food did not like the look of the yellow pink salmon. Their best estimate was that 70 percent of the pink salmon were yellow that year. They had never seen this before. The eyes of one of the female pink salmon I found were bugged out, suggesting enormous pressure in her head. She died as I watched. When I autopsied her, she had a large black mass attached to her brain.

Dr. Miller and Dr. Di Cicco's research on the effects of PRV on chinook salmon included liver damage causing jaundice. These fish turned yellow because their red blood cells, infected with PRV, have ruptured, overloading their bodies with hemoglobin, which damaged their livers. It was a chain reaction: virus invades cells, uses cell machinery to replicate itself; cell bursts and kills the fish. This is not a normal patho-gen/host relationship. The virus needs the fish. If it kills 70 percent of a run, it extinguishes itself.

I cannot yet prove that PRV is killing off large numbers of wild salmon in British Columbia, but clearly the ruination of the 2013 pink salmon, gone yellow in the lower Fraser, should have triggered an intense inves-tigative response from DFO. It didn't. I am hoping PRV isn't killing off all the salmon of this coast. However, hope feels like a stupid response to the plumes of Atlantic viruses pouring into the Pacific out of pens and pipes of Norwegian-run industrial feedlots. Investing in hope is a waste of energy. Better to do what you can to stop what's going on.

On the way home from the Fraser in 2013, I stopped at the Campbell River. As I stood there trying to spot salmon, a twenty-pound chinook swam up to the sandy spot I was on, his eye moving wildly. He pushed himself partway up the bank and slowly died at my feet. He too was yel-low. I stared into his eyes, horrified. He had left this river a fat and sassy little smolt. He'd travelled all his life, evading orca and sea lions, catch-ing fish in the wide-open ocean, growing mature. Now he was dying before he could pass on his rich DNA to the next generation.

After he died, I sampled his gills, which tested positive for PRV. His liver was yellow, his spleen swollen. Everything felt wrong.

23.

Courtroom Drama

IN SEPTEMBER 2018, I was in another courtroom, this time to hear my Ecojustice lawyers, Margot Venton and Kegan Pepper-Smith, argue our second lawsuit against the minister of fisheries for his refusal to screen farm salmon for PRV. Since we had won this case once, I was confused as to why we had to argue it all over again, even though I was the one who filed it. Shouldn't the court take it from here and force Canada's government to follow its own laws? Apparently not. And, while Ecojustice was paying the lawyers, I was responsible for the court costs, which were escalating with every motion submitted by Mowi and Cermaq, who once again had inserted themselves into the process. My bill already stood at $22,000. If I won, DFO and the companies would have to pay these costs. If I lost, I would pay the court costs for DFO and the two fish farming companies. The stakes were high for the coast and for me personally.

If this lawsuit had been argued in the 1990s, the Fisherman's Union, the Steelhead Society and many others, even politicians, would have been in an uproar over the industry farming Atlantic salmon infected with an Atlantic virus here in the Pacific. But now all of them stayed silent. I don't know why. Fortunately, a lawsuit only requires a lawyer, a judge, a plaintiff and the defendants to proceed, and we were all present. Even better, the 'Namgis were here to argue their parallel case, with their lawyers, Sean Jones and Paul Seaman, and a knot of chiefs looking on from the gallery. Natural laws and human laws had been broken. Mowi, Cermaq and DFO were there to make sure they remained broken. We were outnumbered, but we were not outgunned.

The hearing, in front of Federal Court Justice Cecily Strickland, was scheduled to last an entire week. She was from Newfoundland and, like most judges, I found her impossible to read. In these circumstances, I always hope for judges who come from families of fishermen. Did she have a memory of what DFO did to the North Atlantic cod stocks and what happened in her community when that fishery collapsed?

Central to the 'Namgis case were three expert reports stating that PRV in farm salmon poses a risk of "serious and irreparable harm" to wild salmon. There seemed to be an effort to suppress these. First, DFO bureaucrats failed to provide these reports to the federal minister when he was reviewing whether to approve restocking the Swanson Island farm. Because the reports hadn't actually gone to the minister, the fish farm lawyers argued they couldn't be part of the case and asked that three expert reports be struck from the record. When the judge ruled in their favour, the DFO lawyers went on to argue the Department had no "duty to consult" with 'Namgis, because PRV did not cause harm.

We're fighting with cheaters, I thought, remembering the words of the lobster fisherman in Nova Scotia. If Minister Wilkinson had seen this evidence of harm to wild salmon due to PRV, would he still have issued the permit to restock Swanson?

The lawyers on my side got to work removing the DFO scaffolding that was shoring up the preposterous position that PRV was no risk to wild salmon. Sean Jones walked the court through the sequence of events when Dr. Gary Marty, the BC government fish pathologist, recognized the disease HSMI in BC farm salmon in 2008, but didn't report it. Then Jones took the court through Dr. Kristi Miller's contract with Creative Salmon, which had asked her to solve the mystery of why their farmed chinook salmon were turning yellow and dying. And the fact that when Miller discovered the jaundice appeared to be associated with PRV infection, the same Dr. Marty apparently advised Creative Salmon not to allow her to publish her results.

Sitting in that courtroom as lawyers explained the battle between Dr. Marty and Dr. Miller over whether PRV was harming salmon was a long way from the glow of my laptop in the dark house at the water's edge where I'd first read all this and thought, *I need a lawyer*. I couldn't help but wonder what would have happened if Canada's fisheries laws had not been broken. Would so many salmon be dying on the riverbank, turning yellow from the inside out? Would the southern resident orca still be our healthy and content neighbours in the Salish Sea? Would the bears be starving? Would once-thriving coastal communities be struggling with catastrophic loss of fishing industry jobs?

The DFO lawyers argued that the Department was using the precautionary principle—taking a better-safe-than-sorry approach until the harms from PRV were proven. I was dumbstruck that they could actually stand up and argue this: DFO has never taken sufficient precautions to protect wild salmon from salmon farms.

Then the company lawyers really went off the rails. One of them theorized to the judge that to be able to do what I was doing I must be wealthy; another told the judge that I was not a judge, which I am pretty sure the judge already knew. Did I make them so angry that they became more aggressive than smart? How was any of this even relevant?

In January 2019, the Dzawada'enuxw of Kingcome Inlet filed their claim in Federal Court in Vancouver alleging that the ten salmon farms in their territory were infringing their Aboriginal Rights. The federal government was on record as recognizing these rights, and this nation was determined to see them honoured.

Their filing claimed that the farms were exposing important wild fish stocks to harmful viruses and parasites and polluting the waters of their territory. The nation was seeking an order from the court to quash the federal licences of these farms, which were owned by Cermaq and

Mowi. These two companies were now facing challenges to their provincial tenures, suits over their habit of transferring PRV-infected fish into the Broughton and a challenge of their federal licences as well, confronted by a total of four First Nations in three lawsuits and a groundbreaking government-to-government process. Then there was me. Why couldn't they see that it was time to bow out gracefully from the archipelago before things got even worse for them?

A month later, on February 4, the 'Namgis and I won our lawsuits to make the government reassess its policy of transferring PRV-infected farm salmon into the Broughton and all of British Columbia. By now, I had been to court five times to bring the salmon farming industry into compliance with our laws and have never lost; as my winning record reinforces, many aspects of farming salmon in marine net pens are simply not legal in Canada. In a 201-page decision, Justice Strickland ruled to quash DFO's policy not to screen farm salmon for PRV because, among other reasons, it failed to protect wild salmon health. This meant DFO had to draw a new policy. She reaffirmed the 2015 decision on the same matter—the one four fisheries ministers had ignored.

Strickland admonished the sitting minister, Jonathan Wilkinson, directly. She said there was a burden on him to explain why he had appealed the 2015 decision, then withdrawn that appeal and simply refused to screen for PRV. She drew attention to the 'Namgis concern that DFO would continue to allow the transfer of infected fish unless someone could prove that the virus threatened an entire conservation unit with extinction. (A "conservation unit" is defined as a group of wild salmon runs that exists sufficiently isolated that, if extirpated, the fish are very unlikely to come back; the salmon of the Broughton are one such unit.) Waiting to act until DFO was certain that PRV in salmon farms would cause the extinction of the salmon of the Broughton was simply not acceptable. To avoid inconveniencing the salmon farming industry, DFO was playing with ecocide.

Strickland defined the minister's reliance on scientific uncertainty to support his ministry's lack of action as a "badge of unreasonableness."

She found very little evidence that DFO demonstrated concern for wild salmon, citing a recent auditor general's finding that the Department did not monitor wild salmon health. She underlined that DFO still relied heavily on one paper regarding the lack of occurrence of HSMI in farm salmon, the one written by Garver et al. in 2016. This was the paper that Dr. Marty co-authored and then undermined just a few months later when he stated in an email that he had found evidence of HSMI in BC farm salmon and wanted credit for this discovery. The conclusions of this paper were shown to be false a year later when Di Cicco, Miller and colleagues published the evidence that HSMI was present in a BC salmon farm. And yet DFO clung to it like a sinking life raft.

Strickland gave the Canadian minister of fisheries four months to write a new PRV policy that would comply with the law.

During the course of this second lawsuit, the Canada Pension Plan became the sixth-biggest shareholder in Mowi, increasing its number of shares when the 'Namgis filed and then again when the joint lawsuits from 'Namgis and myself were heard. Was this a signal to the industry that despite the growing resistance, both on the ground and in the courts, Canada was still their friend? My overarching question remains: Why would Canada break its own laws, undermine its own commitment to reconciliation with First Nations and subvert its own science to make it possible for this industry to continue?

Three days after Strickland's decision, DFO announced that an expert panel it had convened had found that PRV had minimal impact on the Fraser sockeye. But within minutes of that announcement, one of the experts on the panel, John Werring, a biologist with the David Suzuki Foundation, insisted that no such consensus had been reached. I would learn later through an access to information request that Dr. Miller's edits to this report, which ran contrary to this consensus, had been deleted. A week after the expert panel debacle, Minister Wilkinson did a one-on-one interview with Global TV, on one of Canada's biggest newscasts, expressing his opinion that PRV is not harming wild salmon. Wilkinson's opinion, of course, is a lesser standard than two Federal

Court decisions. His opinion does not excuse his ministry from following the laws of the country.

Two weeks after the decision, on February 18, Wilkinson showed signs of realizing the gravity of the situation and was quoted in the *Globe and Mail* saying, "B.C.'s salmon farming industry should be shifted out of sensitive wild salmon migration pathways." This acknowledgement was unprecedented, but he still did not mention whether he would abide by the court's ruling and initiate PRV-screening of farm salmon.

Four days later, he said, "We need to get beyond this debate that nobody is winning right now," and he blamed the two "camps" for being unable to have an appropriate dialogue. When pressed again by a CBC Radio interviewer about moving the industry off wild salmon migration routes, he wouldn't comment. Now we were back in familiar territory. Perhaps thumbscrews had now been applied to this minister.

The "debate" has been won, twice, in Federal Court. But if the minister responded to the science that reported that PRV is a "disease agent," and screened all farm salmon for the virus, and followed the law that prohibits transfer of infected fish, the industry might not have enough uninfected fish to farm in Canada. Indeed, beginning in the spring of 2018, Washington State prohibited transfer of PRV-infected farm salmon into marine pens. The company operating there, Cooke Aquaculture, agreed to purchase only PRV-free eggs from their source hatchery in Iceland. However, pre-transfer screening found the young salmon reared from those eggs were infected. Cooke Aquaculture tried again, but the fish were still infected, a finding that led to destroying a total of 1.6 million fish. Even though legally they were allowed to continue farming until 2025, they have been unable to stock a single farm since the prohibition on PRV infection.

While three previous Canadian ministers had got away with doing nothing since 2015, Wilkinson was in the hot seat and the federal government of Canada was facing a different crisis. Prime Minister Trudeau and his staff were accused of pressuring the minister of justice, Jody Wilson-Raybould, to go easy on a corporation, SNC-Lavalin, which was facing charges of corruption and fraud. This wasn't proof that the Trudeau government was any worse than previous governments; in fact, it was likely better than previous governments in that it had appointed ministers with integrity who objected to business as usual. However, his government's handling of this Norwegian industry and its viruses raised similar questions about whether someone had been told to go easy.

On June 4, at the end of a four-month extension that Wilkinson had requested from the judge, he made the announcement that yes, Canada would screen for the virus, but only for the Norwegian and Icelandic strains. This put me in a difficult position. This announcement was huge—the first time any minister of fisheries had responded to a virus that could destroy Canada's wealth of wild salmon. But all of the virologists I worked with were clear that *all* PRV in British Columbia is from the Atlantic Ocean. It was DFO and industry virologists who had come up with the unsubstantiated theory that there was a harmless, provincial strain of PRV. This meant there was a mystery strain of PRV that no one I knew had detected and government refused to elaborate on, and fish infected with it would be cleared for transfer. It was hard not to return to the greased pig analogy.

I had to decide whether I would respond favourably to Wilkinson's announcement—as a significant move in the right direction—or take the role of the perpetually angry biologist who is never satisfied with anything government does.

I chose option number one and then made an effort to speak with him, because I felt certain that he was not getting the whole story on this virus from his staff. To his credit, Minister Wilkinson granted me an hour of his time and we had a frank conversation. I could see the difficulty the ministers had faced on this issue. Plucked from a life devoid of anything to do with fish and their diseases and placed in a decision-making position, these ministers had to decide whether to believe their senior staff or try to sort through the merits of what a group of quarrelsome scientists were arguing about. When I presented the evidence, he created a Fish Health Committee and put me on it.

In late September 2019, Justin Trudeau, campaigning for a second term as prime minister of Canada, made a promise to move all salmon farms into closed containment units by 2025, which would put an end to all the risk of impact on wild salmon. The salmon farming industry complained bitterly, saying that raising salmon on land has not been economically proven, even though companies like Atlantic Sapphire in the US and other companies in Norway were rapidly building huge salmon farms on land that will soon rival British Columbia's farm salmon production. Minister Wilkinson responded that the promise by the federal Liberal Party to create a solid barrier between wild salmon and farm salmon "reflects a precautionary approach to a divisive issue." That word again.

On October 22, Mowi's CEO, Alf-Helge Aarskog, made headlines in *IntraFish* with the aggressive comeback, "Trudeau will change his mind on salmon farming." Sure enough, by January 19, 2020, the Liberal government had been re-elected with a minority in Parliament, Wilkinson was transferred out of the Department, and the newly appointed minister of fisheries, Bernadette Jordan of Nova Scotia, said the 2025 deadline was just a deadline for coming up with *a plan* to move the salmon farming industry into tanks. She was photographed smiling with the managing director of Mowi Canada West. The progress made with the previous minister was lost.

In February 2019, the European Commission had conducted a raid on Mowi, Grieg and other salmon farming company operations in Scotland and opened an investigation into whether these companies were acting as a "cartel" engaged in price fixing. In the United States, the Euclid Fish Company, joined later by Cape Florida Seafood, The Fishing Line and Beacon Fisheries, filed a class-action lawsuit on April 24 against Mowi, Grieg Seafood and other salmon farming companies for price-fixing. In June, a consumer, Robin Wilkey, filed a class-action lawsuit on behalf of consumers in twenty-seven states in the US District Court in Maine against several Norwegian-owned salmon farming companies for maintaining artificially high prices.

New York–based Prime Steakhouse also filed a separate purchaser price-fixing lawsuit, and more lawsuits were filed in Toronto. All told, the companies were now being sued for a billion Canadian dollars.

Officials from Mowi and Grieg denied any involvement in non-competitive practices. Then the Norwegian Competition Authority blocked European Commission investigators from raiding their head offices, claiming that only Norwegians could investigate in Norway. In August, Grieg Seafood reported spending $891,960 on legal fees, saying that it hoped the lawsuits would end soon.

All this legal action reminded me that the Norwegian newspaper, *Dagbladet*, had run a front-page story in January 2010 under the head-line: "Here is the salmon farming 'Mafia' network." It had featured the faces of ten people across industry and government, over the caption, "Producers have good control of all the important positions in the Ministry of Fisheries in Norway." One of those faces was the Norwegian minister of fisheries herself.

24.

An Ancient Government Re-emerging

WHEN THE JUNE 20, 2018, deadline to renew all the salmon farm tenures in the Broughton passed without a decision, the minister of agriculture, Lana Popham, said the province needed ninety more days before announcing the outcome of the government-to-government talks with the Broughton nations. Ninety days later, Popham said she and the province needed sixty more days. Sixty days after that, she said nothing.

One more week of deafening silence passed. I was certain the silence was only surface deep and that just below that surface all parties were vying to gain ground.

On December 14, 2018, a press conference to announce the results of the talks was held in the BC legislature. Lined up in front of the cameras were Popham, Premier Horgan, Chief Robert Chamberlin, the then-federal minister of fisheries, Jonathan Wilkinson, and representatives from Cermaq and Mowi, the companies affected. All of them nodded their heads to say that an agreement had been reached between the province, the federal government and three nations of the Broughton Archipelago, the 'Namgis, Mamalilikulla, and Kwikwasut'inuxw Haxwa'mis. The agreement laid out the orderly removal of most of the salmon farms from the archipelago over the next four years. Given the nearly invisible 2018 juvenile salmon out-migration, I thought: *This is not going to be fast enough.*

However, buried in the fine print of the agreement was a sword so sharp the four-year timeline was the lesser win. The nations now had the authority to screen the farm salmon going into their territories for PRV and *all* pathogens. The measure of how much control over the industry had been won by these nations was an addendum to the agreement in which Mowi had to ask permission from the nations to restock its farm at Sargeaunt Pass: "We will seek First Nations agreement . . . for this restocking to occur." Mowi's undertaking was signed by its CEO in Norway, Alf-Helge Aarskog, not by the head of the Canadian subsidiary in Campbell River.

These nations had stepped into the role that the minister of fisheries had abdicated. I am not sure if the minister was aware that he had made room for an ancient government to re-emerge. Robert Chamberlin looked exhausted, and was at the press conference in a wheelchair, suffering from significant health issues that he later recovered from. But going forward, nothing concerning salmon is going to happen in the Broughton Archipelago without First Nations oversight.

Wilkinson mostly studied his shoes.

Ernest Alfred, who had sparked the uprising that had led to this day, had travelled the three hundred kilometres from Alert Bay to be there at the conclusion of what he started. But he remained locked outside the legislature. He was given no reason why he couldn't attend the press conference, but perhaps in this historic moment, government thought it could not be seen as having bowed to the pressure of activism.

I had been warned that "winning" feels differently than one anticipates. In the wake of the announcement, I realized I had no trust left. I couldn't help wondering if we had actually won. Did the industry and the government have other cards up their sleeves? Would the wild salmon survive this?

———

On the next calm day, I untied my boat to go take a look at the first farm in the Broughton that was scheduled for decommissioning. For nineteen years I had witnessed and recorded the suffering, death and catastrophic ecosystem damage at the Mowi Glacier Falls farm site. This is where the tiny silver slips of salmon, freshly hatched from their pebbly winter nests in the Ahta River, met industrial aquaculture and died, their death an "externality" that sweetened shareholder profits. As I've mentioned, the Canada Pension Plan is one of the beneficiaries of four ministers of fisheries ignoring the laws of Canada in favour of this industry; our pensioners are unknowingly stealing from the grandchildren they love more than anything on Earth.

I cut a wake up the inlet in my speedboat towards the farm, relieved that Glacier Falls would be the first one to go, because the Ahta River has my heart. I hoped it wasn't too late for the river; the 2018 outmigration of young salmon had been so weak, there was barely a pulse. The farm structure was still there, all the walkways and buildings, but as I drew alongside I saw there were no nets in the water and no fish. April Bencze, who had come with me, launched a drone and took the last photos of this industrial nightmare. Goosebumps prickled my skin as a weight lifted, and my lungs filled with the wet winter air. As I looked up, the woman's face in the nearby mountainside was looking down, her eyebrows dusted with snow, giving her a restful look.

I opened a small container and released some of Twyla's ashes into the water. *Help heal this place, my friend.*

In a few months, the few surviving Ahta River salmon fry arrived at this site. They were silvery, iridescent blue near their tails, their eyes deep gold and flecked with sparkling black. I silently apologized to them that it had taken so long that there were so few of them left, but this is what people do. We dare the worst to catch us, and then in the face of the worst, we do something brilliant.

CONCLUSION

Department of Wild Salmon

IN 2007, I had co-authored a paper in the journal *Science* that predicted the collapse of the pink salmon in the Broughton Archipelago due to sea lice from salmon farms. In 2019, it happened. A local wildlife photographer, Rolf Hicker, did what the bear tour operators in the area avoided: he posted photographs of grizzly bears in the Broughton Archipelago. They hardly looked like bears. Their ribs were clearly visible through their long shaggy fur. Their legs looked much too long, because their stomachs were drawn up against their spines. They were starving and would not live through the winter. Just one-tenth of 1 percent, 0.1 percent, of the Glendale River pink salmon returned.

After weeks of padding up and down the barren river, the bears entered the ocean and began swimming. They appeared on many tiny islands of the archipelago, where no one had ever seen grizzly bears before. They were desperate to find a river that still had salmon but had no memory of where to go. The paths and the timing of salmon migrations are passed down from mothers to cubs, but this knowledge was useless now. There were no salmon where there should be salmon. By December, many bears were too hungry to hibernate and some boldly tried to enter houses, enticed by the smell of food. First Nation villagers tried to show respect for grizzly bears that were now on their front porches. Government conservation officers intervened and shot them.

These bears were collateral damage from an industry that has never belonged in these waters.

The lowest wild salmon return in the history of Canada happened in 2019. Meanwhile Alaska and Russia to the north and west saw many excellent salmon returns. While all these BC, US and Russian salmon feed in the same general area of the North Pacific, something deadly was plaguing the ones that spawned in British Columbia, dragging local populations down to the hard edge of extinction. The data coming in from people counting salmon in rivers revealed a pattern. Many salmon runs were low, but wild salmon from heavily salmon farmed regions, such as the Broughton Archipelago, the Discovery Islands and Clayoquot Sound were almost non-existent. The Kakweiken, Viner, Ahta, Glendale, Orford and Phillips Rivers were nearly empty.

This season, spawning grounds that had been stroked by female salmon digging nests for ten thousand years lay untouched. A thin film of green/brown algae covered the pebbles in a fine shag carpet that billowed silently in the current. This is a sure sign there are no salmon. When salmon dig nests, they wipe the algae off the rocks. When you wade across a salmon stream in the fall, you can see large circles of bright pebbles swept clear of algae by salmon. These are the redds, or salmon nests. They stand out in contrast to the darker rocks still coated in algae, making it easy to avoid stepping in the nests and crushing the buried eggs.

There were no ravens calling along the rivers, the signature soundtrack of the spawning season. The strong scent of fish was absent from the river valleys. There were no eagles standing in the shallows, their curved dagger claws deep into a salmon carcass as they tore off hunks, threw their heads back and gulped down the nutritious meat—defence against the lean times of winter.

Faced with this evidence of extinction, my positive nature faltered again. Despite more than thirty years of doing everything I could think of—the science, the lawsuits, government processes, the activism on repeat—I was watching extinction in play. After the uprising and all that came after it, were we too late? The magnitude of what I was witnessing dominated my days and my dreams. It was inside me. It was me. There was nothing else. I could not shrug off the brutal cut of extinction.

I tried to console myself by counting my blessings—my two children, grandchildren and other close family, the warmth of my dog sleeping beside me on stormy nights, working in my garden, the joy and awe of experiencing the rebirth of ancient governance among the nations whose territory I lived in. Still, I instinctively wanted to flee the scene of this crime. But where would I go? Australia was burning, along with the Amazon and parts of Africa. Climate change refugees were on the move. Crops were failing in the breadbaskets of the world.

There is nowhere to run. We, as a species, have to face this. Our primary survival strategy has been migration into new territories, but that is over. Wherever we go, we meet ourselves and the damage we have wreaked. There is nowhere to run, nowhere to hide. It is our turn: we either evolve or go extinct. We are the perpetrators and the victims.

Through the winter of 2019–2020, I travelled monthly to Vancouver to sit on the minister's Fish Health Committee, tasked to provide guidance on making salmon farming more "sustainable." There is nothing sustainable about feeding fish to fish, to produce fewer fish, while releasing Armageddon levels of infectious agents into the ocean, but I accepted the volunteer position. Most of the people at the table worked on behalf of the salmon farming industry, either within DFO or directly for the three big companies.

Also on the committee were people from two environmental organizations, the David Suzuki Foundation and the Pacific Salmon Foundation, leading salmon virologist Dr. Fred Kibenge and delegates from two First Nations. When a scientist from the University of British Columbia assured us at one of our meetings that the wild salmon returns in British Columbia were fine, I felt a roar build in my throat and struggled to tame it before it left my lips. "How can you possibly say that?" I asked as calmly as I could, thinking of the dying grizzly bears.

He backed down quickly, but industry partners glanced nervously around the table.

While many industries are directly damaging our planet, they, at least, are fairly clear that their allegiance is to their shareholders. To my mind, shareholders are the most dangerous animals on Earth; their profits relying on a cancer model: relentless growth to the point of killing life.

Governments are less honest in their goals, as they give up in the face of laws designed to protect corporate interests rather than their citizens. I now knew what this was called: *political expectations*. We elect leaders who look brave, but invariably they fall silent once in power and find themselves up against global corporations that are addicted to the consumption of Earth's resources with no view to the future, even their own. I want more from the governments that I vote for, but I have to recognize that I am ignorant of the pressures they face and find myself unwilling to completely write them off.

However, what I have zero tolerance for are the scientists who use their positions of authority and public trust to justify or hide the industrial damage that is now threatening civilization. As a scientist, I recognize the skilled manipulations of the evidence that give their work a veneer of credibility, delivering scientific cover to the senior bureaucrats who are running things in an industry-friendly way. This perverted information is then sent up the line in ministerial briefings. Since ministers are shuffled every few years, changing portfolios or leaving government, they never get the chance to really learn whether to trust the senior bureaucrats who write the briefings; governments come and go, but the bureaucrats largely remain in place. This relationship—between scientists willing to produce the science to shore up industry-enticing policies and the bureaucrats who represent this as the only science to be believed—is killing us.

Similarly, but more subtly, academic scientists depend on external funding of their research. Whether the issue is climate change or salmon farms, we need to weigh the validity of the science against its funding source. If two groups of scientists report opposite results—such as in the case of whether the PRV virus found in BC farm salmon is causing disease in wild salmon—it is critical to note that one group is funded by the salmon farming industry and the other is not. This is not to suggest all scientists bend to the needs of their funders, but it certainly does happen and it is one of the greatest threats to life on Earth.

I dutifully made the twelve-hour round trips to attend the Fish Health Committee meetings held in the black tower of DFO's downtown Vancouver offices. I had learned to understand whales by spending a lot of time watching them. Now I was watching and once again trying to figure out bureaucrats.

Since I had already read their emails through the dozens of access requests that I had made, I knew their positions on matters. Now I observed how they behaved with industry representatives and also with the lower-down-the-hierarchy field staff. I knew from the email correspondence that many field staff are fighting as hard as I am to protect wild salmon, but their concerns are blocked by senior staff and tend not to rise to the surface where the decisions were being made. DFO field personnel were writing very stern emails to salmon farming companies demanding they get their sea lice under control before young wild salmon began migrating past the farms every March. Some of these emails were written in the middle of the night. Their authors' stress was evident as they openly lamented the impact of the lice on wild salmon. When they realized that the salmon farmers were ignoring them, leaving heavily lice-infested fish in pens during the young wild salmon migrations, they tried to convince senior management to strengthen the laws and the conditions of licence.

They complained to each other that senior DFO staff were ignoring their efforts to strengthen regulations to protect wild salmon. The regulatory loopholes they complained about were left in place: all the companies had to do to stay in business was to have a plan to keep their lice under the government limits and execute the plan; it was irrelevant if the plan worked, or if the wild salmon lived or died.

Suddenly I had slipped inside this dynamic, sitting in meetings with both the field and senior staff. I brought the field staffs' emails to the table to allow their information to penetrate the airtight layers of the DFO hierarchy. Instead of only policy-friendly reporting, the bad news also had to rise to the surface so it could be dealt with. Everyone at the table knew the solution to sea lice was to institute fines for exceeding the limits. These fines had to be so high that it became less expensive for the companies to cull the infected farm fish than to allow their lice to kill wild salmon. If the companies met these limits, then British Columbia wouldn't be a profitable place to raise Atlantic salmon in marine net pens. They would put them in a tank. End of subject.

I was told this was impossible, that DFO was not allowed to fine salmon farms. This was a jaw-dropper; I had to ask several times whether it was true. Was it really true that DFO officers can come to my door and threaten to arrest me for catching a handful of juvenile salmon, but salmon farms can kill millions of the same fish through sea lice infections and face zero penalties? Field staff looked at me, perhaps thinking *Welcome to our world*, and in that way we became awkward allies pushing for changes that would protect the fish outside the pens.

However, these discussions failed, as all other consultations before them had failed. Senior staff took our concerns, consulted with industry and their lawyers, and came up with new farm lice recommendations for 2020. They would grant the companies an unlimited number of lice per farm salmon for forty-two days—six weeks to get their lice under control during the highly sensitive juvenile wild salmon migration from March to June. This was a godsend if you were a salmon farming corporation that couldn't control its lice infestation, but a death sentence for salmon runs already reduced to less than 1 percent by farm lice. When you are only a few centimetres long, it's lethal to swim for forty-two days in an ocean teeming with lice.

When the Mowi representative at the table boldly stated that the virus PRV does not cause disease in British Columbia, I countered that Emiliano Di Cicco and Kristi Miller had published finding the disease

HSMI, due to PRV, in a BC fish farm in the Discovery Islands in 2017. The Mowi rep shook her head no, and the DFO meeting facilitator, Carmel Lowe, director of science, said I was getting into too much detail for the committee. I countered that sorting this out was critical to providing effective recommendations to the minister. "What about bringing two veterinarians with opposite opinions—Emiliano Di Cicco and Gary Marty—to this table to explain their opposing views on HSMI?" I asked. There was a murmur of agreement around the table.

As a result, on January 28 and 29, 2020, a veterinarian workshop was held to answer whether PRV causes disease in British Columbia or not, but DFO's deputy minister, Timothy Sargent, prohibited me, the two First Nations representatives, John Werring from the David Suzuki Foundation and Andrew Bateman from the Pacific Salmon Foundation, all members of the committee, from attending. When I asked why we were banned, DFO senior staff said, "This conversation needs to be protected"; a company rep said the company people needed "to feel safe."

The facilitator selected for this workshop, Dr. Ian Gardner, had already gone public in opposition to the finding that PRV is causing disease. I arrived at the workshop as it was getting under way to ask Lowe if she was sure she wanted to make the mistake of excluding us and further destroying the public's trust in DFO. Apparently she was. As they entered, I looked each participant in the eye. Doctors Di Cicco and Kibenge, the only two scientists present who accepted the evidence that PRV is a disease agent in British Columbia, were in for a hell of a fight, with no witnesses. At the end of the workshop, the group were asked to vote on whether PRV is causing HSMI in British Columbia— an unusual method of conducting science. I wasn't there to cast a vote but the managing director of Mowi's BC operations, Diane Morrison was. The final report recommended that DFO refuse to recognize any diagnosis of HSMI in a salmon farm until the disease had reached a "population level"—meaning, they were to wait until the disease was an epidemic within the farm. This destroyed any hope of containing the spread of this exotic virus to protect wild salmon.

The problem, I realized, as I tried to find a path through the obfuscation, was that no one from DFO at the Fish Health Committee was there to oversee the health of *wild* salmon. I began looking for anyone in DFO with such a job description.

DFO is an organization with 11,500 employees. I went online to scroll through the DFO staff to check all the department's directors. There were a lot of them, but no one was in charge of the state of wild salmon. This is despite the fact that salmon support tens of thousands of people in the various fisheries and the growing wilderness tourism industry, bringing in billions of dollars to the province. Salmon are entwined in the legal title and rights of First Nations. The horrifying images of the southern resident orca, carrying her dead baby on her head for seventeen days over two thousand kilometres, made millions of people worldwide aware that this population of orca was starving for lack of salmon in Canada. Salmon are economically, biologically and legally important. Furthermore, people love them and want them to thrive.

I did find a person in the DFO directory in charge of Salmon Management and Client Services. Who were DFO's "clients" and what "services" did they require, and how were these services attached to management of wild salmon? I wrote this person and asked her if she had been invited to sit on the minister's committee on fish health, where the only fish being discussed were farm salmon. She did not answer.

Also not at the table was the one person who had experience measuring the impact of viruses on *wild* salmon health—Dr. Di Cicco, the veterinarian with the Pacific Salmon Foundation who was the lead author on the research with Dr. Miller that reported the impact of the PRV virus on chinook salmon. Actually Di Cicco was at the meetings out of his own interest in what was being said, but he was not allowed to talk. When industry representatives threw his science under the bus, claiming there was no evidence that the PRV virus causes disease in British Columbia, I glanced at him. He looked as if he had been hit. He didn't look up, but sat caved in on himself. How was he able to keep silent?

———

Sick of meetings, I attached a magnetic sign I'd had made that read *Department of Wild Salmon* to the side of my car and went to look at what returning salmon I could find. I needed to be with them, smell the forest, touch the clear river water, feel their energy. I did find salmon returning to some rivers. It wasn't too late yet.

In remote wilderness areas, spawning salmon are shy. A human moving along the edge of the river could be a wolf or a bear, and so the fish rush away if you make the slightest movement. They are not only assessing the gravel for its nest-building potential and sizing up prospective mates, they are also watching the silhouette of the forest through the rushing water, alert for predators. However, in rivers that flow near towns, the salmon ignore people and will dig their nests right in front of you. As always, I marvelled at how completely confident they were even though they had no previous experience with the spawning ritual.

The first river I visited was the Campbell River. Arrow pulled at the leash I used to keep her close so she would not disturb the salmon or the bears. I felt calmed by the sheer beauty of the river flowing through the dappled light of leaves waving fall colours in the cool breeze. There on the dark wet sand of the riverbank I spied a dead pink salmon glowing yellow in the muted light. I leaned down to lift its gill plate. Damn, the gills were pale. I slit its belly with my pocket knife, took a look, then spun on my heel and hurried up the riverbank to retrieve my sampling kit from the car. The fish's spleen was huge, swollen in the act of fighting infection even as the fish died. Its heart was pale and the tough little valve attached to the heart, the bulbus arteriosus, was pale yellow. Yellow is the colour Di Cicco and Miller reported in the chinook salmon dying of PRV.

I took samples, measurements and photos, labelled the vials and bags and popped them into a cooler, then drove south to the next river, the Puntledge. I was no longer sight-seeing. I was tracking yellows.

Dead pink salmon, turned yellow by jaundice, were visible from the bridge, lying on the river bottom. A helpful man in shorts and light blue plastic Crocs waded out and brought them to me. Yellow skin, pale gills, swollen spleens; dead with eggs still in them. I took more notes, samples and photos. I called Brad and Sandy, my friends from the lower Fraser River with the speedboat. We bent over yellows strewn dead the length of Mountain Bar, taking samples from the freshest corpses. The dramatic beauty of the dark blue mountains, the cottonwoods in yellow fall foliage, the hundreds of eagles perched on the trees, their white heads gleaming like blossoms among the leaves, and the bright blue sky could not calm my rising sense of dread.

If these fish were dying of PRV, a virus my own research and the work of others have traced from Norway to the millions of Atlantic salmon in net pens throughout the southern half of the BC coast, this was an epidemic. As I knelt beside a dead fish at the river's edge, I could see tiny young salmon and trout tugging at the fraying flesh of another dead yellow salmon that lay on the river bottom. *Transmission.*

In the natural world, the decomposing bodies of spawned-out salmon feed the world around them. They feed the trees that are sequestering the carbon that is threatening life on Earth. They feed the eagles, fish and bears, and the Indigenous and invading cultures. They feed the insects that lay eggs that will hatch in spring to nourish the next generation of tiny newborn salmon wriggling out of pebble nests. And in addition to all this, they feed us. They represent food security.

In the unnatural world, dying salmon are industrial disease vectors, putting this entire food chain at risk.

As I was walking back to my car from the river, a young man hurried to catch up with me. At first I was apprehensive, but he was in hip waders and carrying a fishing rod, and so I stopped. In a lovely foreign accent he said, "You are Alexandra Morton, aren't you? I am from Denmark and I come every year to BC to fish. I read your posts on Facebook and I love what you do. Please keep it up. We have lost our salmon in Europe."

Everywhere I went, people responded to the sign on my car, pleased to see that the Department of Wild Salmon was on scene. They likely assumed I was with a branch of DFO dedicated to wild salmon. It was just me and my dog, but the Department of Wild Salmon was also a concept I was working on: a step-by-step path to restore wild salmon by intertwining the salmon people, powerful new scientific tools and local Indigenous and municipal governments, in which the fish become the ultimate authorities on their own restoration. They become our guide and teacher.

We love wild salmon, but in over a hundred years of human attempts to force more salmon from the natural system and then to combat the declines that we caused, we have loved them to death. With very few exceptions, we never actually gave the fish what they needed. Instead, we take shortcuts; we do what suits us more than them. The trouble for the salmon, and all that depends on them, is that they run afoul of so many industries, including logging, mining, hydropower, fishing, salmon farming, oil and agriculture, as well as urban development.

Governments in both Washington State and British Columbia thought they could destroy salmon habitat and simply create salmon without a river, and that everything would be fine. Hatcheries seemed like a good idea, but they have not worked out. Still, people cling to the hope that restoring salmon is as easy as building more hatcheries. Some of the most dedicated people working the hardest to restore salmon are hatchery workers. In all weather, including snow, they catch salmon and carefully transport them to hatchery tanks to wait for the females to ripen. Gently feeling the females' bellies, they can tell when the eggs have been released from the skein that holds them in place in the fish's body. They are ready to be fertilized.

With a swift blow to the head, they kill the fish, then slit her belly open and carefully remove the eggs. Since the male salmon are always ready, the hatchery workers then "milk" them for their sperm, which they collect in a cup. Putting the eggs together with the sperm is the next step.

Spawning in the natural world is a carefully choreographed event. Since the outer soft shell of a salmon egg will only allow sperm an entrance for a matter of moments, the male and female have to release sperm and eggs into the gravel together. As the eggs tumble into the river, the sperm fertilizes them, then the eggshells seal up as the mother quickly pushes pebbles over them to prevent them from being swept downstream.

While hatchery workers do think carefully about which males to pair with which females, they are looking through human eyes, not salmon eyes. Humans successfully breed many species, but we have never bred *wild* animals. This is the first problem with hatcheries. They prevent wild salmon from rapidly evolving to keep up with the changes in their environment. With the era of rapid climate change upon us, we would be wise to back off and let the salmon handle this. They know how to ensure that each generation has the best chance to deal with changes in their environment.

The hatchery workers quickly add the sperm to a bowl of translucent orange eggs and gently stir. If the sperm does its job, a light foam appears. The workers add water to harden the shells and seal the dividing cells inside the eggs. Then they place the fertilized eggs in trays they stack in racks, where water gently pours over them to simulate the river flowing over pebble nests. Entire salmon runs made in a bowl.

When the tiny fish hatch, they are protected from predators and fed a specially formulated chow. They swim in a featureless steel tank until they are released back into the rivers their parents were taken from. Unlike the progeny of their wild brethren, weaker fish do survive in the hatchery because there are no predators; since finding food is too easy, they don't learn anything about *being salmon*. But they grow bigger and faster than the wild fry and so compete successfully against the wild fish for food in the rivers. Though they appear healthy and robust, their genetic code is weak; the reproductive success of hatchery-bred salmon can be as much as 50 percent lower than that of their wild relatives. Hatchery fish are dependent on hatcheries.

The second problem with hatcheries is that the disease organisms flourish unnaturally when you raise salmon in the absence of predators. We learned this with salmon farms, but it is also true of hatcheries. They are not self-sustaining.

There may be a place for hatcheries to raise salmon for fishermen to catch. But we'd need to release those hatchery fish away from the wild runs. Big hatchery returns attract big commercial fisheries. If the huge seine nets and kilometres of gill nets are set across truly wild salmon migration routes and the wild fish are caught along with the hatchery fish, the valuable wild runs, with their superior genetics, risk extermination. This is the third problem with hatcheries.

The Department of Wild Salmon would link the hundreds of people who are already on scene on the rivers and in the marine environment working to study or restore wild salmon. We would take tiny non-lethal samples of salmon as they migrate through our regions and read their immune systems. Remarkably, many of the same genes turn on and off in fish immune systems as in human immune systems. For example, the immune system of a Pacific salmon fighting the influenza-family ISA virus looks similar to the immune system of a human fighting an influenza virus. A salmon gets mucus on its gills; a human gets mucus in the lungs. The immune system uses a planet-wide language shared by the cells of all animal life on Earth.

Immune systems are like toolboxes and genes are the tools in that box. When an animal becomes stressed, its immune system picks the right tool to deal with the specific stressor by turning on the genes that will best deal with the situation. This means that looking at which genes have been turned on, or upregulated, tells us what is stressing the animal. In a sense, the pattern we detect allows the animal—in this case the salmon—to talk to us and tell us the water is too warm, it's fighting a virus, bacteria, or pollutants and so on. If we take samples at intervals down the long rivers and along the coast of British Columbia, we could see where salmon immune systems are lighting up to indicate a problem. By looking at which genes are turned on, we could make a good guess at what's wrong. Then this information could be provided to the people in that region and together we could find the cause—the agricultural run-off, the storm drain outfall, the source of viruses, parasites and bacteria, the dam causing elevated water temperatures—and turn our minds to fixing the problem. We could find the bottlenecks and open them up, strategically getting out of the way of the fish where the salmon need it most. As salmon pass this location during the next migration, we could ask the salmon, Did we make it better for you? By sampling again, they can tell us.

This is the really powerful ingredient to this immune-system science. It begins a remarkable conversation between us and the fish. First Nations Elders would say that they used to engage in such a conversation to make sure the life-sustaining salmon populations never faltered. This science would allow the rest of us to catch up. If we do this sampling throughout salmon's coastal migration pathways, we will get a blueprint of how we need to change if we want to keep wild salmon alive. A spinoff benefit to this approach is that we learn how we are damaging the ocean and rivers and what is required to reverse the damage and thus protect ourselves from the destruction of these ecosystems.

Kristi Miller is the world leader in applying this science to salmon and DFO is trying to stifle her; every time she checks in with the salmon in British Columbia, the fish tell her something else about salmon farms that the current DFO regime does not want to hear. Miller's work is at odds with policy, and so they try to shut her up, but it turns out she is remarkably resilient and determined. Norway, the home of the salmon farming industry, has tapped her to work with them, but Canada pretends her work should be ignored.

The Department of Wild Salmon would pay close attention to the people trudging up rivers, climbing over logs, and crawling through dense brush to reach salmon runs throughout British Columbia—the eyewitnesses. This science depends on them, and so I would take them into the labs to see what happens with the samples and data they so arduously collect. As field workers visited the labs, they would find out why was it was so important to use sterile tools on each fish and to take each sample exactly two kilometres apart along the river. Samples taken at precise intervals allow for higher degrees of confidence in statistical results; we would learn more. But forcing a field crew to do the impossible destroys morale and weakens the results, so the lab technicians working on the samples would need to pull on their own hip waders, try to anchor a boat on a falling tide where it will go aground in exactly ninety minutes and help in the gathering. In this way, the technicians in the labs would also gain respect for the challenges faced by the collectors in the field; working together, they would streamline methods to find a balance between what is optimal and what is possible. The Department of Wild Salmon would facilitate annual gatherings where all teams could share ideas, successes and failures—where they could eat together and perhaps hold a salmon dance, and create a community among the people learning the language of salmon.

And finally, all of this would have to be gathered under the auspices of the local First Nations. While giving control over what happens to salmon runs to First Nations scares some people, consider this: Indigenous governments are entirely focused on very specific regions, without the need to consider international trade. This difference is critical to life on Earth. While the big picture is important, it immobilizes governments who are trying to satisfy international corporate needs *and* keep complex ecosystems functioning to produce clean air, water and food. We are extremely lucky that the First Nations of British Columbia were not extinguished by colonialism and that they are combing through the ashes, revisiting the secret places, reviving their languages and seeking wisdom from their Elders to rebuild governments based on human and nature as one.

I know that many Indigenous people reject the word *science*. I saw the horror on the face of one woman in the ancient salmon drying shack on the banks of the Fraser River in Lillooet as I pulled on blue latex gloves and opened a sterile blade to sample the fish she was preparing for the drying racks. But they are scientists in the truest sense of the word. They observe, remember, ponder, see and feel that all life is connected.

The sacred dances of the animal kingdom are cultural, but they are also biology lessons. All the animals that appear around the fire in the Big House—from bears to bottom-dwelling fish like sculpins—are part of what happens in this place and why it happens.

Here on the western edge of the North American continent, salmon are masters at the art of thriving. Through the concept of the Department of Wild Salmon, salmon would become our teachers, ensuring that we finally learn how to thrive, because we will only thrive if the world around us thrives.

I wrote to the facilitator of the Fish Health Committee, Carmel Lowe, just as I entered self-isolation against COVID-19: "I am resigning to ensure that my name does not endorse the outcomes of this committee. . . . It is unforgivable at this moment in history for DFO to pretend they don't understand the risk of allowing a highly contagious virus to spread through Canada's wild salmon."

The collapse of the 2019 wild salmon runs worsened in 2020, showing us that we are down to the wire, with no time to repeat mistakes. Sitting in the black tower of DFO, watching field staff waving red flags as their superiors ignore them, I realized those staff needed a pathway to the decision makers.

DFO is deaf to their field staff. DFO is broken because they have severed their own nervous system, blocking the information flowing from field staff to the decision makers. How DFO manages salmon is not based on salmon, it is based on politics. This is not working.

I realized it was time to try something else.

Dear Minister of Fisheries,

If Canada is going to keep her salmon, your department needs a Director of Wild Salmon, Pacific Region, someone whose sole mandate is keeping wild salmon alive, who you can trust to tell you what the

*fish need. This person has to be someone who doesn't really want the
job, who isn't looking for advancement, a political career or academic
tenure and who knows not only what is going on, but more importantly knows the people who know what needs to be done. This person
needs to possess an honest working relationship with First Nations and
understand the powerful science that can allow salmon to talk to us.*

*I am writing to ask you to consider creating a new position in response
to the 2019 wild salmon collapse, the Director of Wild Salmon, Pacific
Region, and name me as the first occupant in this role.*

Alexandra Morton

I am waiting for the answer.

On April 2, 2020, I headed out in my speedboat to begin my twentieth
year of counting sea lice on young wild salmon as they passed the salmon
farms in the Broughton Archipelago. I stopped at the research station
to load my net into my boat. I had to work alone this season because my
boat was too small to safely bring any crew on board during a pandemic.

Since 2001, every year, from April to June, I have made sure to take
weekly samples near two Mowi salmon farms, Wicklow and Glacier,
and one Cermaq site, Burdwood.

Few adult wild salmon had returned to the nearby Ahta and Viner
Rivers the fall before, so I knew there would be very few little fish.
When I finally found a school in the Burdwood Islands, I nosed my boat
up to the rocky shoreline and began my routine, catching about forty
salmon, mostly chum and a few pinks, in the bunt of the net. I scooped
them gently into a bucket and, once back aboard, I began the process of
recording data.

I lifted each fish and slid it into a plastic bag with a little seawater
then held it against a piece of graph paper to measure it. They were so

tiny, less than 4 centimetres long. Using a hand lens, I examined all sides of each fish through the bag. Their skins were smooth and slivery—no lice, no lice wounds, no scars. Their eyes were jet black, so dark it felt like I was looking into another world. In recent years the eyes of the little fish I'd sampled had become disturbingly cloudy, a grey veil between them and their world, almost certainly making it harder for them to see, to find food and avoid predators.

My heart began ringing like a bell and the sensation grew stronger with each fish I examined. As I was finished with the fish, I slipped it out of its bag and back into my bucket. At the end, I poured them all out of the bucket into the ocean, wishing them well. I breathed deeply, maybe a little shakily, unfamiliar with the sensation of joy. Sea lice were still ravaging juvenile salmon elsewhere on the coast, but this place was safe for wild salmon again.

I don't know if there are enough wild salmon left to rebuild the rivers of the Broughton Archipelago, but for the first time in a long while I knew that everything I had done was worth it.

The power of one is all we have, but we all have it.

Acknowledgements

SO MANY PEOPLE have helped me over the years. They were the silver lining, my safety net, teachers, inspiration and shelter in the storms. Every twist and turn of this seemingly endless road made me ask, What should I do now? Looking for answers, I found mentors, people whose perspectives added valuable depth and dimension. Thank you to Rick Routledge who has been endlessly generous with his time in not only designing sampling regimes for the many studies, but also offering thoughts on how to communicate with government and why I should not give up.

Thank you, Damien Gillis, for your political insight, Andrew Nikiforuk for shedding light on the dark side of politics and Helen Slinger for sharing a dram of whisky, humour and wisdom on how to communicate with people. Thank you to my sister, Woodleigh Hubbard, who checked in on me relentlessly and tried to get me to remember that I needed to take care of myself.

Thank you to Bob and Nancy Richter, who made it possible for me to stay in Echo Bay after my husband died, and to my dear friend Billy Proctor, who has taught me so much about the place I came to call home and took me on as his deckhand so that I could support my son.

Thank you to Dr. Daniel Pauly for telling people that I did not stick the lice on young wild salmon—that the lice epidemics were real. Thank you to Harvey Andrusak for being the first person in government to openly share my concerns. Thank you to Sabra Woodworth for

334 NOT ON MY WATCH

so generously opening her home to me, taking care of my dogs when I had to leave them behind and, more than anyone, listening to me and providing feedback. Thank you to Bill and Donna MacKay for making it possible for me to get across Blackfish Sound no matter how hard the wind was blowing, and for opening their house to me and my children, as we waited for weather to get home.

Thank you to Paul Watson for sending me a ship and to the remarkable people who crewed that ship, in particular Carolina Castro, who knew how to protect the first sparks of the occupation that led to the removal of so many salmon farms. Thank you to the lawyers: Jeff Jones for steering me through the legal minefields that sought to destroy me and Greg McDade for all the progress we made at the Cohen Commission, for taking salmon farm regulation away from the province of BC, for so much advice over the years and for putting an end to the strange ruling that I could only approach Mowi salmon farms in a toy boat. Thanks to Margot Venton, Kegan Pepper-Smith, Morgan Blakely and Lara Tessaro at Ecojustice for winning the lawsuits that tried to stop the spread of piscine orthoreovirus from salmon farms. Thank you also to Sean Jones, whose work with the 'Namgis to stop the spread of PRV brought the experts together to create a record of the true and terrible impact of this virus.

Thank you to Sarah Haney for making it possible to create a research station out of my home and to all the brilliant young scientists and volunteers who put so much time and effort into making the Salmon Coast Field Station into a scientific powerhouse. Thank you to Drs. Fred and Molly Kibenge for their bravery and hard work in tracking fish viruses with me. Thank you to Rudy North and Dick and Val Bradshaw for contributing the funds to make it possible for the Kibenges and myself to publish the first research on the ISA virus and piscine orthoreovirus in BC.

Thank you to Don Staniford and Anissa Reed for your unparalleled creativity, stamina and humour, which built all this into a movement to save this coast.

I want to thank Ernest Alfred for taking the step that set in motion the removal of salmon farms from the Broughton Archipelago. While many, many people were involved in making this happen, Ernest's first step onto the farm at Swanson Island was the tipping point.

Thank you to William Wasden Jr. for teaching me about First Nation governance and to Millie Willie for her stark honesty on the relationship between the Indigenous and non-indigenous here in BC. Thank you to George Quocksister Jr. for his bravery in boarding the farms and bringing us the images of what was going on in their pens.

Thank you to the women who stood on the farms: Karissa Glendale, Nabidu Willie, Lindsey Mae Willie, Sherry Moon, Cassandra Alexis, Tsatsaqualis, Sii-am Hamilton, Julia Smith, Molina Dawson, Tabatha Milian, Maia Beauvais, Tidi Nelson, Andrea Cramner and Nic Dedeluk. Your determination, endurance and grace under fire formed a protective circle around the archipelago that no one could destroy!

Thank you to the leaders: Chiefs Don Svanvik, Robert Chamberlin, Willie Moon, Arthur Dick, Eric Joseph, Chaz Coon, Wesley Smith, Rick Johnson, Robert Mountain, and Richard Sumner. You walked through fire in service of your people.

Thank you to Minister Jonathan Wilkinson for hearing me out and taking a chance on me. Thank you to Minister Lana Popham for having the courage to stand up to the salmon farming industry and do what was right.

Thank you to Karen Wristen, Stan Proboszcz, John Werring, Craig Orr and Will Soltau for your decades of painstaking effort to make it easy for government to understand the mistruths perpetrated by their own bureaucracies. Thank you to Eric Hobson for decades of work to move the salmon farming industry into tanks on land to preserve jobs *and* wild salmon. That they ignored your work speaks to the dangerous alliance between industry and government, an alliance that is rapidly killing our planet.

Thank you to Dr. Larry Dill, who used his standing as a senior scientist to speak in plain terms to debunk the junk science in this territory.

Thank you to April Bencze and Tavish Campbell, who generously donated their hard-won images to save the salmon of BC. Thank you to Sally Allan, who demanded financial order through the storms (I fear you and don't dare to lose a receipt!). Thank you to Brad Crowther and Sandy Bodrug for all the hours you sampled the salmon of the Fraser River.

Thank you to Tony Allard and John Madden, who may have thought it would be easy for businessmen to bring politicians up to speed on the truth, and then did not give up. You have made a real difference.

And, finally, thank you, Anne Collins, for taking 120,000 words and making them readable.

SOURCE NOTES

INTRODUCTION: WONDER AND RESISTANCE

The Access to Information Act (https://atip-aiprp.apps.gc.ca/atip/welcome.do) gives Canadian citizens, permanent residents, and any person or corporation present in Canada a right to access records of government institutions that are subject to the act.

Part 1: Into the Wilderness

1. THE ROAD TO ACTIVISM WAS PAVED WITH SCIENCE

Morton A. 1986. Sound and behavioral correlation in captive *Orcinus orca*. In: Kirkevold BC, Lockhard JS, editors. Behavioral biology of killer whales. New York: Alan R. Liss. p. 303–333.

Dr. Michael Bigg's photo-identification research was published in Bigg MA, Ford J, Balcomb K, Ellis M, Ellis G. 1987. Killer whales: A study of their identification, genealogy, and natural history in British Columbia and Washington State. Phantom Press.

2. FINDING HOME

The water dwellers, a short fifteen-minute NFB film, was shot in 1963 about life in Echo Bay (www.nfb.ca/film/water_dwellers). While some things had changed by the time I arrived, much of what appears in this short documentary remained the same.

3. THE INVISIBLE FORK IN THE ROAD

Since the writing of the Magna Carta, English common law has recognized public rights navigation over tidal waters. Rockwell DR, VanderZwaag DL, editors. 2006. Towards principled oceans governance: Australian and Canadian approaches and challenges. New York: Routledge.

The United Nations Convention on the Law of the Sea, Article 19, further defines "innocent passage" (www.un.org/depts/los/convention_agreements/texts/unclos/unclos_e.pdf)

Morton v. British Columbia (Agriculture and Lands), 2010 BCSC 100. Decision of the BC Supreme Court (Justice Hinkson) ruling that salmon farms are fisheries, January 26, 2010.

Morton AB, Symonds HK. 2002. Displacement of *Orcinus orca* (L.) by high amplitude sound in British Columbia, Canada. ICES Journal of Marine Science. 59(1): 71–80. doi:10.1006/jmsc.2001.1136.

4. THIS WAS NO "MISTAKE"

Much of the material in this chapter came from the newspaper *The Fisherman* and is more extensively cited in my blog (https://alexandramorton.typepad.com): Salmon feedlots—this was not a mistake, January 2013.

5: THE CLEARANCES

The provincial government study that zoned the Broughton Archipelago for salmon farms: Coastal resource interests study: Finfish aquaculture opportunities. 1989. Broughton Islands. Victoria, B.C.: Ministry of Crown Lands.

The discovery of the parasites in the eyes of the sole caught near salmon: Blaylock RB, Overstreet RM, Morton AB. 2005. The pathogenic copepod *Phrixocephalus cincinnatus* (Copepoda: *Pennellidae*) in the eye of arrowtooth flounder, *Atherestes stomias*, and rex sole, *Glyptocephalus zachirus*, from British Columbia. The European Association of Fish Pathologists. 25(3): 116–123.

The research into the fate of escaped Atlantic salmon: Morton AB, Volpe J. 2002. A description of escaped farmed Atlantic salmon *Salmo salar* captures and their characteristics in one Pacific salmon fishery area in British Columbia, Canada, in 2000. Alaska Fishery Research Bulletin. 9(2): 102–109.

The memo on importing Atlantic salmon eggs from an Icelandic hatchery that was not certified under Canadian regulations is Cohen Commission exhibit 1683, p. 2. The Cohen Commission of Inquiry into the Decline of Sockeye Salmon in the Fraser River website (http://commission-cohen.ca/) has been archived by the Internet Archive (https://archive.org).

The provincial Salmon Aquaculture Review (http://www2.gov.bc.ca/ assets/gov/environment/natural-resource-stewardship/environmental-as-sessments/eao-project-reviews/salmon-acquaculture-summary-report.pdf) was created in an attempt to address rising concerns about the impact of the new salmon farming industry on British Columbia. It focused on the Broughton Archipelago.

6. SALMON COAST FIELD STATION

Morton AB, Williams R. 2003. Infestation of the sea louse *Lepeophtheirus salmonis* (Krøyer) on juvenile pink salmon *Oncorhynchus gorbuscha* (Walbaum) in British Columbia. Canadian Field Naturalist. 117: 634–641.

Morton AB, Routledge R, Peet C, Ladwig A. 2004. Sea lice (*Lepeophtheirus salmonis*) infection rates on juvenile pink (*Oncorhynchus gorbuscha*) and chum (*Oncorhynchus keta*) salmon in the nearshore marine environment of British Columbia, Canada. Canadian Journal of Fisheries and Aquatic Sciences. 61(2): 147–157.

The provincial Pink Salmon Action Plan (https://archive.news.gov.
bc.ca/releases/archive/2001-2005/2003agf0004-000137-attachment1.
htm) cleared the juvenile wild salmon migration route of adult Atlantic
salmon farms.

Morton AB, Routledge R. 2006. Mortality rates for juvenile pink
Oncorhynchus gorbuscha and chum *O. keta* salmon infested with sea lice
Lepeophtheirus salmonis in the Broughton Archipelago. Alaska Fishery
Research Bulletin. 11(2): 146–152. http://www.adfg.alaska.gov/static/home/
library/PDFs/afrb/mortv11n2.pdf

Krkošek M, Ford JS, Morton AB, Lele S, Myers RA, Lewis MA. 2007.
Declining wild salmon populations in relation to parasites from farm
salmon. Science. 318: 1772–1775. doi:10.1126/science.1148744.

Egler FE. 1977. The nature of vegetation: Its management and mismanagement: An introduction to vegetation science. Norfolk, CT: Aton Forest
in cooperation with Connecticut Conservation Association.

Films that Twyla Roscovich made with me:
Discovery of sea lion drowned in salmon farm nets, April 24, 2007
(https://youtu.be/ofDaDumu9vM).
Introduction to Alex Morton and her research, April 26, 2007
(https://youtu.be/NJQu9o2UfOg).
What's so great about pink salmon, May 4, 2007 (https://youtu.be/
mZvob2PJ_Wg).
Message to Cermaq shareholders, May 17, 2007 (https://youtu.be/of3
URNlMLMk).
Salmon going down on DFO's watch, June 1, 2007 (https://youtu.be/
1BcRBwCh6BA).
Dear Marine Harvest part 1, June 4, 2008 (https://youtu.be/7eC3Y2mUK98).
Dear Marine Harvest part 2, June 4, 2008 (https://youtu.be/TCBI3Qj1krM).

The problem with salmon farms in a nutshell, October 21, 2008 (https://youtu.be/yTYhQAN9BWo).

Salmon farm diseases, October 21, 2010 (https://youtu.be/vekW4FgXefo).

Salmon confidential, 70-minute documentary, May 2013 (https://youtu.be/fTCQ2IA_Zss).

My lawsuit against minister of Fisheries and Oceans and Marine Harvest, May 8, 2013 (https://youtu.be/LEp8dIvk_lQ).

Hard evidence, August 27, 2016 (https://youtu.be/gnzqvfpvc7A).

The Salmon Coast Field Station (www.salmoncoast.org) continues to operate.

7. NORWAY, THE MOTHER COUNTRY

The email from Georges Lemieux, senior trade commissioner with the Canadian embassy in Oslo Norway is part of Cohen Commission exhibit 1976, p. 60.

Other scientists in Norway felt the consequences of trying to rein in and report on the fish farming industry.

In 2003, the Norwegian Institute for Nutrition and Seafood Safety (NIFES) hired the American scientist Dr. Claudette Bethune, a senior seafood toxicologist, to ensure that fish sold in Norway was safe. She loved the work, loved the country and soon fell in love with a Norwegian man and became engaged to be married.

Then, in the autumn of 2004, a twenty-ton shipment of animal feed ingredients entered Norway from China. It was contaminated with 1.5 tons of cadmium, a heavy metal that causes cancer. A few months later, Bethune reported that her testing had revealed high cadmium levels in farmed salmon feed. Recent studies had found that of all farmed animals, such as cows, pigs and chickens, salmon absorbed the highest percentage of whatever toxin might be in their feed. While beef and pork products contaminated by the cadmium were taken off the market, the farm salmon

that were eating cadmium-contaminated feed remained for sale because
the European Feed Manufacturers Federation requested that the European Commission double the maximum allowable limit of cadmium in
fish feed. Bethune's institute assisted in this request and so cadmium-
contaminated farm salmon feed became legal.

Bethune is one of the rare breed of scientist who cannot live with the
knowledge that people are unaware of a risk to their health, like Canada's
own Shiv Chopra, who blew the whistle on the human health impact of
the bovine growth hormone (BGH) used to boost milk production. He
was fired from Health Canada for insubordination.

Bethune became Norway's first such whistle-blower when she handed
over the cadmium data to a reporter, who wrote a story that accused
Norway of withholding food safety information. Bethune also warned
the public about the high levels of flame-retardants and dioxin-like
PCBs, potent cancer-causing agents, in farmed salmon. The government
was not at all pleased. Export of farm salmon was a money maker and
soon Russia had slapped a temporary ban on the importing of Norwegian
farmed salmon.

Branded a "traitor" in the Norwegian media, she lost her fiancé and
her job. When she left the country, she discovered there were no jobs for
a "troublemaker" in the field of food toxicology in the European Union.
She returned to the US, where she was able to at least find work in a small
lab in the Midwest before working her way back to the level at which she
had been previously employed.

Bethune's Norwegian colleagues were concerned about what her
treatment meant for all of them and the freedom to communicate scientific results. They brought enough pressure to bear on the Norwegian
Parliament that it passed legislation to protect academic freedom in 2007.
However, concerns persisted regarding toxins in farm salmon. Eleven years
later Bethune co-authored a paper on the concentrations of carcinogenic
toxins in farm salmon.

Dr. Anne-Lise Bjørke Monsen, a pediatrician with the Haukeland
University in Norway, has conducted research over the past twenty years

on the influence of micronutrients in mothers on the development of fetal brains. She was not looking for a fight when the parents of an autistic child came to her wanting a second opinion on some tests done on the boy in the US screening for pollutants, a lot of which Monsen realized were in farmed salmon.

Dr. Bjørke Monsen was aware of three US studies that had analyzed large quantities of farmed salmon and concluded that the levels of PCBs, dioxins, dieldrin and toxaphene (insecticides) found in the farmed salmon was a cancer risk. Dr. David O. Carpenter, one of the scientists involved said, "One should avoid farmed salmon like the plague."

These toxins were elevated in the test results from the autistic child, and caused Dr. Bjørke Monsen to look at the potential risk from eating farmed salmon, which appeared to contain more environmental toxins than any other food eaten regularly in Norway. These were toxins stored in fat cells, she realized, which could stay in the human body for up to twenty years. She knew from her own work that women's bodies release these toxins when their bodies draw on fat reserves during pregnancy and nursing, with their first child receiving up to 98 percent of the mother's lifetime toxin load. The concern for the pediatrician was that these toxins were passing to the baby during the critical phase in development of the human brain.

Since in Norway farmed salmon was heavily promoted to women and children, Dr. Bjørke Monsen issued a public warning to pregnant women and children that was picked up and published in 2013 in *VG*, one of the country's leading newspapers, under the headline, "Doctors and professors—'Do not eat farmed salmon.'" The story set off a political firestorm. Fortunately the whistle-blower legislation that was Dr. Bethune's legacy protected Dr. Bjørke Monsen, and she didn't lose her job.

At first the health minister, Jonas Gahr Støre, refused to comment, but then he said perhaps there should be a review. The minister of fisheries, Lisbeth Berg-Hansen, who actually owned a salmon farm, declined to be interviewed, but assured Norwegians that farm salmon was safe. Then the news broke that Norway's Scientific Committee for Food Safety had known about the risks to brain development and overall health associated with eating farmed salmon for seven years. They hadn't gone public with it even as farm salmon sushi consumption was skyrocketing among young Norwegians.

Six days after the article appeared, Norway issued an official health warning to limit consumption of fatty fish, though it did not specify farmed salmon.

In November 2018, the European Union Food Safety Authority set the tolerable weekly intake of dioxins and dioxin-like PCBs to a level seven times lower that what had previously been viewed as safe, in part due to their dramatic impact on sperm quality in men. This caused the debate in Norway about how much farm salmon is safe to eat to reignite once again; some in government arguing that up to 1.3 kilograms per week is safe, while others believe the safe limit is no more than 200 grams.

Even for a country enamoured with the industry, the relationship with salmon farms is troubled.

Twyla Roscovich made videos on my request to DFO to medevac young wild salmon past the salmon farms.

Plan to medevac juvenile salmon past salmon farms, April 1, 2008 (https://youtu.be/gHOkeEYGPUs).

DFO says no to medevac, April 12, 2008 (https://youtu.be/Iq2hTfKaCOs).

The full letter written to Canada by Georg Fredrik Rieber-Mohn can be found on my blog (https://alexandramorton.typepad.com): Please heed this warning from former attorney general of Norway, February 2010.

Article on Claudette Bethune: Cherry D. 2006. Scientist questions Norway's advice on cadmium. IntraFish, January 16. www.intrafish.com/news/scientist-questions-norways-advice-on-cadmium/1-1-556646.

Article on Dr. Anne-Lise Bjørke Monsen: 2013. Pressure grows on farmed salmon. NewsinEnglish.no, June 11. www.newsinenglish.no/2013/06/11/pressure-grows-on-farmed-salmon.

These non-English articles can be read using Google Translate:
Article (in Norwegian) on legislating academic freedom as a
result of the case of Claudette Bethune: Korneliussen SO. 2006. Vil
lovfeste akademisk frihet. abcnyheter, October 2. www.abcnyheter.no/
nyheter/2006/10/02/32188/vil-lovfeste-akademisk-frihet.

The *VG* article on Dr. Monsen's concerns: Pedersen TR, Ertesvåg F.
2013. Stiller spørsmål ved lakse-eksperts motiver. VG, June 10.
www.vg.no/nyheter/innenriks/i/BO19v/stiller-spoersmaal-ved-lakse-
eksperts-motiver.

Norwegian article titled Eating us sterile: Kvifte B. 2019.
Spiser oss sterile! TVHelse.no, July 5. www.tv-helse.no/miljogifter-
spiser-oss-sterile.

"The world's most dangerous fish": Nordgård K. 2018. «Verdens
farligste fisk». Nordnorsk Debatt, December 4. https://nordnorskdebatt.
no/article/verdens-farligste-fisk.

Part II: Activism

8. GROUND-TRUTHING

I documented my conversations with Trevor Rhodes, director of the
Aquaculture branch of the provincial Ministry of Agriculture, on my blog
(https://alexandramorton.typepad.com): Dialogue with the fish farm
regulators, March 21, 2010.

Morton AB, Routledge R, Krkosek M. 2008. Sea louse infestation
in wild juvenile salmon and herring associated with fish farms off
the east central coast of Vancouver Island, BC. North American
Journal of Fisheries Management. 28(2): 523–532. doi: 10.1577/
M07-042.1.

9. GET OUT MIGRATION

Morton v. Heritage Salmon Ltd et al. Private prosecution under the Fisheries Act, Court File No. 13381, Port Hardy Registry, June 30, 2005.

Morton v. British Columbia (Agriculture and Lands), 2009 BCSC 136. BC Supreme Court (Justice Hinkson) ruling that returned the management of salmon farms from the Province of BC to the federal government.

10. COMPASS BEARING

Stickleback cannot be the source of sea lice on juvenile wild salmon because the lice are unable to reach maturity on stickleback; this species of fish is not a suitable host for sea lice. Krkošek M, Ford J, Morton A, Lele S, Lewis M. 2008. Sea lice and pink salmon declines: A response to Brooks and Jones (2008). Reviews in Fisheries Science. 16(4): 413–420. doi:10.1080/10641260802013692.

Testimony by Dr. Kyle Garver on August 25, 2011, in the Cohen Commission transcript (p. 6, line 25) states that "650 billion viral particles" can be shed per hour from a salmon farm; he later requested a correction to read "65 billion."

My report to the Pacific Salmon Commission—Hypothesis: Salmon farm-origin pathogens as a dominant driver in Fraser Sockeye declining productivity—can be found on the Pacific Salmon Commission website (www.psc.org/publications/workshop-reports/fraser-river-sockeye-decline-workshop) in download 04 - Fraser Sockeye Decline Workshop Appendix C, Part 2.

An example of the chilling effect on scientists: In 2008 Dr. Martin Krkošek was awarded a Governor General's Gold Medal for his doctoral dissertation on his sea lice research, yet no university in Canada would hire him. He went to New Zealand. Eventually he did become a tenured

professor at the University of Toronto, but the career-dampening effect
of research into the impact of salmon farms permeated the scientific
community. Very few scientists were willing to step into the crosshairs
of this aggressive little industry and its big friends.

The paper reporting the spread of the IHN virus via the salmon
farming industry: Saksida SM. 2006. Infectious haematopoietic necrosis
epidemic (2001 to 2003) in farmed Atlantic salmon *Salmo salar* in British
Columbia. Diseases of Aquatic Organisms. 72(3): 213-223.

Paper showing decline of wild salmon in all regions of the world
where salmon farms exist in wild salmon habitat: Ford JS, Myers RA.
2008. A global assessment of salmon aquaculture impacts on wild
salmonids. PLOS Biology. 6(2): e33. doi:10.1371/journal.pbio.0060033.

Decision document on whether provincial farm salmon health
records are public information: Office of the Information & Privacy
Commissioner for British Columbia Order F10-06. 2010 BCIPC 9.

11. MISSION FOR SALMON

Manuel A, Derrickson RM. 2015. Unsettling Canada: A national
wake-up call. Foreword by Naomi Klein. Toronto: Between the Lines.

Hume M. 1992. Run of the river: Portraits of eleven British Columbia
rivers. Vancouver: New Star Books.

12. COHEN COMMISSION

The Cohen Commission of Inquiry into the Decline of Sockeye
Salmon in the Fraser River website (http://commissioncohen.ca/) has
been archived by the Internet Archive (https://archive.org).

Senior DFO biologist fails to report rotting farm salmon: Cohen
Commission exhibit 1976, p. 58.

Norwegian research tracing the ISA virus from Norwegian hatchery, Aquagen, into Chile: Vike S, Nylund S, Nylund A. 2009. ISA virus in Chile: Evidence of vertical transmission. Archives of Virology. 154: 1–8.

Confidential memo from Dr. Mark Sheppard, August 01, 2007: Cohen Commission exhibit 1679.

Many of the documents listed below are in the 60-page report, "What is happening to the Fraser sockeye," that I submitted to the Cohen Commission. It became exhibit 1976 and is posted on my blog (https://alexandramorton.typepad.com): "My report to Cohen—There is a serious issue with disease," October 2011.

Internal DFO conversation regarding import of Atlantic salmon eggs into British Columbia: Cohen Commission exhibit 1976, p. 53–56.

Internal DFO conversation regarding pre-spawn mortality of Fraser River sockeye salmon: Cohen Commission exhibit 1976, p. 4–9.

Dr. Kristi Miller reporting on the paper Epidemic of a novel, cancer-causing viral disease may be associated with wild salmon declines in BC: Cohen Commission exhibit 1976, p. 21.

Discovery of salmon leukemia virus in farm salmon by DFO: Eaton DE, Kent ML. 1992. A retrovirus in chinook salmon (*Oncorhynchus tshawytscha*) with plasmacytoid leukemia and evidence for the etiology of the disease. Cancer Research. 52: 6496–6500.

DFO research reporting Harrison River sockeye DNA never detected on the primary sockeye migration route through the Discovery Islands: Tucker et al. 2009. Seasonal stock-specific migrations of juvenile sockeye salmon along the west coast of North America: Implications for growth. Transactions of the American Fisheries Society. 138(6): 1458–1480. doi:10.1577/T08-211.1.

Craig Stephens PhD thesis, "The evidence supporting the hypothesis that marine anemia is a spreading infectious neoplastic disease could have profound regulatory effects on the salmon farming industry": Stephens C. 1995. A field investigation of marine anemia in farmed salmon in British Columbia [thesis]. Saskatoon: University of Saskatchewan. Available on Salmon Farm Science blog (https://salmonfarmscience.files.wordpress.com).

What is happening to the Fraser sockeye?: Cohen Commission exhibit 1976, see the archive link (https://archive.org) for this report.

Video of my examination at the Cohen Commission: The unofficial trial of Alexandra Morton, 2016 (https://thegreenchannel.tv/film/the-unofficial-trial-of-alexandra-morton).

13. FEAR AND SILENCE

Many articles have been written about the collapse of the North Atlantic cod stocks and how DFO scientist Ransom Myers discovered why the fish were vanishing and was ignored by senior DFO staff. Read Dr. Ransom's obituary in the journal *Nature* written by Dr. Daniel Pauly (www.nature.com/articles/447160a).

Part III: Virus Hunting

14. A REPORTABLE VIRUS

Unpublished ISA virus results: Kibenge M, Jones S, Traxler G, Kibenge F. 2004. Asymptomatic infectious salmon anaemia in juvenile *Oncorhynchus* species from the North West Pacific Ocean. Cohen Commission exhibit 2045.

November 9, 2011, email chain, Dr. Cornelius Kiley, CFIA: Cohen Commission ISA hearings exhibit DFO-599910.

November 4, 2011, email, Nelle Gagne: Cohen Commission exhibit 2040.

October 25, 2011, email from Gary Marty describing ISA virus test designed by master's student: Cohen Commission exhibit 2048.

November 9, 2011, email from Joseph Beres: Cohen Commission exhibit DFO-599910.

Testimony of Dr. Kim Klotins (CFIA) that if ISAV is confirmed, exports of BC farm salmon would cease appears in the documentary by Twyla Roscovich, *Salmon Confidential*.

May 30, 2012, email from Alf Bungay (DFO) regarding "stream of commerce": Access to Information and Privacy (ATIP) request A-2012-00770, p. 3662.

The internal CFIA conversation regarding removing ISA virus surveillance samples from federal labs and sending them to the BC Animal Health Centre in Abbotsford: ATIP A-2015-00315.

Kibenge MJT, Iwamoto T, Wang Y, Morton A, Routledge R, Kibenge FSB. 2016. Discovery of variant infectious salmon anaemia virus (ISAV) of European genotype in British Columbia, Canada. Virology Journal. 13:3. doi: 10.1186/s12985-015-0459-1.

The ISA virus retesting done by the CFIA on my samples appears in Appendix 9 – RT_PCR data analysis spreadsheet in ATIP A201300119_2014-05-08_08-26-45, p. 410–412.

15. LOCK HER UP

The proposed Animal Health Act, Bill 37, is discussed on West Coast Environmental Law's Environmental Law Alert Blog (www.wcel.org/blog): The rise and fall of the Animal Health Act, June 3, 2012.

The Province newspaper wrote: "The minister said he's having his staff look at options to deal with the perception that the new act will restrict free speech by citizens and journalists": http://www.theprovince.com/news/intent+muzzle+media+public+Minister/6689093/story.html

Letter to Agricultural Minister Don McRae from Elizabeth Denham, Information and Privacy Commissioner for BC: https://www.oipc.bc.ca/public-comments/1140.

The Cohen Commission Final Report is available at http://publications.gc.ca/pub?id=9.652609&sl=0.

16. DAMAGE TO THE HEART

The provincial lab report of HSMI-type lesions: Case 08-3362 appears in Cohen Commission exhibit 1549-309.

Kibenge MJT, Iwamoto T, Wang Y, Morton A, Godoy MG, Kibenge FSB. 2013. Whole-genome analysis of piscine reovirus (PRV) shows PRV represents a new genus in family *Reoviridae* and its genome segment S1 sequences group it into two separate sub-genotypes. Virology Journal. 10: 230.

Asking Norway about piscine reovirus: 15-minute video by Twyla Roscovich, July 18, 2013 (https://youtu.be/3scxcIDuEOo).

Correction: Siah A, Morrison DB, Fringuelli E, Savage P, Richmond Z, Johns R, et al. 2016. Correction: Piscine reovirus: Genomic and molecular phylogenetic analysis from farmed and wild salmonids collected on the Canada/US pacific coast. PLOS ONE. 11(10): e0164926. doi:10.1371/journal.pone.0164926.

Section 56 (b) of Canada's Fishery (General) Regulations: https://laws-lois.justice.gc.ca/eng/Regulations/SOR-93-53/index.html.

Garver KA, Johnson SC, Polinski MP, Bradshaw JC, Marty GD, Snyman HN, et al. 2016. Piscine orthoreovirus from western North America is transmissible to Atlantic salmon and sockeye salmon but fails to cause heart and skeletal muscle inflammation. PLOS ONE. 11(1): e0146229. doi:10.1371/journal.pone.0146229.

Dr. Gary Marty, May 21, 2016, email is found in ATIP A2016-203, p. 998.

Dr. Gary Marty, May 23, 2016, email is found in ATIP A2016-203, p. 1011.

"the histopathologist from the province convinced the industry not to sign off on the report . . . if PRV was to be included in the analyses." A-2016-01097, p. 59.

Publication on piscine orthoreovirus in farmed chinook: Di Cicco E, Ferguson HW, Kaukinen KH, Schulze AD, Li S, et al. 2018. The same strain of *Piscine orthoreovirus* (PRV-1) is involved with the development of different, but related, diseases in Atlantic and Pacific Salmon in British Columbia. FACETS. 23 April. doi:10.1139/facets-2018-0008.

Morton v. Canada (Fisheries and Oceans), 2015 FC 575. Federal Court decision (Justice Rennie) ordering DFO to develop new policy regarding PRV screening of farm salmon, May 6, 2015.

Morton v. Canada (Fisheries and Oceans), 2019 FC 143. Federal Court decision (Justice Strickland), reaffirming 2015 decision, February 4, 2019.

Paper on starving orca: Wasser SK, Lundin JI, Ayres K, Seely E, Giles D, Balcomb K, et al. 2017. Population growth is limited by nutritional impacts on pregnancy success in endangered Southern Resident killer whales (*Orcinus orca*). PLOS ONE 12(6): e0179824. doi:10.1371/journal.pone.0179824.

Racing a virus, short video by April Bencze (https://vimeo.com/258135790).

Part IV: The Uprising

17. A SHIP

Margaret Wente calling me a "folk hero": Wente, M. B.C.'s fishy salmon science. 2010 (updated 2018). Globe and Mail, September 2. www.theglobe andmail.com/opinion/bcs-fishy-salmon-science/article1369928.

18. KEEPING UP THE PRESSURE

Morton A, Routledge R, Hrushowy S, Kibenge M, Kibenge F. 2017. The effect of exposure to farmed salmon on piscine orthoreovirus infection and fitness in wild Pacific salmon in British Columbia, Canada. PLOS ONE. 12(12): e0188793. doi:10.1371/journal. pone.0188793.

Letter of Understanding regarding a government-to-government process to address finfish aquaculture in the Broughton Area, including recommendations on Provincial Tenure Replacement Decisions. June 27, 2018. www2.gov.bc.ca/assets/gov/environment/natural-resource-steward-ship/consulting-with-first-nations/agreements/broughton_nations_and_bc_letter_of_understanding_june_2018_final_signed.pdf.

Namgis First Nation v. Canada (Fisheries, Oceans and Coast Guard), 2018 FC 334. Federal Court decision (Justice Manson), denying injunction to stop Mowi from restocking the Swanson farm, March 23, 2018.

Di Cicco E, Ferguson HW, Kaukinen KH, Schulze AD, Li S, et al. 2018. The same strain of *Piscine orthoreovirus* (PRV-1) is involved with the development of different, but related, diseases in Atlantic and Pacific Salmon in British Columbia. FACETS. 3: 599–641. doi:10.1139/facets-2018-0008.

23. COURTROOM DRAMA

Morton v. Canada (Fisheries and Oceans), 2019 FC 143. Federal Court decision (Justice Strickland), reaffirming 2015 decision ordering DFO to initiate PRV screening of farm salmon, February 4, 2019.

24. AN ANCIENT GOVERNMENT RE-EMERGING
News release on government agreement to decommission the Broughton salmon farms: Government, First Nations chart path for aquaculture in Broughton Archipelago. December 14, 2018. https://news.gov.bc.ca/releases/2018PREM0151-002412.

CONCLUSION: DEPARTMENT OF WILD SALMON
Regarding the second problem with hatcheries, in the Cohen Commission documents, I saw emails from DFO-run hatcheries saying that they would not reach their release quota unless they could release fish they knew were infected with bacterial kidney disease, BKD. And so they did. Today, given DFO mismanagement of salmon farm pathogens, I think it would be impossible to bring wild fish into hatcheries as broodstock without bringing PRV in as well. Allowing viruses and bacteria to flourish in unnatural settings where predators are excluded is so dangerous because it removes the natural limits that prevent escalating virulence.

INDEX

ALEXANDRA MORTON IS a field biologist who became an activist who has done groundbreaking research on the damaging impact of ocean-based salmon farming on the coast of British Columbia. She first studied communications in bottlenosed dolphins and then moved on to recording and analyzing the sounds of captive orcas at Marineland of the Pacific in California, where she witnessed the birth, and death, of the first orca conceived in captivity. In 1984, she moved to the remote BC coast, aiming to study the language and culture of wild orca clans, but soon found herself at the heart of a long fight to protect the wild salmon that are the province's keystone species. She has co-authored more than twenty scientific papers on the impact of salmon farming on migratory salmon as well as several books, including *Listening to Whales*. She founded the Salmon Coast Research Station, has been featured on *60 Minutes*, and has been key to many legal and protest actions against the industry, including the recent First Nations-led occupation of salmon farms on the Broughton.